THE RENEWAL FACTOR

THE RENEWAL FACTOR

ROBERT H. WATERMAN, JR

BANTAM PRESS

LONDON · NEW YORK · TORONTO · SYDNEY · AUCKLAND

TRANSWORLD PUBLISHERS LTD
61–63 Uxbridge Road, London W5 5SA

TRANSWORLD PUBLISHERS (AUSTRALIA) PTY LTD
15–23 Helles Avenue, Moorebank NSW 2170

TRANSWORLD PUBLISHERS (NZ) LTD
Cnr Moselle and Waipareira Aves,
Henderson, Auckland

Published 1988 by Bantam Press,
a division of Transworld Publishers Ltd
Copyright © Robert H. Waterman, Jr. 1987

Grateful acknowledgment is made for permission to reprint the following excerpts:

Chapter 1: Albert Bandura, SOCIAL LEARNING THEORY, © 1977, p. 12. Reprinted by permission of Prentice-Hall, Inc., Englewood Cliffs, New Jersey. Myron Magnet, "Restructuring Really Works," FORTUNE, © 1987 Time Inc. All rights reserved. Chapter 2: "Notes and Comment," reprinted by permission; © 1986 The New Yorker Magazine, Inc. Ralph E. Gomory, "Technology Development," Vol. 220, pp. 576–580, 6 May 1983, © 1983 by the AAAS. Harvey M. Wagner, PRINCIPLES OF OPERATIONS RESEARCH: With Applications to Managerial Decisions, © 1969, p. 7. Reprinted by permission of Prentice-Hall Inc., Englewood Cliffs, New Jersey. David Ogilvy, OGILVY ON ADVERTISING, text copyright © 1983 by David Ogilvy. Used by permission of Crown Publishers, Inc. Chapter 3: Philip Caldwell, "Cultivating Human Potential at Ford," from JOURNAL OF BUSINESS STRATEGY SPRING 84, Vol. 4, No. 4, Copyright © 1986, Warren, Gorham & Lamont, Inc., 210 South St., Boston, MA 02111. All rights reserved. David Bradford and Allen R. Cohen, MANAGING FOR EXCELLENCE, copyright © 1984. Reprinted by permission of John Wiley & Sons, Inc. "Management by Walking Away," reprinted with permission, INC. magazine, (October 1983), copyright © 1983 by INC. Publishing Company, 38 Commercial Wharf, Boston, MA 02110. James F. Fixx, THE COMPLETE BOOK OF RUNNING, copyright © 1977 by James F. Fixx and Random House, Inc. Chapter 4: Geoffrey N. Smith, "The Yankee Samurai," excerpted by permisson of Forbes magazine, July 14, 1986, © Forbes Inc., 1986. Brenton R. Schlender, "Daisy Admits Guilt on Tax Case Filed in Massachusetts," reprinted by permission of The Wall Street Journal, © Dow Jones & Company, Inc., 1986, all rights reserved. Chapter 5: Excerpt from CAR AND DRIVER, January 1986. Copyright © 1986, CBS Magazines. Chapter 7: John W. Gardner, SELF-RENEWAL, W.W. Norton & Company, Inc., copyright © 1980, 1964, 1963 by John W. Gardner. Chapter 9: James Brian Quinn, "Strategic Goals: Process and Pitfalls," SLOAN MANAGEMENT REVIEW, Fall 1977, p. 26, by permission of the publisher. Copyright © 1977 by the Sloan Management Review Association. All rights reserved.

British Library Cataloguing in Publication Data

Waterman, Robert H.
  The renewal factor: building and
  maintaining your company's competative edge.
  1. Management
  I. Title
  658   HD31

  ISBN 0-593-01501-0

Printed in Great Britain by
Mackays of Chatham Ltd, Chatham, Kent.

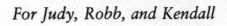

For Judy, Robb, and Kendall

ACKNOWLEDGMENTS

A team, like those we write about in this book, made both the research and the book better than it possibly could have been otherwise. Each member was crucial to the effort. They were the hearty band that left the security of big business to form Waterman & Company, whose principal business for the first year or so of its existence was to finance the research and writing of *The Renewal Factor*. All of them starred in this production. My main acknowledgments and thanks go to these four adventurers:

Sue McKibbin, a Ph.D. organizational anthropologist from the University of Illinois, contributed greatly to every part of the project. She pointed us to the relevant research in the academic world—research that would later be essential in supporting our main theses. Her knowledge of the various streams of research is matchless. In fact, she takes such delight in digging a new piece of material out of an obscure and, to my mind, just-this-side-of-unreadable publication that one of our main problems was to get her to stop uncovering new information. Sue accompanied me on much of the fieldwork, made friends with most of the top executives, middle managers, and factory workers she met, wrote better interview notes than any of us, and helped in all phases of the writing process, from original draft to detailed edits. She kept us going during the rough middle part of the process with her upbeat, irritating response to every challenge: "That'll be easy." Sue radiates, and makes the rest of us shine.

Kay Dann, my assistant for close to eight years, keeps us all organized and in fine spirits. Kay had shepherded Thomas J. Peters and me through *In Search of Excellence,* knew what it took to get a book like this researched and written, and kept us on track throughout the process. Kay is the flywheel in our small machine. She ensures we are taking our own advice on financial control. She makes sure the momentum is there and stays in place. Her combination of irreverence and good cheer seems to work magic with all the people we encounter on a venture of this magnitude, from the potentially exasperated top executives, and their assistants trying to match their own hectic schedules with my own, to the clients who help pay for research of this kind, to the occasional oddball who is attracted to causes like ours—well-meaning, to be sure, and not to be put off but to be deflected nonetheless. Kay works a charm—both inside our own organization and at the interface with us and the rest of the world—that is hard to fathom and would be impossible to replace.

Sally Hudson is pure delight. She is the quintessential example of the power of an idea we talk a lot about in this book: directed autonomy. I first met Sally when she crawled out of the depths of McKinsey & Company's secretarial pool and allowed that she would like to work with my small group. Just like other groups, we like being liked. Sally seemed capable. She clearly was eager. We said yes. Sally took over the organization of our research files, learned to use the computer, put us on data base, learned how to download financial information on companies and industries into our own financial models, learned how to use all the marvelous library services available to the microcomputer user, and got us all working facilely with Microsoft Word, a powerful word processor but overwhelming to some of us who were unfamiliar with the wonders and perplexing idiosyncrasies of such programs. During the course of the project, Sally became a full-fledged field researcher. She continues to grow and embodies the spirit of this book—continued learning, continuous renewal.

David Graulich is the fourth member of our small pride of searchers for renewal and excellence in business. David is a graduate of Dartmouth, of the staff of *The Wall Street Journal,* and of McKinsey's public relations department. His background makes him a fine field researcher. He has a keen sense of humor and his extensive outside reading of everything from the business press to books of current interest helped keep our work tied closely to the issues of the day. David stays in touch with his friends in the business community. Through that, and his reading, he was often the source of an interesting story in support of what we learned on our field trips, a good reality check on the companies we picked to study, and sometimes the champion for adding a company that the rest of us would not have thought of.

Many others were outrageously helpful along the way. Our major debt goes to the companies and people in them who supported the project. We expected that organizations would be interested in our renewal topic, but we had no feel at the outset for the enthusiasm that would greet our efforts to study and write about this important topic. With very few exceptions, the companies opened themselves completely to our research and gave us access to anyone we wished to interview, from chief executive to union leader, from secretaries to factory workers. If we missed anything about the companies we looked at, it was due to our own time constraints, not their willingness to be studied. Though we studied more than forty companies, there are many others, all over the world, who deserve to be included, who serve as elegant models of renewal, and who got left out for no better reason than our own inability to get around to them.

Of the other noble searchers for renewal in organizations, I owe special thanks to Charlie Wilson. He was of incalculable help in designing the analytic side of our method for identifying the companies we would approach and in teaching Sally Hudson how to track this information and keep it up-to-date. Others who helped get us going include Janet Abrams and Alan Sussna, Philippe Kaas, Quincy Hunsicker, Lukas Muhlemann, Brian Humphries, and Phil Cuneo were particularly gracious in helping to arrange my interviews in Europe. Special thanks go to Christopher Dann, Don Potter, and Clara Richardson. All read early drafts of the manuscript and fed back an appropriate blend of enthusiasm and criticism, strengthening the manuscript thereby.

No effort of this kind is without roots somewhere else. Of the special people in my own background who have had a profound impact on my thinking on the subject of renewal and its importance, the list starts with Susan Reed, an artist and my sister, who got me started with painting, first as a hobby and then as a serious avocation. Art is my own continuing adventure in renewal. It keeps me fresh and the business side of my life in balance. The other coach on this side of my life is Charlie Reid, a great artist, teacher, and good friend. Others on the list are people I know who set fine personal examples of renewal: Pauline and Rich Richardson, my parents-in-law, who have been knocked down by more nasty shocks in life than most of us would survive, but who bounce back from them all, always in good spirits. Ann Waterman, my stepmother, who keeps my father young and renewed, and my father, who continues to model the kind of integrity in business that we talk about in this book. Sharon Monsky, one of the best consultants I've worked with, a reader of the manuscript, and a person who, rather than being done in by a rare disease called scleroderma, renews herself and the medical profession by organizing a foundation to put research money to work against the disease. Vicky and Roger Sant, who make it their business to keep themselves, me, and most people they meet renewed in some way.

I still owe a great debt to the three who, with me, launched the research into effective organizations. Particular thanks go to Tom Peters, but also Tony Athos and Richard Pascale. Thanks also to John Stewart and Jon Katzenbach, who put me in touch with these people and both of whom are sources of clear thinking on most subjects.

The people at Bantam Books have been wonderfully supportive. My prime tribute goes to my editor, Linda Grey, who believed in the book from the beginning and contributed greatly to both its structure and its wording. Thanks also go to Alberto Vitale, who took an extraordinary interest in the book and its subject matter, and to Harriet Fier, who joined the project late but contributed much.

Rafe Sagalyn is a gem. Officially he is my agent; in reality he is much more. Champion. Coach. Contributor of many superior ideas to the manuscript. Thanks also to Philip Durbrow, Patrice Kavanaugh, and others at Landor Associates who volunteered time to help me brainstorm the subject of renewal and title ideas.

Special tribute goes to John Gardner, who has had a clear and direct impact on my thinking. In 1962 he wrote a book called *Excellence,* and in 1963 he wrote *Self-Renewal.* Though his emphasis was on the individual, with implications for the institution, and my emphasis is on the corporation, with implications for the individual, his influence is obvious.

For those to whom this book is dedicated, my family, I can offer only my most heartfelt thanks. We are close. Much of that is because of their willingness to follow and lead a continuing search for renewal and adventure. Robb's spirit, sense of humor, own writing style, and zest for adventure often set the example. Kendall's combination of wisdom, knack for humor, continuing reaction to the manuscript, spirit of support when my own spirits are low, and artistic sense keeps me going. My wife, Judy, is my best friend and coach. By early training I'm an engineer. Over the years she has taught me more than I think even she appreciates about people, the use of the language, enthusiasm, and the human side of enterprise. Judy is special.

INTRODUCTION

In today's business environment, more than in any preceding era, the only constant is change. Somehow there are organizations that effectively manage change, continuously adapting their bureaucracies, strategies, systems, products, and cultures to survive the shocks and prosper from the forces that decimate their competition. They move from strength to strength, adjusting to crises that bedevil others in their industry. They are masters of what I call *renewal*.

This book is the result of an extensive research project on the subject of managing organizational change and renewal. We spent over seven person-years doing the research and then writing *The Renewal Factor*. The project started with a list of five hundred companies in fifty-three industries. Tight financial analysis laced liberally with good judgment narrowed the list to the forty-five organizations we studied in depth. We talked to executives, managers, and employees in organizations in the United States and abroad, large and small, for profit and not. The companies we studied have two things in common: First, all are among the best in their industries or fields. Second, they have renewed. The two factors are related. Some renew with seeming ease, others with difficulty.

Our research led us to conversations with forklift drivers, bowling-ball designers, X-ray technicians, a football coach, computer scientists, potato growers, explorers for gold, and a juggling puppet at Children's Television Workshop who talked like Marlon

Brando in *The Godfather*. We obtained a foreign perspective from interviews in Europe, where a French executive advised that the key to renewal was taking baths, not showers, since baths took longer and were more conducive to creative thinking. Our extensive data collection included the *Maytag Employee Cook Book* (with recipes for Fern's Pecan Pie and Easy Does It Lasagna), a smart collection of company baseball caps, and the lyrics to a country-and-western song written by a Steelcase truck driver in honor of his truck. ("Well I took a lot of pride in my ride, but I cried, when this shiny truck pulled right up next to me.") We gained unexpected insights into the success of Humana, the health care company in Louisville, when my associate missed a step on a stairway, injured her ankle, and had to be taken to the emergency room of a Humana hospital.

From our original field research we derived eight general themes or principles for organizational renewal. Under each is a bouquet of examples, subsidiary ideas, and "how-to's." Other researchers looking at the same subject might come up with a different set of observations, or at least use different labels to describe ones similar to ours. But we seriously doubt that any managed renewal effort strays far from the themes we introduce here.

Many of the qualities that Tom Peters and I talked about in *In Search of Excellence* also help organizations renew. This is a complementary, but different, book. A strong emphasis on people as sources of renewal underlies both works. *The Renewal Factor*, however, explores the strategy dimension in more depth. It celebrates a management style that combines direction and empowerment. It stresses the liberating nature of good financial controls and a reliable fact base. *The Renewal Factor* faces squarely the political nature of companies—where politics hinders renewal and where it helps. This book deals specifically with the challenges of staying competitive in today's environment: the multiple ways renewers stay in touch, how they break bureaucracy, restructure, and yet maintain stability. Throughout, *The Renewal Factor* speaks to the challenge and the opportunity in uncertainty—how you manage when one of the few things you know for sure is that change will occur in unpredictable ways.

This book takes up where the search for excellence left off. It might be aptly subtitled *The Search Continues*. No organization can maintain excellence without renewing. No organization can strive for excellence, or even attempt to improve, without the ability to renew.

ONE

Renewal:
The Challenge

My family and I travel extensively. We like variety, new experiences, and rarely go back to a place we've been. The exception is Kona Village in Hawaii. We have been there ten times and will probably keep going back as long as it retains its special charm. I asked Alex Smith, one of Kona's managers, how they maintained such amazing constancy over the fifteen years we had been vacationing there. He smiled and said, "You've changed a lot in those years, haven't you?" We admitted that we probably had. He continued: "There's your answer. Kona Village is not the same as it was. The guests run the place. You only see it as unchanging because we have been lucky enough to do a good job of tracking the tastes and needs of people like you." Kona Village is both old and new. General Manager Fred Duerr and Alex Smith know how to retain the best of the past and still change with the times. They are a fine example of renewal.

It is more urgent today than ever that we try to understand the dynamics of renewal. There was a time in this country when, if you depleted what you had, the solution was easy. You moved somewhere else, tapped into a new set of resources, and started fresh. You walked away from the old structures. That doesn't work anymore. There's nowhere else to run; the frontiers themselves have been exhausted—with one exception: the challenge of renewal.

There was a time in this country when business was easier. We set the pace for the rest of the world. We were immune to serious foreign competition. Many of us were regulated, therefore protected. No longer. Today's leaders must re-create themselves and their ways of doing business in order to stay on top, or to stay competitive.

There was a time when people were "factors of production," managed little differently than machines or capital. No more. The best people will not tolerate it. And if that way of managing ever generated productivity, it has the reverse effect today. While capital and machines either are or can be managed toward sameness, people are individuals. They must be managed that way. When companies dispirit individuals they defeat their ability to change. When companies encourage individual expression, it is difficult for them *not* to renew. The only true source of renewal in a company is the individual.

There are great examples of renewal all around us. You see it in the faces of nurses at Humana's Louisville Hospital, where despair has been replaced by hope. Or at Nucor's mini-mill in South Carolina and at Ford's South Chicago plant, where people are prospering and building good products in industries that others have left for dead. There was renewal in the words and actions of assembly workers in the furniture factory of Steelcase in Grand Rapids, Michigan, as well as among the puppeteers of the *Sesame Street* television show and the grocers who are part of the Super Valu network of independent food stores. And then there are the companies with magnificent traditions and equally fierce determination to reverse the effects of entropy—great names such as IBM, Citicorp, J.P. Morgan, Maytag, and Hewlett-Packard.

Renewal is practiced at GE's Appliance Park in Louisville, Kentucky, where today General Electric Company manufactures some of the highest-quality refrigerators and dishwashers in the world and maintains a first-rate service organization. It wasn't always like this. "Well, back in the seventies our business was going to pot," said one employee. "People didn't care one bit. We'd build good appliances, bad appliances. It didn't matter; management didn't care."

Appliance Park was a candidate for sale or closure. It was an old plant, with old equipment, horrible relations with the union, appalling work-force attitudes, awful quality. GE was losing money on $2 billion in sales. Quality standards were so low that of every

100 appliances GE shipped, they expected 135 service calls within the warranty period. Management considered the service operation a profit center; they made money (or so some thought) on poor quality.

Within six years Roger Schipke and a small team changed that. Quality today is exemplary. Market share is up twelve points in a fiercely competitive industry. Customers are getting good products *and* great service. The union was among the first to support the new approach. Schipke and other members of the management team are rightly proud of the turnaround they've pulled off at Appliance Park.

Look at renewal's effects: the Ford automobile ten years ago versus the Ford Taurus today. Brunswick Corporation, once about to close down, now newly profitable with outboard motors and fishing reels. How a team led First Boston Corporation from nearly disappearing in 1978 to the top of investment banking today. Or how the city government of Scottsdale, Arizona, replaced factionalism and divisiveness with cooperation and a sense of shared mission.

The excitement in the potential for positive change is also apparent in smaller organizations. Chantiers Beneteau, a shipbuilding business with a proud, century-old history, was originally a manufacturer of fishing trawlers. Today they make sailing craft. Chief executive, Xavier Fontanet, quickly learned that product quality was his main problem, challenge, and opportunity. The work force had lost interest. Perhaps building pleasure boats paled in comparison with designing commercial ships. Or maybe it was the withering of an old company. The vessels produced by Chantiers Beneteau were seaworthy, but no great shakes on the fits and finishes—the trim and detail that distinguish a fine pleasure craft from an ordinary one.

Within a year Fontanet had completely changed work-force attitudes. Chantiers Beneteau was turning out ships any of us would take pride in owning. And the way they did it was annoyingly effective—annoying in its simplicity, effective in its elegance. Since ships are not mass-produced but custom-ordered, Fontanet encouraged customers to send some personal information with each order. This might include background on the family, a description of their home, photographs, and a paragraph or two on the adventures they planned with their new craft.

Workmanship began to improve at once. Photos of the customer families were pinned up next to workbenches. No longer were ships being built in the abstract. Now the men and women of Chantiers Beneteau were helping the Bancrofts in Portland, Maine, find a new, exciting dimension in their lives. They were setting a course to help Ted Hall become an accomplished racer on San Francisco Bay. They were providing the means for the family Schmidt in Hamburg to enjoy a summer sailing vacation. Fontanet had renewed his company, the builders had renewed their product, and the sailing families had renewed their lives.

There are no easy solutions to the renewal challenge. But the issue is crucial for everyone in management and it cries out for more attention. You rarely open a newspaper these days without reading of a new bankruptcy, a hostile takeover of a once proud corporation, or relentless currents of losses from companies that seemed invulnerable only a few years ago. It is a lesson to us all. Companies that fail to revitalize are easy targets. We need to learn from those who have done it well. We need to understand the best practices.

Learning from the Best

The process of learning from the best is similar to the two-part method by which most people learn to ski. The novice skier tries something new, makes mistakes, probably falls down. Then the instructor tells him what went wrong. He tries again, maybe getting it right, and the instructor says, "Good job." The psychologists call this kind of learning *behavior modification*.

But the student in ski school learns only half the lesson this way. The other half happens when the instructor does it right, the student follows the expert down the hill, and the student improves. Imitative learning. A few psychologists, most notably Albert Bandura at Stanford, have studied this kind of learning. In one well-known experiment, Bandura exposed children via taped pictures on television to violent behavior in adults. Later the children were more violent, and the means they chose to express their violence were copies of the behavior they'd seen in the videos. Bandura states:

In actuality, virtually all learning phenomena resulting from direct experience occur on a vicarious basis by observing other people's behavior and its consequences for them. The capacity to learn by observation enables people to acquire large, integrated patterns of behavior without having to form them gradually by tedious trial and error.

Bandura further points out: "Learning would be exceedingly laborious, not to mention hazardous, if people had to rely solely on the effects of their own actions to inform them what to do." His studies show that we learn most from those we regularly associate with and from those we admire.

We underutilize this powerful notion. Psychologists, as a general rule, don't do as much with it as they might. In a widely used current psychology text there are twenty pages on trial and error—behavior modification-type learning—and only two pages on learning by imitation.

Business schools depend heavily on the case method. The class debates issues while the teacher acts as moderator. The case method is trial-and-error learning for the most part—learning that tends to center on the negative aspects of the case: "What's going wrong here? What do we do about it?"

Every day we are exposed to the negative view of business. Flip on the television and watch business portrayed in the news by *60 Minutes* or by *Dallas* or *Dynasty*. What we see is the vaguely evil, sinister, mistake-making side of life in the world of organizations. Power politics and shady deals. Where are the role models, the examples—which in fact abound—of those who are doing it right? We don't see enough of the good side, and we seriously limit our ability to learn about management as a result.

But there are people who *do* do it right and they seem to have a common vision. They are the renewers, and while their lessons can be organized in many ways, the eight themes that emerge as most important are:

1. INFORMED OPPORTUNISM

Renewing organizations set direction for their companies, not detailed strategy. They are the best of strategists precisely because they are suspicious of forecasts and open to surprise. They know the value of being prepared, and they also know that some of the most important strategic decisions they make are inherently unpredictable. They think strategic planning is great—as long as no one takes the plans too seriously. They often see more value in the process of planning than in the plan itself.

Wells Fargo executives, who do plenty of planning, never would have guessed they would be acquiring Crocker Bank. And when Porsche's newly appointed CEO, Peter Schutz, was asked to prepare a ten-year plan, he says, "I thought about that assignment for a while and then started calling peer CEOs, asking about their ten-year plans, *the ones from 1972.* What do you suppose was in those plans? Did AT&T anticipate the Carter phone decision? Did IBM predict the PC market? Did United Airlines forecast deregulation? Of course not."

The renewing companies treat information as their main strategic advantage, and flexibility as their main strategic weapon. They assume opportunity will keep knocking, but it will knock softly and in unpredictable ways. Their ability is to sense opportunity where others can't, see it where others don't, act while others hesitate, and demur when others plunge. They behave as *informed opportunists*—equal emphasis given to both words in the phrase. One very successful executive in the minerals business captured the points on information and opportunity beautifully: "I tell my geologists I want them to be 'Fred Astaires'—intellectually quick, nimble, and ready to act."

The process of planning has multiple purposes; for many the process was more important than the plan itself. While poking good-natured fun at some of their own past plans that went awry, the renewers seem to know how important the process can be in generating information, in identifying issues, in improving communications, in reinforcing the culture, in supporting the financial control system, and in identifying possible crisis points.

2. DIRECTION AND EMPOWERMENT

The renewing companies treat *everyone* as a source of creative input. What's most interesting is that they cannot be described as either democratically or autocratically managed. Their managers define the boundaries, and their people figure out the best way to do the job within those boundaries. Steelcase, the nation's premier office furniture company, designs and makes its own factory equipment. They admit to being fanatics when it comes to efficient manufacturing. But they won't bend metal on a new machine until the operator has had a chance to review the design, make modifications, and approve the final design. Their management style, like that of many of the renewing companies, is an astonishing combination of direction and empowerment.

They give up a measure of control in order to gain control over what counts: results. When Ford embarked on the program to build the highly successful Taurus, management showed the tentative design to the work force and asked for their help in devising a car that would be easy to build. The Ford designers and engineers willingly lost tight "control" in the classic sense. What they got in return was a winning product.

When people are treated as the main engine rather than interchangeable parts of the corporate machine, motivation, creativity, quality, and commitment to implementation well up. Maytag estimates that 20 percent of their productivity gains come from worker ideas; the rest come from improvements in technology. But Maytag managers hasten to add that focusing on the other 80 percent is missing the point. Maytag wouldn't get any productivity improvement *unless* they were asking for ideas and getting the whole company on the same side of the productivity issue.

3. FRIENDLY FACTS, CONGENIAL CONTROLS

The renewing companies treat facts as friends, and financial controls as liberating. Morgan and Wells Fargo not only survive but sail through the troubled waters of bank deregulation because their control systems are sound, their risk is contained, and they know themselves and the competitive situation so well.

Renewing companies have a voracious hunger for facts. They see information where others see only data. They love comparisons, rankings, measurements, anything that provides context and removes decision-making from the realm of mere opinion. Meanwhile, the renewers maintain tight, accurate, real-time financial controls. Their people don't regard financial controls as an imposition of autocracy, but as the benign checks and balances that allow them to be creative and free.

4. A DIFFERENT MIRROR

Habit breaking, the prerequisite for change and renewal, needs more than a simple decision to do it. It takes motivation, desire, and will. Crisis can provide that. But the leaders of renewing organizations seem to get their determination from their singular ability to anticipate crisis. That stems from their continuing willingness to look into "a different mirror."

IBM looks at "best of breed." The Ford Taurus team looked at "best of class." Maytag put wooden models of a proposed new product in shopping malls to gauge customer reaction. Steelcase executives publish their home phone numbers to emphasize their open door policy, get feedback from the folks. David Jones, CEO of Humana Corporation, attends public meetings on health care in order to tape-record and analyze the question-and-answer sessions. The techniques are more numerous and varied than the companies we talked to, but the intent is the same.

These renewing companies get their passport to reality stamped regularly. Their leaders listen. They are open, curious, and inquisitive. They get ideas from customers, suppliers, front-line employees, competitors, politicians—almost anyone outside the hierarchy. An executive at a high-tech company said that one different mirror for him was serving on the board of a declining company in smokestack America. "That whole industry seems trapped in a disastrous set of habits," he remarked. "It has made me especially sensitive to the habit patterns that will make or break us."

5. TEAMWORK, TRUST, POLITICS, AND POWER

A high level of backbiting politics, no teamwork, no set of shared business values, and maybe vast business diversity combine in a sure recipe for stagnation. This is a deadly combination. Purposeful change becomes almost impossible. Even well-meaning individuals cannot afford to trust one another's agenda. Dana continues to be one of the most successful companies in the truck and auto parts business. They continue to set the pace for enlightened management of a unionized work force. One of the reasons Dana works, say their top executives, is that trust is a given: You don't have to earn it; you start with it.

Renewers constantly use words such as *teamwork* and *trust*. They are relentless in fighting office politics and power contests, and in breaking down the we/they barriers that paralyze action. They are heroic leaders, but not lone rangers: little emphasis on charisma; rather, they are outstanding people, supported by others with complementary skills. Most of the renewing companies had a calm at the center; there was quiet intensity and determination without the helter-skelter behavior, slamming doors, shouting voices, frenetic movement, and general bedlam that poses for productive activity at stagnating companies.

While it seems manifest that those who make change happen are politically skilled and understand the use of power, in a positive sense of that word, still the words themselves—*politics, power*—are so loaded, so rightfully suspect, that those who are good at politics and power often deny it. And because their denials suggest their ambivalence on the skilled uses of politics and power, they confuse the hell out of the young in their organizations. Unless our management vocabulary is enriched on the good and bad uses of power and politics, vacuums will continue to be created, then filled by idealistic innocents who can't get much done, and by manipulators who get themselves advanced but stand for nothing.

6. STABILITY IN MOTION

The renewing companies know how to keep things moving. If they share a habit pattern, it's the habit of habit breaking. Sometimes they seem to change for its own sake. IBM's chief executive, John Akers, smiles and says that they never reorganize except for a good business reason, but if they haven't reorganized in a while, "that's a good business reason." Renewing companies are deliberate bureaucracy-busters. They delight in smashing the pettifogging encumbrances that printing entrepreneur Harry Quadracci calls "playing office." But they do that against a base of underlying stability.

In many of the renewing companies we found all sorts of devices to keep the organization fluid. People move more often and with greater degrees of freedom across functions, divisions, from line to staff and vice versa. They move laterally. Some move down, but without the stigma that moving down means moving out. Promotion from within is the rule, but key skills are brought in when needed from the outside. Unusual budget and organizational arrangements are used to promote creativity—at Heinz's Ore-Ida division, it is a Fellows program; at Super Valu, a cross-pollination of ideas from the hundreds of independent grocers who are the company's customers and partners; at Steelcase, James River, and Dana, a determination to keep manufacturing plants small.

Renewal requires a constant interplay between stability and change. Morgan or Hewlett-Packard can move people around with relative ease because there is a safety net, a home base. Nucor, the mini-mill steel company, is absolutely dependent on producing more with fewer people. So is Maytag. Both have been able to automate continuously *because* they don't lay people off. They retrain them. They grow. They let attrition take its normal course. Most of the good companies look for the best people, enforce high performance standards, and then hold a very large safety net under them. They offer security of employment, not position.

There was a nice expression of bureaucracy-busting when Grace Hopper, Navy rear admiral and co-author of the Cobol computer language, retired after a forty-two-year military career. The Secretary of the Navy said she "challenged at every turn the dictates of mindless bureaucracy." In her retirement speech, her advice to the rest of us expressed the secret of her accomplishments: "Go ahead and do it; you can always apologize later."

7. ATTITUDES AND ATTENTION

Visible management attention, rather than management exhortation, gets things done. Action may start with the words, but it has to be backed by symbolic behavior that makes those words come alive. When GE was having massive quality problems with their refrigerators, production manager Don Kelley bought traffic lights, installed them in the factory, and programmed them to go red every time quality dropped to unacceptable levels. Assembly lines would shut down, regardless of the production schedule, and wouldn't reopen without Kelley's inspection and approval. Moreover, he risked censure from the corporate auditors by continuing to pay incentives *even though* the lines were shut down because of poor quality. He was trying to say: "Quality counts, and I really mean it. We're not trying to attach blame, just get it right." Words would not have been half as powerful as his actions.

Attention makes a difference, and so do attitudes and expectations. If I expect you to do well, you probably will do well, and if I expect the reverse, you probably won't do as well. Psychologists call it the Pygmalion effect. Managers who renew companies seem to understand it. When Carlo De Benedetti took the helm in Ivrea, Italy, to try to rescue the fast-sinking Olivetti Corporation, he raised prices. He explained that the last thing he needed was to intensify the efforts to cut costs. The people already thought of themselves as losers; he believed he had to find a way to reverse that attitude. He did, and it worked.

8. CAUSES AND COMMITMENT

Man is a maker of meanings in a world that sometimes seems without meaning. Few things help us find meaning more than a cause to believe in, better yet, about which to get excited.

Renewing organizations seem to run on causes. Quality is the most prevalent cause, even for longtime champs like Maytag and Hewlett-Packard. At Ford, it's employee involvement *and* quality *and* the customer. At Club Med, the cause is to make each person's vacation an escape, "an antidote to civilization." Dana Corporation has always rallied around "productive people"; now they've added the need to become more responsive to the market-place, to be "market-driven." The cause that brought alive the San Francisco Symphony was its aspiration to be among the world's great orchestras and to be recognized as world class. Renewers seem able to pick causes and communicate them in a way that conveys an element of risk—of challenge—but not fool-ishly so. Renewing companies constantly review their causes in light of the issues: the major problems and opportunities that shift with time. They seem to be able to turn tedious issues into noble causes. With effort, they do so in ways that enhance the dignity of the people they employ.

Causes are one thing; commitment is another. Commitment is not something that emanates from management edict. Instead, it results from extensive communication and management's ability to turn grand causes into small actions so that people throughout the organization can contribute to the central purpose. But there's a trap in moving from cause to commitment. In taking small steps, people often become more committed than they realize. The business of engendering commitment has to be approached thought-fully on two dimensions. First, the very commitment that caused renewal at one time can blind a company to the need to renew along other dimensions at another time. Second, management's efforts to gain commitment must stem from solid, worthwhile values. Leaders use the same means to gain commitment that others use to manipulate.

Surrender the Memories

Historian J. H. Elliott composed an epitaph to describe the de-cline of Imperial Spain during the seventeenth century:

Heirs to a society which had over-invested in empire, and surrounded by the increasingly shabby remnants of a dwin-dling inheritance, they could not bring themselves at the moment of crisis to surrender their memories and alter the antique pattern of their lives. At a time when the face of

*Europe was altering more rapidly than ever before, the coun-
try that had once been its leading power proved to be lacking
the essential ingredient for survival—the willingness to change.*

Elliott might just as easily have dedicated his epitaph to an
uncomfortably large number of U.S. businesses in the 1970s and
1980s. Simply stated, these have not been fun years for many an
American businessman. With frustrating regularity the Japanese,
the Germans, the Koreans, the French, and the Italians have
beaten up on American companies in industries that the United
States used to *own*. Why?

It's all well and good to speak of Japan Inc., unlevel playing
fields, cheaper labor, or tariff protection. Rationalizations abound.
The reality is that we deserved to get whipped. The Japanese were
never magic. We were snoozing; we were arrogant; we didn't
care. We were getting thrashed, battered, knocked, whacked, and
blasted, because our managers didn't care about quality, had
stopped investing in technology, had developed disdain for the
people who worked for them and for the customers who bought
their products. Maybe not in all cases, but in some very big, very
important ones.

As the only major economy spared the destruction of World
War II, the United States enjoyed a remarkable hegemony after
1945. It was hard *not* to make money. Europe was primarily a
second-tier dumping ground for excess domestic goods; Asia meant
cheap cigarette lighters and tinny knockoffs. Many U.S. basic
industries were sheltered from competition by dense regulation.
It was too good to last, and it didn't.

Starting in the late 1960s, American managers—who had
been telling the rest of the world how good they were—were
smashed by wave after wave of change that was unprecedented in
their collective experience. Inflation and interest rates shot up like
Chuck Yeager in an X15 as the United States tried simultaneously
to wage war in Vietnam and underwrite the Great Society. We
left the comfort of the gold standard, and somewhere between
there and the oil embargo, the United States was thrown into
global competition. We had to surrender two and a half decades
of memories.

The huge North American market had previously swallowed up almost everything a domestic producer could produce. Now we had to compete seriously in non-U.S. markets, going head-to-head against determined, patient, well-financed foreign companies that often had state backing. Hewlett-Packard, for example, primarily domestic a few decades ago, now generates more than half its revenues abroad. And because our overseas competitors—the Europeans, Australians, Japanese, the "Little Dragons" like Taiwan and Hong Kong—have always been dependent on foreign trading partners, they tend to be better at international collaboration than Americans.

Meanwhile, the Carter and Reagan administrations were introducing large-scale deregulation, reconfiguring such industries as banking, savings and loans, trucking, airlines, telecommunications, and securities. The ensuing upheaval demonstrated that the onus for economic decline could not be solely on American manufacturers. There was plenty amiss in the highly touted service sector also. In the banking industry, for example, deregulation ended decades of comfortable, predictable, profitable routine. In the 1960s one personnel director of a bank had a policy of hiring "C" (or below) students because "not much happens in banking. We have trouble with the brighter folks, who get bored." Today bankers must compete across state and national lines with foreign banks and with unlikely new adversaries, such as Sears and American Can, (Primerica) both of whom have diversified into financial services. Thus, global banking mirrors other industries. Twenty years ago, a list of the world's ten largest banks had American names at numbers 1 through 10. The same list today has only two U.S. banks. There are more Japanese banks in the top fifty financial institutions of the world (sixteen) than American (seven).

For some observers, the American decline was inevitable, unavoidable, and unlamentable. Like the Spanish empire, we had our day in the sun. This line of thought gave rise to public policy questions: Should we pull the plug on mortally wounded industries, like steel? Erect stiff protectionist barriers to protect ailing ones, like semiconductors? Berate our trading partners and threaten to retaliate because they dared to make products preferred by American consumers?

Then, a generation of young Americans came of age and began careers with the conviction that the business of buying and selling companies was a quicker path to riches than working for them. How mundane merely to run a department or a division of a corporation. How exciting to use the magic of junk bonds or other creative paper to swap and sell entire corporations in the role of investment banker, or takeover attorney, or securities trader, or, yes, management consultant. Why wait tables in the lounge when you can roll dice in the casino? Why take a job where you have to manage assets, when trading them is so much more lucrative? No employees to worry about. No tiresome products that need quality engineering and caring workmanship. Not even any customers, in the conventional sense of the word. Just a Quotron screen, some numbers to crunch, an airline ticket, and a voracious client with capital to spend (not too much cash, though, since vertigo-inducing leverage is the name of this game).

John Gardner wrote in *Self-Renewal* that institutional arrangements of a society are not themselves the means for renewal. Their redeeming virtue—the main reason a free society bothers to keep institutions around—is that they nourish the free individual, and such people are inexhaustible sources of renewal.

In concept at least, we build organizations to meet our needs as individuals. *Our needs*—as customers, as employees, as managers, as shareholders, as citizens. But all too often, quietly and slowly, and while we're not really watching, we're trapped by the very thing we've built to serve us. Suddenly we find ourselves enslaved by mindless bureaucracy, by habit, or simply by comfort. People, the only real sources of renewal, stop trying. Customers vanish. The best employees lapse into apathy, or vote with their feet and leave.

The challenge is a tough one and not unique to corporations. We are commonly trapped by the things we seek: material possessions, fame and glory, the good life. Governments, including elected ones, often ignore or suppress the will of the governed. The challenge is never completely solved; it recurs like weeds in a garden. But the challenge is far from impossible. The essence of living, really living, is renewal. And the highest expression of management art is the manager's ability to renew a department, a division, a company, himself. Without renewal there can be no excellence.

The Habit Trap

Organizations, like people, are creatures of habit. For organizations, the habits are existing norms, systems, procedures, written and unwritten rules—"the way we do things around here." Over time these habits become embedded like rocks in a glacial moraine.

For example, IBM is a company with as strong a culture and as good a knack for renewal as any, but its managers admit that in the mid-1970s they just plain missed the market for minicomputers, the refrigerator-sized machines that would give customers an alternative to IBM's tractor-sized mainframes. IBM had a mainframe habit, and for a long time even this superbly managed company could not bring itself to compete effectively against upstart minicomputer companies like Digital Equipment Corporation or Hewlett-Packard.

Psychologists and physiologists call the phenomenon *habituation* and have measured its effects through brain waves, eye movements, and skin resistance to electricity. Repeat a sharp noise every five seconds; then measure its effect on an animal or a human. The first sound will cause a sharp drop in skin resistance. The second sound will cause a smaller drop, the third still less, as the response of the skin becomes "habituated." When we see an unfamiliar image, our eyes tend to move in a new pattern around it, but as we view it repeatedly, we tend to look in a fixed way at the same portions of it and ignore the rest. Stanford University researcher Karl Pribram has pointed out what he calls "the Bowery El effect." A noisy elevated train used to run along Third Avenue in New York City. After it was torn down, "many people in the neighborhood began to call the police quite late to report 'something strange' occurring—unusual noises, suspected thieves or burglars. . . . The police determined that these calls took place at about the time the former late-night train would have passed these people's houses. What they were 'hearing,' of course, was the *absence* of the familiar noise of the train."

The renewal dilemma is that habits are useful. With habits you and I navigate daily through life's jungle of complexity. They enable quick responses to routine—everything from brushing your teeth in the morning to handling payroll checks at the office every two weeks. The displacement of habits can be terribly unsettling for people, whether it be the neighbors of the Bowery El, a stranded commuter trying to figure out a new train schedule, or the train company itself adjusting to a new organizational structure. A friend who was close to the formation of Conrail, the company created by the shotgun wedding of several regional railroads, observed that the lack of habits in the new entity drove people crazy. "Every problem that came up was being solved for the first time," he said. "They were so new that there were no standard ways of doing anything."

But as useful as habits are in one sense, they are also the main obstruction in the constant struggle to respond to a changing world. Most of us have bad habits we'd like to lose, but if they appeared on last year's list of New Year's resolutions, they'll probably reappear on this year's list. To paraphrase Mark Twain: Habits can't be flung out the window; they have to be coaxed downstairs, a step at a time. Most habits are as difficult for organizations to break as for individuals. For companies, the better they have done in the past, the more deeply grooved they are apt to become in their habits.

Psychologist and philosopher William James, writing in 1890, stated the case for habit in a smoothly functioning society, but also drew a bleak picture of entrapment and despair:

Habit is thus the enormous fly-wheel of society, its most precious conservative agent. It alone is what keeps us all within the bounds of ordinance, and saves the children of fortune from the envious uprisings of the poor. It alone prevents the hardest and most repulsive walks of life from being deserted by those brought up to tread therein. It keeps the fisherman and the deck-hand at sea through the winter; it holds the miner in his darkness, and nails the country-

*man to his log-cabin and his lonely farm through all the
months of snow; it protects us from invasion by the natives
of the desert and the frozen zone. It dooms us all to fight out
the battle of life upon the lines of our early choice, and to
make the best of a pursuit that disagrees, because there is no
other for which we are fitted and it is too late to begin again.*

As James suggests, habits draw from something primitive and raw
within ourselves, some primal source so deeply rooted that we
experience animal fear when renewal requires massive change of
habit. A mid-level manager once said, "Sure it's a jungle in here,
but it is the jungle I live in, and I know my way around." People
in an organization may know painfully well how flawed their
work world is, but it is a world they know, and therefore one that
is comfortable.

J.P. Morgan regularly appears at the top of *Fortune's* "most
admired companies" list in terms of "quality of management"
and "ability to attract, develop, and keep talented people." Perhaps one reason is their understanding of the fear that accompanies
change. Recently they went through a big reorganization that
broke a lot of habits and had major implications for everyone's
career. The Morgan people said that both Chief Executive Lewis
Preston and President Dennis Weatherstone realized the importance of being visible and articulate about the proposed change.
They spent an unusual amount of time listening, explaining, and
listening some more before reorganizing in order to allay the fear
of the unknown that always is a partner to change.

Not the least of the fears about change is that, deprived of
the protective cushion of habit, you might do something that
looks foolish. You might have to make what billionaire investor
Warren E. Buffett calls "the intelligent-but-with-some-chance-
of-looking-like-an-idiot decision." Strip away the habits and you
can feel stripped of your identity. Jack MacAllister, chief executive officer of US West, can attest to that. When the Bell System
was broken up in 1984—one of the momentous changes in American business history—AT&T named MacAllister to run one of
the seven independent new companies. MacAllister seems to thrive
on change; he takes pride in having been a rebel inside the old

AT&T system. While he could have operated the new company out of Northwestern Bell offices in Omaha, he chose to start fresh at a new location in Denver. "When I got to Denver," Jack recalls, "I was applying for a department store credit card. The lady behind the counter asked me to fill out the standard application, and I had to explain that I was the designated president of an unnamed company with no address and, as yet, no employees. She thought about that for a moment, frowned, and said, 'Look, it would be easier if you just put *unemployed.*' "

A short-term loan from the science of physics helps explain the true nature of the renewal challenge. *Entropy* is a principle of physics that measures the disorder in a closed system. A derivative of the second law of thermodynamics, entropy says that everything that is organized will break down or run down unless it is maintained. Science writer Boyce Rensberger explains:

Examples of entropy's workings can be found throughout the everyday world. Desks will get messy. Cars will wear out. Stars will blow up. Without librarians, books get scattered and jumbled. Lacking nutrients, organisms die and rot. In each case, a highly organized system will inevitably proceed to a state of disorder and chaos unless energy (which is equivalent to work) is brought into the system to re-establish order.

A company, even one with a long history of good performance, needs to introduce fresh management energy into its system to stave off the inexorable forces of decay. One way to think about renewal, then, is as the antidote for corporate entropy.

Some challenges are for solving and others are for living with, as Tony Athos, author and former Harvard professor, keeps reminding us. Renewal is one for living with. It's a constant challenge, never . . . quite . . . solved. But renewal can be just the thing to put the fun and adventure back into business. Renewal is an alternative to the dreary stuff that seems to constitute many jobs: the meetings, reports, routines, and monotony that rob the spirit and dull the soul. Instead of being a daily drudgery, work in a renewing organization becomes a form of expression, a vehicle for excitement, a source of energy and drive. You know you are in a renewing organization when people use words like *purpose* and *meaning* and *adventure*.

One key distinction: Renewers are not zealots on crusades. If recent history has taught us anything, it is about the danger to all societies when persons construct missions that serve their own designs and then set out indiscriminately to fulfill them. The driving force for renewal is an agreeable combination of hope and realism, a spirit that philosopher John Gardner calls "tough-minded optimism." It is a spirit that more closely represents the thinking of an astute, prudent, and perceptive builder than that of an impassioned extremist.

The wave of restructuring, spinoffs, mergers, and acquisitions is no fluke. That phenomenon states plainly that entropy in corporate America had reached an intolerably high level. As a recent *Fortune* article says, "So far, the evidence overwhelmingly shows restructuring to be a powerful force for economic improvement despite its painful and regrettable human cost." That we should have to pay that cost is more than regrettable. It's an indictment of management's past. It clearly says that we did not know how to manage renewal. For any future management team it would be unacceptable performance. Crucial as it is, renewal resists any quick fix or easy delineation. Louis Armstrong's reply to a question about the definition of jazz offers tempting refuge: "Man, if you gotta ask, you'll never know."

Still, to further describe the endeavor, here are a few things renewal is *not*:

Renewal is not change or change management. Change is the lubricant for renewal, but change by itself is not enough. An organization in eclipse changes. Companies change if enmeshed in internal political battles or enslaved by the great gods Growth and Quarterly Earnings. Acquisitive executives, betting big bucks on businesses they don't know, change things. Executives who take on massive, maybe imprudent, debt to stave off takeovers are changing things. But changes like these don't necessarily renew; they often leave companies less able to serve customers, their own employees, and eventually their shareholders.

Renewal is not the binges of conglomerateurs who buy and

sell businesses they don't understand. It certainly isn't the poorly managed large company that buys a well-managed, profitable smaller company to bolster its own sagging cash flows, suffocating the acquired company in the process. On the other hand, there are many companies like James River who use acquisitions to enact renewal. James River buys paper mills that are the neglected stepchildren of other companies, reenergizes the work force, improves the paper-making technology, and creates better jobs for the employees, better products for the customers, and wealth for the James River shareholders.

Renewal is not the greenmail tactics of corporate raiders who, with the collusion of acquiescent managements, play games of self-interest with shareholders' money and then make eloquent speeches about the glories of the free-market system. The fact that the greenmail opportunity exists at all is a compelling case for renewal. The takeover wave in this country is only partly due to relaxation of regulatory pressure. Much of it stems from opportunity: the opportunity created by sleepy companies that did not renew. Corporate raiders can help the renewal cause by busting up a stagnant company, or one that never should have been put together in the first place. But when the outcome of a hostile raid is management's repurchase of shares from the raider at a price far in excess of prior market value, the whole thing has the suspicious smell of managers acting in their own interest, not the shareholders'.

Renewal is not the actions of an entrenched corporate management that suddenly wakes up to the need for cost containment and invokes "cost control" to make wholesale layoffs, reneges on pension and retirement plans, waters down product quality, short-changes suppliers, and slashes research. Some situations do get so grave that desperate measures have to be taken to salvage the company. But you have to wonder why these companies reached such a state of crisis in the first place.

Renewal is not growth for growth's sake. Growth can be renewal, but the motives for it have to be closely examined, because growth can also be decay expertly disguised. Too often the pursuit of growth is nothing more than a combination of executive ego, executive boredom, and the reality that the size of the executive paycheck is more closely correlated to company size than to anything else.

Renewal, after all, is about builders. Many people can introduce change for change's sake and call it renewal. That is illusory. A builder, on the other hand, leads an organization toward renewal that outlives the presence of any single individual and revitalizes even as it changes.

There are three kinds of managers. First, there are the custodians, the ones who are just there. Their main concern is what British diplomats used to call "masterly inactivity"—to make sure nothing happens on their watch. Since the world is changing fast, something does happen; their unit atrophies.

The second kind is a manipulator of wealth. He is busy doing financial deals. He may get rich. But no wealth is created. He contributes nothing to growth in gross national product. At best, wealth is merely transferred from one set of hands to another; at worst, wealth is destroyed. The sorry record of most attempts at diversification, painted by the conglomerates in colors no one could miss, bears strong witness to the impact of the destroyers. Warren Buffett calls the syndrome "gin rummy management" and describes its practitioners as "revolving-door capitalists." He's taking verbal aim at the teeming deal-doers, both those willing to discard their least-promising business at each change in competitive fortunes and those whose main interest is to see businesses "put in play," to use the phrase currently hot among the investment bankers.*

Custodians on the one side, gin players on the other. Fortunately for us all, there is a third kind of manager. These are the builders, the transforming leaders who go to work with the belief that they can make things somehow better. This book is about this third type, the builders and the beamish, the managers who make a difference. They are not content with "just being there," nor are they preoccupied with the corporate gin rummy games. Some of the builders are entrepreneurs, the new American folk

---

* As Buffett knows from tough personal experience, sometimes a business has to be discarded. He had to take Berkshire Hathaway out of the textile business, and, as he describes it, the decision was personal agony for Buffett and his partners. He has profited hugely from acquisitions like See's Candies and Precision Steel. But Buffett creates—not just transfers—wealth for his shareholders and the economy.

heroes, of whom we ought to be justly proud. Some of the builders are the deal makers who kick sleepy companies into this decade. But the majority of the builders are—and always will be a much larger and more significant number—everyday corporate managers who simply find ways to renew and refresh their units, their departments, their companies. These are the leaders who generate excellence, the ones we need to study, to emulate, to understand.

TWO

The Informed Opportunists

Chance favors only the mind that is prepared.

—LOUIS PASTEUR

*As a general rule the most successful man in life is
the man who has the best information.*

—BENJAMIN DISRAELI

*To prophesy is extremely difficult—especially with
respect to the future.*

—CHINESE PROVERB

Following the true strategic path of a company is a little like
watching a butterfly make its way through a sunny meadow. It
may be going somewhere but its path looks random, inefficient,
irrational. The reason for the erratic, seemingly haphazard behavior of companies is the elusive nature of opportunity, which
knocks frequently, it seems to me, but often in disguise and
usually unexpectedly. What's more, bad deals dress up like opportunity and seduce some of the most deliberate strategic thinkers.

Not long ago, in an issue of a business magazine, one president of a successful company declared that an organization cannot move ahead without a clear picture of where it is going.

Strategists often make a similar point by paraphrasing the Cheshire Cat's advice to Alice: If you don't care where you're going, any road will take you there. But these folks seem to be asking for a clarity that just isn't there. *The New Yorker* made this observation about strategy: "When it comes to forecasts—of the weather, of the price of oil, of hemlines—we're so used to surprises by now that if there is no surprise that's the biggest surprise." Exactly! It certainly has a more honest ring to it than the call for "clear direction." But strategy *is* important. The problem is, how do you resolve, even think about, the dilemma? Strategy is needed; the future is mainly unpredictable.

So, what do successful corporate strategies look like? It's common for the big decisions made by companies or divisions to come as a surprise—not just to the company's competitors or the business press, but to the company itself.

Wells Fargo Bank is a wonderful case in point. Five years ago they had the lowest return on their portfolio of any major California bank; today they have the highest. Five years ago they were among the highest cost operators in their industry. Today they are the lowest among the large West Coast banks. Today their market capitalization—the company's stock price multiplied by the number of common shares outstanding—is fourth in the nation, just behind perennial giants like Morgan, Citicorp, and Bankers Trust. In 1985, Wells capped its amazing surge by spending just over a billion dollars to buy Crocker Bank, in what has been acclaimed as one of the most skillful deals in post-deregulation American banking.

CEO Carl Reichardt says, "You talk about strategies. Who would ever have guessed that we would acquire Crocker?" Now, Wells Fargo does plenty of planning, but the biggest strategic decision they have made in years—the Crocker acquisition—was unplanned. It started with a low-key inquiry by Wells Fargo about buying a few Crocker branch sites. This modest inquiry set events in motion that led to Wells's purchase of the entire bank in what was the largest U.S. bank offering ever. Both the acquisition itself and the great speed with which it was completed were entirely unanticipated by Wells's top management.

On a smaller scale, but strategic nonetheless, we have the case of the Dreyer's Grand Ice Cream Company, a thriving firm in Oakland, California, often cited as one of America's most dynamic small businesses. Its main strategic event, and a major source of renewal, came when its current CEO, Gary Rogers, was driving by Dreyer's headquarters one rainy afternoon in 1977. Gary had been a consultant, then an entrepreneur who was failing in the theme restaurant business. He was casting about, and on a whim wandered into the Dreyer's office to ask if there were any materials on ice-cream franchising or ice-cream shops. "I asked the receptionist, and she told me: 'No, we really don't have anything like that, but why don't you talk to our president about it?' I said, 'Okay, fine.'

"So I sat down with this man I had never met before and he began to answer my questions. Then the phone rang. He took the call—it was obviously an important conversation—and when he hung up the phone he was quite emotional. I started to excuse myself. He said, 'Don't leave. Let me tell you what just happened. Dreyer's has started to grow fast and I am out of capacity in my plant here. I am desperate to build a new plant, and I went to the bank to apply for a loan to build it. They just called to turn me down. I don't know what I am going to do.'

"It was in that moment, knowing nothing about the ice-cream business, that I blurted out, 'Have you ever considered selling your company?' Two days later I had an option to buy it." Gary raced about to line up the financing, depending on his many contacts in investment banking from his previous ventures in food service and restaurants. "What changed my life—call it ability or instinct or just willingness to play at the table—was that most people, having just met someone for twenty minutes, wouldn't have said, 'Hey, do you want to sell your business?' "

The phenomenon is general; it goes beyond acquisition. It applies, in retrospect, to every strategic move made by companies, divisions, departments, and people. The well-known story of the Post-it note at 3M best illustrates the point. Post-it may be the product 3M is best known for these days; with sales of more than several hundred million dollars, it has to be counted a grand strategic success. Its origins were a series of happy accidents, anything but carefully planned.

Art Fry, the champion behind the Post-it, recalls that he got the idea when he was singing in a church choir. The pieces of paper he used to mark his place in the hymnal often would fall out before the second service. Why not, he reasoned, develop a marker with sticky stuff on the back, one that would stick to a page but could be removed without damaging the hymnal?

Meanwhile, Spence Silver in another 3M division had been trying to produce a supersticky bonding agent. What he actually produced was some goo that was sticky but didn't stick all that well. A failure in terms of Silver's plan. Just what was needed for Fry's Post-it. Two happy accidents. One grand strategic success.

Banking, ice cream, note pads. Stories like these are common among renewing companies. The big opportunities that lead to renewal, and the strategic decisions that capture them, seem more like the whimsical flight of a butterfly than the path of a carefully aimed arrow.

In an essay by Herbert Simon, "The Psychology of Thinking," the author asks us to imagine an ant making its way across a windswept beach. Wells Fargo, Dreyer's, and similar examples come to mind. Simon, a Nobel laureate in economics, describes the ant's laborious path—angling to the right to ease the climb up a steep dunelet, detouring around a pebble, stopping for a moment to chat with a compatriot:

> *Thus [the ant] makes his weaving, halting way back to his home. So as not to anthropomorphize about his purposes, I sketch the path on a piece of paper. It is a sequence of irregular, angular segments—not quite a random walk, for it has an underlying sense of direction, of aiming toward a goal.*

The ant metaphor, writes Simon, provides a good model for behavior by non-ants. "Viewed as a geometric figure, the ant's path is irregular, complex, hard to describe. But its complexity is really a complexity in the surface of the beach, not a complexity of the ant." In the same sense, much of corporate behavior is fairly simple. It's the complicated environment that makes what we do look complex.

When an organization seeks renewal, it resembles an ant on the beach. Renewal tends not to be a straight-line process that gets executed by the numbers according to a master plan. Instead, it's irregular, angular, hard to describe, yet pulled by an underlying sense of direction. The process of renewal is complex, but it is a complexity of the environment, not of the strategy. The problem for the manager, as usual, is what to do.

A quiet revolution has taken place. It goes beyond conventional models of planning and implementation. It's a revolution unmarked by a signal event or a philosophical center. But somewhere between the groundbreaking work of organizational thinkers like Herb Simon, and the firsthand experiences of the executives we interviewed, there is a way of managing—call it "informed opportunism." It's a fusion of the rational and the random; it is a salient energy source for organizations as they strive to renew.

For years Shell has been one of the top-performing oil companies. What was most interesting about them was their exploration record offshore, which was among the best in the world—perhaps *the* best. The reason was their unusual ability to renew oil resources. Charlie Blackburn, now president of Diamond Shamrock Exploration, was in charge of oil exploration for Shell U.S.A. A modest man by nature, he defined their success this way: "Lots of information. We know more than others." Using the Gulf of Mexico as illustration, he said they had massive amounts of information on subsurface geology. He talked about "thousands and thousands" of seismic lines shot, he waxed almost poetic about the numbers of possible interpretations of the resulting data, and he enthused about their methods for encouraging more interpretation than other companies, putting the data on Cray supercomputers, simulating possible geologies, past and future.

Information as strategic advantage. Information as the *real* strategy. It should have been obvious. You learn it in business school. The role of the manager is to be right more often than wrong. You learn it in physics—we live in a probabilistic world, not a deterministic one. But if the strategists know it, they behave as if they don't. Their focus is on finding the "right strategy" rather than the right information—information that will lead them to be right more often than wrong.*

---

* This is different from the analyze-it-to-death syndrome Tom Peters and I talked about in *In Search of Excellence*. That syndrome is risk aversion: avoid decisions by studying them forever, hoping for perfection. What I'm talking about here is a process that welcomes risks but comprehends it, manages it, and contains it.

Shell's general strategy—find oil—doesn't make them different from a host of other oil companies. Even their specific strategic variant—find oil offshore—doesn't make them unique. But in the Gulf geology we have the perfect example of the complex environment faced by Simon's stalwart ant. It's a very complex geology under the Gulf waters. On any given well, neither Shell nor their competitors know whether they will find oil, let alone discover a highly profitable play. They have, much more often than any of them would prefer, the agonizing experience of sinking tens of millions into a dry well. But their odds of failure are lower than others'. They know more.

They are informed—they drill in places more likely to yield oil. They are opportunistic—they drill lots of wells despite the high cost of drilling and the high probability of coming up wet from Gulf storms but dry otherwise. Blackburn went on to say that they choose to explore offshore because that's where, based on some lucky hits in the early 1950s, they had an information advantage. He commented further: "We wouldn't be much good in the Permian Basin [the oil-rich region around Midland, Texas], where the geology is simple and where two thousand wildcatters, all talking to each other, would put Shell, with its way of doing things, at an information disadvantage."

Not long ago, Andy Pearson, former president of PepsiCo, now full professor at the Harvard Business School, was talking about the introduction of the Sting tennis racket by Wilson Sporting Goods, a PepsiCo subsidiary at the time. He said that Wilson had developed a new way to make a graphite racket. "With it," says Pearson, "we could produce a great racket for one hundred dollars less than our major competitor, Prince." Despite the price advantage, the racket didn't sell well. Although it looked and played like a Prince Graphite, very few people who could afford to buy a graphite racket believed they could pay $100 less and get the same quality. On the face of it the strategy was a bust. According to Pearson: "That high-end market segment just wasn't interested in our claim, even though it was true."

But Wilson had good market information. Pearson says, "We uncovered another segment—a bigger one at that—who wanted graphite, but thought they could only afford an aluminum-frame racket." Wilson quickly revised its strategy, and developed an ad campaign featuring teaching pro Vic Braden. He urges, "A graphite racket for the same price as aluminum—you've gotta go with graphite!"

The Sting was a success even though the original strategy was wrong. Or putting it differently, the real strategy was not the plan to sell a graphite racket in competition with the Prince; rather, it was the information and Wilson's willingness to move quickly on what they had learned. Information. Unpredictable event. Opportunity.

It's a Stochastic World

Recently, in a meeting with a group of senior Hewlett-Packard managers, Lynn Phillips, a member of the Stanford Business School faculty, used the phrase *stochastic shocks*.* Most everyone seemed to understand the word *stochastic*—it describes a process that is driven by random events—and as soon as the phrase rolled off his tongue, an otherwise polite and attentive audience really sat up and took notice. Why? They saw their own frustrations with strategy mirrored in that phrase. All too often they would get a sensible program going, only to have it blown out of the water by some capricious turn of the environment, some unpredictable move by a competitor or the economy, some stochastic shock.

Tom Theobald, vice-chairman of Citicorp, has a direct manner of speaking that parallels the bold way he has led at Citicorp. "I don't believe in the necessity of any kind of futurism," he says. "In fact, I believe we are all relative degrees behind current reality, and all we have to do is be less behind our current competitor to win the game." Theobald smiles and confesses to having "a retrograde view of the whole thing." When interrupted and asked if he doesn't actually mean "retrospective," he insists, "No, I mean retrograde. The object of the game is to be less backward than your competitor. This applies not only to banking, but to any business."

An extreme position, perhaps, but one that captures what we heard repeatedly at the renewing companies: In a curious way a

* The term *stochastic shock* was originally coined by macro-economist Josef Schumpeter.

healthy respect for the limits of forecasting shifts attention to the opportunities that elude the most astute forecasting mechanism. IBM's John Akers: "You cannot forecast oil prices, economic dislocations, currencies. Let's admit it! . . . Short-term aberrations have happened, are happening, and will always happen."

Akers's observation was portentous. Lately, short-term things have been happening to IBM, and the company is experiencing its well-reported share of problems. But even those are relative. To get things in perspective, for decades IBM has generated return on capital of almost 20 percent. Last year, which was a bad one for IBM compared with expectations, return on capital dropped below 15 percent. Digital Equipment Corporation, today's stock market favorite and a renewing company in its own right, has typically generated a return on capital of just over 11 percent.* IBM has been continuously successful for decades, it still generates more profits than any other company in the world, and it is one of the best-managed companies I've seen. We have a great deal to learn from them, including how to ride out the heavy weather without losing sight of fundamental business principles.

Tom Theobald's colleague at Citicorp, Dick Huber, reflects on his years of experience in Brazil: "Knowing for sure that the sun is going to come up tomorrow is about the extent of the forecasting that you want to do in Brazil. Totally new monetary system, new economic system—wow, literally over a weekend!"

The late Dan Lundberg, widely admired for his insights into gasoline prices: "People think that I'm prescient. You can make projections, you can make forecasts and you can make predictions, but I don't do any of that. I compile data and I draw conclusions. That's it. I don't have a crystal ball."

Lynn Phillips, Tom Theobald, John Akers, Dick Huber, and Dan Lundberg capture one of the main problems in strategy. Most companies try to overlay a rational, linear, deterministic technique, which they call strategy, on an underlying process that is random, full of surprise . . . in other words, stochastic. It doesn't work. The essential nature of big events defeats our attempts to tame them. What we have to do, if we're to be any

* In 1986, with IBM's drop and Digital's rise, return on equity for the two companies was about the same, and Digital just nudged out IBM in return on capital.

good at all at renewal, is go with the flow. We must adopt strategic methods that fit the unpredictable forces at work.

And that's not easy. Most of us are not that good at dealing with random events and probabilities. Most of us don't think easily in terms of the odds, probabilities, and statistics. Herb Simon, as usual, puts the issue in perspective. The basis for much of contemporary forecasting and the way corporations frame their expectations stems from the introduction of game theory in 1944 by Von Neumann and Morgenstern. "But far from solving the problem," says Simon, "the theory of games demonstrated how intractable the task is to prescribe rational action in a multi-person situation where interests are opposed." This may sound like a gloomy prognosis, but Simon has a pragmatic answer: "Although uncertainty does not therefore make intelligent choice impossible, it places a premium on robust adaptive procedures instead of strategies that work well only when finely tuned to precisely known environments." In other words, renewal itself should be part of the plan. And big plans should be broad, directional, roomy, adaptive—not detailed strategies or complicated long-range plans.

There is an important distinction between forecasting the future and determining probability for a particular event, but the relationship between probabilities and forecasting is often misunderstood. As a simple illustration, imagine a set of seven assumptions leading to a single conclusion. Each assumption has a 90 percent chance of being right. Intuitively we think that with such high probability for each assumption we'd enjoy a very good chance of our conclusion's being correct. In fact, the odds are less than fifty-fifty (47.8 percent, to be precise, or $.9 \times .9 \times .9 \times .9 \times .9 \times .9 \times .9$). Psychologists Daniel Kahneman and Amos Tversky, in their research on decision-making, find that people consistently overestimate the probability of future scenarios that are constructed from a series of individually probable events. Says Tversky:

How do people formulate strategy? First they decide what their opponents, say, the Russians, are likely to do. Then they plan how they will react. Then they decide how the Russians will react, and so on. It sounds like the right thing to do . . .

*[but] it may not be wise to choose the course of action that's
the best reponse to what you think the Russians are most likely
to do. You may not know what the Russians are up to. Even
the Russians may not know what the Russians are up to!*

Tony Burns, Ryder's CEO, is a master at both probability and
informed opportunism. "I wouldn't have dreamed six months ago
that we would have $500 million invested in aviation." Since the
1980 deregulation in trucking, Ryder has been shifting its focus
from trucking to a more general interest in the transportation
business. In the past four years Ryder Systems has purchased
forty-five companies in a move to redefine its markets and services. Most of the acquisitions have been winners; those that
weren't were sold when it became clear that they had little chance
of becoming profitable. Note the way Ryder combines opportunism and information here: small deals in related areas; learning
from both the winners and the losers; dumping the losers.

Burns, in talking about informed opportunism, emphasizes
Ryder's ability to get out of deals as much as their ability to get
into them. They learned it the hard way: "We had to sell five
businesses in 1974 and 1975 just to survive. That was tough but
we had to do it. Now we still have the ethic that if you're not
profitable, you don't stay in the company." He comments that
they are far more selective today in their acquisition program
than they were earlier, but even so they make mistakes.

During the 1984 planning cycle, Ryder's small aviation division identified ways that it might provide customers more value-
added services. They decided to explore the engine overhaul
business, and by April 1985, Aviall and another firm had been
identified as interesting acquisition candidates. Of the two, the
second outfit seemed the more interesting and was being pushed
harder. Market research done one month later determined, however, that Aviall was the better candidate.

When Ryder learned that Aviall was in the Citicorp portfolio,
they knew they would have to move rapidly to keep Citicorp
from making a public offering. Ryder quickly mobilized its staff
and resources to review the various aspects of a potential Aviall
deal. According to one of their executives: "When Aviall appeared,

we had very mixed emotions, because we had been looking so hard at the other company. But every staff department that came in did its analysis and in turn got excited about the deal. With each new bit of information, we felt better. People developed an honest and sincere excitement about the quality of the business at Aviall and the fit with Ryder Systems. We knew Aviall would live up to Ryder's standards."

Ryder's many acquisitions seem to contradict the stick-to-your-knitting principle from *In Search of Excellence*. But the argument for sticking to your knitting mainly takes issue with huge acquisitions in unrelated areas that take management teams completely out of fields they know. Witness, for example, the oil industry's sad record outside the petroleum business: Exxon's ill-fated ventures into office equipment, Mobil's agonies with Montgomery Ward, or Atlantic Richfield's struggles with Kennecott Copper.

In contrast, what Ryder is doing, like many others with their acquisition programs, is a form of experimentation within their own transportation industry. It's a way of shaking up the company and learning—a way of defining strategy on the run. Most of the acquisitions are small in relation to Ryder's total size. If they work, Ryder can build them into its culture. If they don't work, the company spins them off. Opportunity. Information.

Humana is another example of a lurching combination of opportunity and information at work, longer on opportunism than information during the early years. Few industries provoke as much debate and controversy as the $400 billion health care industry. The bulk of costs in health care are hospital costs. Humana, headquartered in Louisville, Kentucky, stands out both in financial performance and in its ability to control hospital costs while delivering higher-quality service than you would get in the average U.S. health care institution. By and large, the medical establishment views profit-making health care firms with deep suspicion. The charge is that in order to run themselves efficiently and cut costs, quality and service will be sacrificed. But, as is true in every other industry, quality in health care does not cost more; in fact, it's cheaper. Far from the villain that most doctors suspect, Humana struck us as among the most ... well, human of organizations.

The company's top brass, David Jones and Wendell Cherry, are a lawyer and an accountant by training—not members of the medical establishment. They got their start on a golf course when one of the foursome mentioned what a growth industry the nursing-home business would be. By 1968, Jones and Cherry had the largest nursing-home business in America. Within one year their stock had hopped from $8 per share to $84. "Then the bubble burst," says Jones. They then decided to go into mobile-home parks, reasoning that this industry (fast-growing, houses people) would be similar to nursing homes. But it wasn't; it felt to them too much like selling cars.

By then the nursing-home industry was maturing, so Jones and Cherry decided to go into the hospital business. They spent two and a half years selling off all their nursing homes. "Throughout that period," says Jones, "we disagreed on how fast we wanted to move into the hospital business and whether we wanted to buy or build hospitals. We ended up doing both—buying and building.

"We learned a valuable lesson from it all. Decisions never turn out to be right. Incrementalism is the best way to describe the way we run the company now. We have no trouble shifting gears." Adds Wendell Cherry: "We have perspective now. We realize that no trend lasts very long. Everything is cyclical." Humana always had the opportunism part of the strategic equation, and now it looks as if the information part is playing a bigger role.

Even financial strategy—how a company raises capital and services debt—can be an extension of informed opportunism. According to Ed Fontaine, chief financial officer at Newmont Mining, there was one thing he and former chief executive Plato Malozemoff always agreed on: "We would finance the company so we could move like that"—he snaps his fingers—"on a large opportunity without betting the company." Newmont got its start in the copper business but has successfully diversified into gold and coal mining. (The company recently acquired and helped turn around the ailing Peabody Coal Company.) If you look at Newmont's impressive track record in the mining business over the years, it is all informed opportunism.

So one big slice of being better strategists—and a real challenge for most of us—is being better at dealing with probabilities. That is the only way that managers can be effective opportunists.

Being Informed

A related challenge is staying informed. Information, as the investment community has known for years, is the real strategic advantage. The source of more than a few fortunes made on Wall Street has been the inside knowledge that a stock would move before it was known to the general public. These days, use of inside information can land you in jail, which doesn't seem to stop the particularly avaricious. They carry to a despicable extreme an underlying principle of investment—and business—strategy. It's based on a knowledge advantage: a reason to believe that you can do more with an opportunity, or protect yourself better from a stochastic shock, than the competition.

Knowledge is precisely the story of the Wells Fargo acquisition of Crocker. Although the availability of the bank for purchase came as a stochastic shock to the Wells management, they were in fact only a few degrees away from being prepared for something like that. Having successfully executed their expense-control and portfolio-restructuring strategies, and having the results of that reflected in the market value of their stock, they were able to start thinking about where to invest. The obvious choice, with interstate banking becoming a higher probability, was to buy another West Coast bank—maybe one in Portland or Seattle. But Wells had always been weak in Southern California, so Carl Reichardt suggested thinking of Southern California as a state. "When you do that and run a few numbers, you realize that Southern California is a 'state' with the tenth-largest gross domestic product in the world. We had no business considering Oregon or Washington if there was any way we could build position in Southern California."

What they also knew, from rigorous analysis of their own experience, was what sort of branch networks would best serve a given market area at the lowest cost. They had identified the kinds of branch concentrations in a specific city, suburb, or outlying town that would best build market share. They understood that building a branch network from scratch in Southern California would be prohibitively expensive. They also had a good feel, based on their own experience, for which branches in Southern California were not doing well. So Wells knew the following: They wanted to buy some branches there, and other California banks had more branches than they could afford after deregulation. What Wells did *not* know was which bank, or several banks, might be willing to sell branches.

That's when opportunity took over. When one of Wells's top management found himself in Hong Kong seated next to an executive from England's Midland Bank, which owned Crocker, he asked him whether they might ever want to sell branches. Midland's executive replied that he didn't know; they were doing some strategic thinking about the whole Crocker situation at the time. On several ensuing occasions, Wells's top managers found themselves in contact with their peers from Midland. They repeated the question, but Midland was as noncommittal as ever. Then, in November 1985, another Midland executive was in San Francisco at a bankers' convention. Two Wells executives met him for breakfast and asked their perfunctory question. But this time the response was radically different: "Well, no, we do not want to sell any branches. We would like to sell the whole bank."

"That," says Reichardt, "took us totally by surprise; we were in no way prepared for an offer like that." Actually they were more prepared than they thought. They had a mountain of information. They had to recast the data, but it didn't take them long to figure out which branches they would keep and which they would close if they bought the bank outright. Their own experience in cost cutting helped them determine whether the price Midland was asking—a little over a billion dollars for a bank that was just barely in the black—made any sense. For most banks it would not have. But Wells had accurate estimates of how much cost they could reduce from the existing Crocker operation. "Our only concern then," says Reichardt, "was that their portfolio be clean [relatively free of bad loans]. Hazen [Paul Hazen, Wells's president] and I could, and did, look at all the big ones ourselves; it was another California bank and we had personal knowledge of most of the big credits [more information]." It's a great story. It shows, about as clearly as any we encountered in this research, how information and chance combine to make for true strategic advantage.

Lots of companies do well in consumer goods. But one of the best examples of renewal in this field is Heinz, recently energized under the leadership of one-time Irish rugby star Tony O'Reilly, and the billion-dollar Ore-Ida division, which for years has been a jewel in the Heinz crown.

Ore-Ida's acquisition of a small frozen-foods company in Philadelphia called Gagliardi is a close parallel with the Wells story. Gagliardi makes the Steak-Umm. For those who don't know the product, it is a thin-sliced frozen steak that cooks up in a hot frying pan in a minute—forty-five seconds on one side, fifteen on the other—and serves as the building block for a pretty good steak sandwich. Gagliardi had been around a long time but had remained small. Paul Corddry, at the time Ore-Ida's chief executive, consumes market research information the way some families devour Ore-Ida's frozen potato products. As Corddry recalls the story, Charlie Strauss, a market researcher whom Corddry regularly retained, was routinely flipping through some field market reports and noticed that in the Northeast a product he had never heard of was growing like crazy and rapidly taking market share. He brought that information immediately to Paul's attention. Together they figured out what the product was and that its basis for success was solid market appeal. The two caught the next plane to Philadelphia to meet with the Gagliardis and find out whether the company was for sale or might be. If so, they wondered if the family would be interested in a partnership with Ore-Ida. Gagliardi was in fact quite interested and a deal was struck quickly.

Reporting on the purchase of Gagliardi after the fact, you would be tempted to attribute it to the brilliant foresight of the Ore-Ida management team, but if you probed what really happened you would find that chance played a major role. The principal ingredients of the strategic recipe at Ore-Ida, like PepsiCo and the Wilson Sting, Shell and offshore exploration, or Wells and the Crocker deal, seem to be information and flexibility. In this case the information came from Ore-Ida's constant market surveillance.

The same phenomenon is at work in smaller companies. Harry V. Quadracci, who runs Quad/Graphics, perhaps the most successful printing company in the United States, describes the acquisition of John Blair Marketing Inc., a related business, which doubled his company's size in one stroke. First, Harry grew up in the printing business and knows who's who and what's what. That's the informed part. Now the opportunism part: "I bought that company before anybody else knew what was happening. I went in and said, 'How much do you want for the company?' He said, 'I want this . . .' and I said, 'Sold!' My competitors were of course studying the situation but simply couldn't move fast enough." The year before the Quad/Graphics deal, John Blair lost $17 million on sales of $150 million, but like the Wells management team, Quadracci and his people pretty much knew—which is to say they had good information based on their own experience— how to make John Blair successful. Recently they posted quarterly earnings of $1.5 million.

It's a lot like stud poker, where each card dealt buys you more information. The information gets more expensive as you go along. In a business deal, a new-product development, an exploration program, or an investment program, each milestone along the way only buys you more information on how well the deal is likely to succeed. Each milestone gets more expensive. And in the immortal words of Yogi Berra, "The game isn't over till it's over." No one hand, or even a small series of hands, will disclose who is the poker shark and who is the novice. The novice can look brilliant on any one hand. The expert is the expert because he wins big over a series of hands—not because he's smarter in any abstract sense, but because he's got poker smarts. He has a better poker intuition. Some of this ability may be a trait he is born with; the rest is acquired through experience.

The business strategists—meaning the best of the informed opportunists—are like the poker experts. They can be very wrong on any one deal and, in that narrow context, will look like amateurs. They, too, are no brighter in the abstract than many of us. They have business smarts—deal-making smarts, exploration smarts, or product introduction smarts. Like the card shark, the renewing managers can look bad on any given hand, but they are careful never to let too large a slice of their stakes ride on any single outcome. They are humble before the inherent randomness of events, but like Herb Simon's stalwart ant, their actions have an underlying sense of direction.

Herb Simon once gave a talk on the subject of management information systems. He started by reaching under the podium and pulling out a telephone. "This is the main system," he said. He elaborated: In his own field he probably stays in touch with 1,000 people. Each of them in turn is in touch with another 500 to 1,000 people he doesn't know—a network of 500,000 to 1 million people. He explained that he was, at most, a few phone calls away from anything he wanted to know. Most successful people make it their business to build contacts. It is their way of staying informed and part of what makes them good strategists.

Inventions of Opportunity

As the Post-it and Wilson Sting stories suggest, the phenomenon of informed opportunism applies not only to high-level strategy but to routine innovation as well. In fact, the concept of informed opportunism is as germane to individual careers as to an organization's strategy. One place where the phenomenon hangs on so tenaciously that it resists our best efforts to rationalize history is in the development of new products.

Hewlett-Packard's co-founder Bill Hewlett writes about it in the introduction to *Inventions of Opportunity,* a collection of articles about the inventions that were the lifeblood of HP as it grew and prospered. One of Hewlett's main points in the introduction, and an observation that comes through over and over in the body of the book, is the apparently random, opportunistic nature of invention. Even so, he emphasizes the importance of staying informed. Of his own career, Hewlett notes that he and Barney Oliver, who was later to become the first head of HP Laboratories, were friends at Stanford. Hewlett says that in the years just after World War II, Oliver was working at Bell Labs, and Hewlett says, "I always made it a point to visit Barney when I was in the New York area." On one of those trips Oliver asked Hewlett whether he had ever thought of using a "three-phase ring circuit" to get around some of the problems HP had been having in extending the frequency range of one of their test and measurement products. Hewlett writes that "it was at once obvious" that this idea was the path to a product that stayed in the line for twelve years (long for HP) and contributed greatly to profits.

A wonderful book called *The Sources of Invention,* by John Jewkes, which meticulously documents case histories of big, commercially successful innovations, talks repeatedly about the same phenomenon. Jewkes finds that it is typical for the inventions that will affect the destinies of corporations, and sometimes entire industries, to come from all the "wrong" places. Kodachrome was invented by a couple of musicians who were interested in color photography but had only a loose association with Kodak at the time. Catalytic cracking, the process that makes oil refining efficient, was invented by a fellow interested in automobile racing.

Similar stories emerge from many of the renewing companies. Hewlett-Packard's rise in the business computing market, for instance, happened almost by accident. They had developed a computer, the HP 3000, for scientific use. It turned out to be just the ticket for the minicomputer, distributed-data-processing business market, a place where IBM was weak.

The course of innovation seems just like the strategic processes we've just seen. Stochastic shock is as prevalent here as it is in grand corporate events. Both innovation and strategy defy all attempts at careful planning. In fact, our efforts to carefully "manage" innovation may contribute more to driving out innovation than helping it. Innovation is critical to renewal; it's crucial that we manage it right. But managing it right means picking a method that fits the stochastic nature of the underlying process rather than trying to force it into a management system that seems rational but just doesn't fit. The right technique is informed opportunism.

Uncertainty and randomness may seem typical of specific inventions, but it's easy to assume that a more linear, certain strategy guides the development of big products. With so much at stake, wouldn't that have to be the case? Not necessarily. The Ford Taurus, for instance, could never have been predicted upfront. Initially its proponents were sure about only two things: They didn't like the products Ford currently had on the market, and they wanted to build a better-quality product. That was the extent of their "strategic plan." The car that eventually rolled off the assembly line was the product of thousands of little inventions and suggestions—from customers, engineers, workers, and designers.

Random as they are, all the stories on innovation share an

important characteristic. The person or team behind the innovation was both current with the relevant technology and had a feel for what might be useful in the marketplace. This is just a variant on the information theme. The specific invention happened in a random, impossible-to-predict way. But it never would have occurred without the technology to support it.

Ralph Gomory, IBM's vice-president and director of research, discusses the relationship between basic research and scientific breakthroughs. "A breakthrough occurs when the technological knowledge and a way to apply it to meet a need come together in one person's head. Everything else is just a means to that end. Incremental steps forward are more pervasive than breakthroughs, but both are important." In an article on industrial research Gomory expressed it this way:

Science can be thought of as a large pool of knowledge fed by the steady flow from the tap of basic research. Every now and then the water is dipped out and put to use, but one never knows which part of the water will be needed. This confuses the funding situation for basic science, because usually no specific piece of scientific work can be justified in advance; one cannot know which is going to be decisive. Yet history shows that keeping water flowing into the pool is a very worthwhile enterprise.

Even at the level of science—as opposed to technology development—Gomory does make a distinction between the research taking place in the IBM labs and what you might see in a university. Like the others at IBM, Gomory keeps his eye on what the best are doing around the world in fields that could affect his company. He also insists that, although the researchers need not justify what they are up to in financial terms, they must be working on things of potential interest to the company.

The policy implications of this are huge. Research can provide a major strategic edge. But because it's impossible to compute the payback on investment in an area like research, all but a few companies are inclined to underinvest. What decision makers don't realize is that, compared with the big-ticket investments like plant, equipment, and product development, *research is cheap*. Steady investment in research is a powerful information generator that supports product-oriented opportunistic action.

Columbo as Strategist

So far the case seems compelling that information and opportunity combine to make for the most important strategies. There is a third factor. Gary Rogers pinpointed it when he described his decision to offer to buy Dreyer's: "I had an instinct for the opportunity that is hard to quantify or even understand." No one seems to know exactly how this third factor relates to being informed and being opportunistic, but everyone we talked to is relatively sure the relationship is there and that it's important. This factor is intuition.

"I depend on my gut," says Tom Theobald. "But I don't mean to use 'gut' in an unscientific way. For God's sake, after twenty-five years in a certain position, you ought to have absorbed a whole lot of dictionary that gives you the meaning of what's going on." H. Ross Perot, the founder of Electronic Data Systems, is also aware of his extensive dictionary, which he calls simply "knowing your business." He says, "It means being able to bring to bear on a situation everything you've seen, felt, tasted, and experienced in an industry."

Henry Schacht, chief executive of the Cummins Engine Company, calls it his sixth sense: "When the hair on the back of my neck has just given me an unpleasant sensation, either because of a recommendation or a set of facts in front of me, I know that something is wrong. We are trying to teach our managers that when you have a sixth sense that says something is screwy, pay attention to it."

A manager's informed side of things is fed from two sources: left-brain analysis and right-brain intuition. They work together to nudge people toward or away from an opportunity. Alone they're not as effective; computer analyses by themselves can be just as misleading as an uninformed gut. But as complementary perspectives that serve as check and balance, analysis and intuition work in tandem for the informed opportunist.

Harvey Wagner, professor of business administration at the University of North Carolina and a distinguished scholar in the world of decision science, puts it well:

A trust in science does not imply the abandonment of hunch and intuition. On the contrary, the history of science itself is studded with cases of important discoveries made through chance, hunch, serendipity, even dreams. . . . Most executives who use their hunches well also seem to possess a high level of knowledge and understanding about their activities. So the question is not when to apply science and when to rely on intuition, but rather how to combine the two effectively.

Critical as the element of intuition is, it is contrary to what most of us have been taught: We "should" trust the numbers and mistrust the gut. Intuitive feelings seem errant, deviating from what we believe is true and accurate (read: measurable). Managers often talk about these feelings in terms of "fittedness." The numbers might seem solid as a rock, presenting an airtight case for moving in a certain direction, but sometimes the analyses and the conclusion they lead to rationally don't "fit" instinctively. An elusive, nonquantifiable consideration arising from an intuition informed by years of experience says, "Hold it!"

Call it the Columbo factor—the quality, other than the dirty raincoat and cigar, that made the irreverent detective played by Peter Falk in the television series so colorful. Columbo solved mystifying mysteries by jumping on information that didn't fit— that didn't make sense somehow. He always had one more question that occurred to him as he started to leave any given scene. Something didn't seem to fit, and the thing that made Columbo so good was that he trusted his gut enough to ask that last question.

Philosopher and author Arthur Koestler's explanation of the creative process sounds a lot like the Columbo factor. He sees it as an intuitive leap that connects two previously unrelated facts or ideas to form a single new one. Sometimes it's not so much a matter of coming up with new information as it is of looking at familiar facts in new ways. Polaroid's founder, Edwin Land, maintained that every significant step in every field "is taken by some individual who has freed himself from a way of thinking that is held by friends and associates who may be more intelligent, better educated, better disciplined, but who have not mastered the art of the fresh, clean look at old, old knowledge."

Dreyer's Gary Rogers expands on the importance and the elusiveness of the intuitive quality: "Often people look back in retrospect and say, 'I knew about that, I talked about that,' and yet they didn't have the ability to see something there." He feels, as did many others we talked to, that a major part of being a good strategist is simply being aware, picking up on clues, noticing things, asking the naïve "Why?" or "Why not?," being constantly curious. But unfortunately, writes researcher Willis Harman, "Most of us . . . still deal with it [intuition] as though it were marked 'for emergency use only.' "

Our language breaks down when we try to justify a feeling we have about something, especially if it goes against a direction that's already been set. We speak vaguely of vibes, a hunch, a feeling in our bones, a sensation in the gut, a sixth sense, or else we say nothing at all and tap the forehead, clutch the stomach. Even the most thoughtful definitions evade being too specific about the intuitive mode, calling it "the capacity to make correct guesses without knowing why."

During the investigation that followed the explosion of the space shuttle *Challenger,* an engineer at Morton Thiokol testified that he advised his superiors that weather conditions at Cape Kennedy were too cold to guarantee the safety of the space craft's O-ring sealants. He urged them to delay the launch. Management pressed for more explanation: How cold was too cold—forty degrees? Thirty-seven degrees? Could they launch at forty-one degrees? The engineer resisted pinning down an exact temperature that was dangerous. He didn't have the facts to be that precise. All he could tell his superiors was that the weather predicted for launching time was "away from goodness." What he knew about the O-rings and the proposed launch during cold weather didn't "fit." But because the most accurate way he could describe this lack of fit was "away from goodness," his warnings went unheeded.

British psychologists Peter Watson and William Hartson, the latter an international chess master, lend their version of "away from goodness" by re-creating how two chess players analyze a particular move:

WEAKER PLAYER: *What's wrong with it?*
STRONGER PLAYER: *It's not good.*
WEAKER PLAYER: *Why not?*
STRONGER PLAYER: *It's not the sort of move you play in this sort of position.*
(End of Conversation.)

Like the chess masters, having an ample storehouse of information and experience helps managers trust their intuition when it comes calling. It also helps to know how to open the intuitive channels that support creative behavior. David Ogilvy, founder of the advertising firm that bears his name, writes:

I doubt if more than one campaign in a hundred contains a big idea. I am supposed to be one of the more fertile inventors of big ideas, but in my long career as a copywriter I have not had more than twenty, if that. Big ideas come from the unconscious. This is true in art, in science, and in advertising. But your unconscious has to be well informed, or your idea will be irrelevant. Stuff your conscious mind with information, then unhook your rational thought process. You can help this process by going for a long walk, or taking a hot bath, or drinking half a pint of claret. Suddenly, if the telephone line from your unconscious is open, a big idea wells up within you.

A French company called BSN—the one that markets Dannon

yogurt in America—is a dramatic example of change and renewal. Originally a flat glass manufacturer, this company has gone through a complete, successful transformation from flat glass to consumer goods. Antoine Riboud, the man responsible for it all, recommends, quite literally, management by taking a bath. "What do you do when you take a bath? First, you wash yourself. But second, you think. You *think*." He then adds with a wry smile, "That is the problem with managers today—too many are taking showers; too few are taking baths. No time to think."

Simple Strategy

Luxuriously long baths notwithstanding, no one can predict some of the most important events that affect companies, divisions, departments. No matter how much planning you do, you can't plan for some things. *Develop a corporate direction, not a strategy.* Keep your basic strategy fairly simple, straightforward, even dull. The strategy itself is important—crucial, as a matter of fact—but it's not where the action is.

Wells Fargo's strategy is about as simple as they come. Reichardt remembers: "We had a bank examiner in here several years ago talking about how great our strategy must be. I told him: 'Yes, we have a threefold strategy—expense control, expense control, expense control.'" How did Wells get to that point? It started at a strategy meeting five years ago. Both Reichardt and then-CEO Richard Cooley could see expenses continuing to grow at about 15 percent per year, a slight slowdown of the past decade's trend in operating expense growth, which had been in the vicinity of 20 percent per annum. They could also see that deregulation, particularly the lifting of Regulation Q, the one that put a lid on what banks could pay for deposits, would have a disastrous impact on their earnings. They made two strategic decisions. The first was to control expense growth. Since then their goal, which they are the first to admit is arbitrary, has been to hold the line on expenses. No growth. Not 20 percent, not 10, not 5. Zero. The second strategy was to restructure the loan portfolio. Most of their lending was in the consumer arena, where margins are small-to-nonexistent in inflationary times. They wanted to get out of that and into a more profitable, better balanced credit portfolio. The fundamental strategies were simple and haven't changed, except maybe to be reinforced, since that meeting.

Like Wells, other companies expressed their strategies in terms that were simple, self-evident, almost bland. They talked about general directions, statements of corporate aspiration and value, the importance of attitudes toward change, and the value of communications in the planning process.

IBM seems thorough in planning and articulate about strategy. But their success is *not* a function of a complex, clever game plan. That's why CEO John Akers made his remark "There is a lot more that is obvious here than meets the eye." He elaborates that his predecessors Frank Cary and John Opel laid out four strategies for IBM in the 1980s: to grow with the industry, to have technological leadership, to be as efficient as anybody else, and to have enough profit at the end of the year to fuel future growth of the business. Akers asks rhetorically, "Pretty simple?" It is. At IBM the four goals are repeated over and over and over. When Akers assumed the CEO position from John Opel in 1985, business reporters kept asking him what his new goals were. "I said, 'Come on! Can you think of four better goals than this? If we could, we would have chosen them!' "*

An effective strategy *has* to be simple. Huge efforts invested in finding and articulating the ultimate strategy that is going to give one company a "sustainable competitive advantage," to borrow from the strategist's lexicon, are probably wasted. Amar Bhide, a former colleague of mine at McKinsey, likes to startle his strategist friends with this question: "If all your competitors gave their strategic plans to each other, would it really make a difference?" His point is that, in a world where there are no secrets and where innovations are quickly imitated or made obsolete, *complex* strategies are often just exercises in self-delusion.

---

* In January 1987, Akers did announce an additional goal: to enhance their customer partnerships.

The Planning Process Chokes
These Things

Beyond keeping the statement simple, the next step toward robust strategy is looking outside the planning system for opportunity. The renewing companies recognize the value of the planning process even though they don't believe it generates their companies' major strategies. That sounds like a contradiction. One of the first places most of us would look for big strategy is "the plan." But paradoxically, if a company has a buttoned-up planning system, it probably is also one that regularly misses opportunity. Just as economics has Gresham's law—bad money chases out good—so organizations follow a dismal law in which tightly structured strategies chase out opportunity.

Bernard Puckett, who has spent many years working with IBM's planning system, understands how planning chokes out new ideas that could mean big strategic opportunity for the company. "Our planning process will not point out the new opportunities. It kills them by design; it grinds them down. But we know that." Puckett remembers that one year after the strategic plan was completed, John Akers asked him to identify the opportunities that had been left out but still deserved a second look. That's a great way to keep good ideas from getting lost in the shuffle.

A company in Cambridge, Massachusetts, called EG&G enjoys a low profile, although they have consistently ranked among the top one hundred U.S. companies for total return to investors. EG&G's business is high-tech: electronics, space, defense. Founded in 1947 by three MIT professors—Edgerton, Germeshausen, and Grier—the company has prospered since 1967 under the gregarious, iconoclastic leadership of Bernard O'Keefe. "Planning systems are inherently risk averse," O'Keefe says. "They cannot give you *the inspiration* that tells you where you go next."

Warren E. Buffett had a more whimsical way of expressing the same idea to shareholders of Buffett's Berkshire Hathaway company in February 1985. Buffett said he was looking for "a few big ideas" and added, "I do not have any such ideas at present, but our experience has been that they pop up occasionally." (How's that for a strategic plan?) A few weeks after writing that, Buffett bought 3 million shares of Capital Cities Communications to help finance Cap Cities' $3.5 billion takeover of American Broadcasting Company—a fairly big idea. On another occasion, Buffett used a touch of overstatement to make his point: "We have no master strategy, no corporate planners delivering us insights about socioeconomic trends, and no staff to investigate a multitude of ideas presented by promoters and intermediaries. Instead, we simply hope that something sensible comes along—and when it does, we act."

Communicating with the Plan

While planning acts a part in the renewal story, its role is subtle, quiet, and indirect. If planning is no longer the matinee idol it was thought to be a decade ago, then it remains an all-important supporting actor who makes the whole production hang together.

Still, many executives understandably say "Yuk" when the subject of strategy comes up. Dana's normally reserved Gerry Mitchell, who does a fair bit of insightful strategy himself, states, "I hate strategic plans; it [the concept] gives me such a bellyache I can't stand it." Even John Willemssen, who is in charge of strategic planning at US West, is quick with the melancholy alliteration: "The worst plans are the plans planned by planners." The thought that "planners don't plan" came up over and over in our discussions. You begin to wonder what planners should do other than call themselves something else. As long as they are called "planners" and put in that role, they will probably have the distressing tendency to want to plan.

Yet, Steelcase has recently been busily *installing* a strategic planning system. Inaugurating a planning system, for God's sake! The company is as profitable as all get-out and is a world-class manufacturing outfit by any standard you'd want to use. Either these guys were nuts, or they knew something. Since they'd been so successful without one, the logical question was "Why now?"

The same question surfaced at IBM. Since many have regarded this company as the best-managed in the world, it seemed strange that while others were cutting back on planning, IBM was planning with zest on both the corporate and division levels and was waxing fervent about their planning process.

Most renewing companies have moved away from rigid planning methods and fat planning books laden with numbers. What has evolved, instead, is planning that better comprehends the realities of change. It is more fluid, more flexible, more realistic than the old ways.

Even so, these companies were engaging in a number of radically different activities under a general banner that goes by the name "strategic planning" (or "long-range planning"; most use the phrases interchangeably). The concept suffers from massive confusion of purpose. Just below the surface, the words *strategy* and *planning* blanket things that are as different as stopwatches and ice cream.

What planning is really used for in renewing companies varies all the way from control to opportunity generation, with a good dose of communication thrown in as well. S. I. Hayakawa points out, in his classic *Language in Thought and Action,* that if we are both talking about mammals, but you are talking about Bessie the cow and I am talking about Moby the whale, we are not yet really in close touch. Even at a lower level of abstraction, Hayakawa says, $cow_1 \neq cow_2$. Bessie the cow is not the same as Rosie the cow. By the same token, $strategy_1 \neq strategy_2$. What one person means by strategy, strategic planning, or long-range planning often is radically different from what another means. Behind the planning perplex is nothing more mysterious than confusion of intent.

IBM's John Akers has an entirely different approach to planning. "You shouldn't call it a planning process," he says, "although what you get out of it is a plan. What you have accomplished is communication." Other IBMers amplified: "In IBM we use our planning system to communicate with each other. That part's *really* important to us because we have so many interdependencies. We will develop a technology in Burlington that will go into our largest computer, or personal computer, or in nine other products all over the world. And people deciding whether to hire marketing reps in Japan find themselves dependent on whether Burlington will have the technology ready that will go into a product that, in a year and a half or two years, will allow us to enter a new market in Japan."

There is a similar focus on the communications side of planning. US West has set up something called the *Forum,* where about seventy employees are pulled together once a month from different parts of the organization to talk about the company's strategies. Dow Jones also stresses the link between communication and planning. Ray Shaw, the company's president, argues that their planning sessions bring people within Dow Jones closer together—editorial people, advertising people, circulation people. "The planning process," he stresses, "makes them work together."

At Steelcase, a main reason for formalizing planning is to remind people down the line what the company stands for. The company's fundamental mission hasn't changed, they explain, nor do division objectives change that much from year to year. Paul Witting, senior vice-president in charge of sales and distribution, has five major objectives in his plan; four are highly qualitative, and the fifth is to increase market share by a little bit every year. He says they need something that lets everybody know the general direction of the company. It also helps lay potential conflicts to rest.

For example, there is always the temptation to sell direct rather than through dealers, although the company has historically been committed to its dealer network. "The continuing re-articulation via the planning process that we will sell only through dealers keeps everyone on track and focused," he emphasizes.

"The importance of planning is the *process,*" people often say, and then go on to explain that the plans themselves don't appear to matter as much as the fact that they have a planning process. Now, on the surface that seems odd. Suppose you took the end products away and left the organization with only process—no plans, just a planning system. People would resist.

But thinking of planning as communication resolves the mystery. Of course the process is important. That's the way people all over a company confer. IBM's Puckett says, "We talk to each other by plan. I have a sheet right here, and the top line on it is the plan and its status. You can go to a product manager and say, 'How's business?' Within the first four sentences he or she will tell you how things are going compared to the plan. The same thing happens if you go to a territory representative—how things are going versus quota. So we use the plan all the time to communicate formally and informally with each other."

My own first encounter with planning as communication, when I wasn't smart enough to recognize what was plainly before me, took place when I was directing some work in Australia for a coal mining company. This outfit was a fifty-fifty joint venture between two larger mining companies. Because of the disparate interests of the different owner groups at board level, they couldn't agree on much of anything. Not knowing what else to do, and following my own instinct to be analytical, my team put together an extensive "fact pack" on the situation.

The fact pack took the form of about fifty pages of charts and exhibits that traced the economic history of the coal mine, analyzed its cost position, analyzed its past record of labor disputes, and outlined some of the broad risks and opportunities in various diversification alternatives. What intrigued me when the team presented this to the board was how interested they were in the data on their own history. There were, in fact, two parts to the intrigue, both related to communication. First, because of the divided ownership structure, there was a we/they split at board level that had prevented effective communication. The fact pack was truly newsworthy. Second, in the absence of fact, everything had been treated as subject for debate.

The fact pack repeatedly comes forth as one of the main strengths of a planning system. This seems strange, since one can collect solid facts only on the past. But past is prelude. Facts are the basis for a good debate on values, and the currency for good communication. The evolution of a fact pack has everything to do with a good planning system.

Take, for example, the emergence of a long-range planning system in the Fine Arts Museum in San Francisco. Although the top executives pressed the obvious point—a museum is its collection—few on the board's long-range planning committee understood the collection. The committee spent the better part of a year listening to the curators of the various parts of the collection present and assess what was there. Not only did the committee learn enough to start doing the planning job right, but the staff itself began to better understand the totality of the museum.

A singular manifestation of planning as communication is in what IBM calls its contention system. IBM's Tom Liptak says, "It's fairly formalized. Sometimes we call it the rules of dissent. The staff is explicitly required to take positions on matters that come up via the planning system, and they must do so in writing. They are not allowed the luxury of saying, 'Maybe.' They must say 'Yes, I agree with that' or 'No, I disagree.' If it's no, they have to fight it out with the line people who are proposing something else, and by dint of superior argument get them to change. If that fails, they and the line people appear before John Akers and the management committee [to argue it out]."

The contention system, Liptak says, "causes a rigorous challenging to occur all the time." He elaborates that the importance of the challenge process is that it is institutionalized. People can take each other on when they have an honest difference of opinion without appearing to be rude or political. The staff can challenge the line, the line people can challenge one another, and feelings are not hurt—at least not too badly.

One of the main values of a contention system is that it provides an open forum for disagreement. In too many organizations honest disagreements come up all the time, but there is no institutional way of airing the differences. Then people who feel strongly are forced to "get political" and become terminally polite: On the surface they are nice to one another, and below the surface they fight like cats and dogs. They have no way of separating disagreement from disrespect.

At IBM the corporate staff is responsible for monitoring developments around the world that might affect IBM's business, quantifying their impact where possible and making sure that information gets factored into the line manager's plans, either directly or through the system of dissent.

Something else that is "crucial, absolutely crucial" is the idea that if you are on the staff with a general authority over manufacturing, you are assumed to represent the chairman of the board with a corporate perspective, rather than being someone who has only the interests of manufacturing in mind. You are expected to change hats, allegiance, and point of view. "You can become a captive of the audience you serve unless you're objective," Liptak says.

This consent/dissent system seems to be a *modus vivendi* all over IBM. It's a function of their size and their being in a single worldwide business, which enables one division to contract with another one for a certain technology. Liptak comments that the two divisions "must agree, using the rules of consent: 'Yes, what I'm going to supply is cost-competitive, and I will deliver the quality and volume . . . to meet your schedule.' So we've constantly got people with great dependencies . . . banging on one another."

Skill Building

Another place where strategy can be particularly important, although few we talked to expressed it this way, is in building a company's capabilities or skills. Once again, habit is the main adversary of renewal. Habit resists change, and therefore is an important part of any company's stabilizing base. But precisely because habit resists change, it is the bog that mires even the most energetic leaders of renewal.

We humans, it seems, don't break habits by setting out to break habits. Rather, we change habits by substituting a better habit for the one we're trying to change. The same thing happens in business. The trick is to think in terms of adding a new skill, fresh proficiency, different competence, more muscle to the organization. The point is to make the organization *as a whole* good, or better, at something that it did not do as well before.

Companies can be thought of as bundles of skills, capabilities, and competencies. One of the main differences between two companies, even ones in the same business, is the difference in their collective skills. In banking, Morgan's historic strength has been serving the needs of the major corporate client. Citicorp has also been good in this area, but their main strategic dream is to become overwhelmingly competent in serving what banks call the retail market (in other words, the consumer). Digital Equipment Corporation has always been strong in the field of minicomputers, had trouble with personal computers, and only recently tried to compete with mainframe computers. IBM, by contrast, has been awesomely powerful with mainframes, and suddenly got that way in the personal microcomputer area. But IBM still has trouble competing in the minicomputer market.

The notion of skill building is what starts to put meat back on the bones of some strategy and organization ideas that got bleached white by the last decade's glare of economic reality. The first framework for capability building was the "happy atom"—the 7-S framework—that was introduced in *In Search of Excellence.**

For those who are unfamiliar with the 7-S framework, the following summary will help. In the center is the dependent variable, skills. The idea is that an organization as a whole will be skilled at something to the degree that the other six sibilants support that skill. A tale from a training classroom at Hewlett-Packard illustrates the point. One of HP's main skills is innovation. One day a group of young engineers got together and brainstormed all the attributes present in the HP culture that support their innovation prowess. They were able to list at least a few dozen items under each category. The next skill picked was marketing, one that HP is building. The engineers were much less able to fill in the framework. The message was clear: HP's marketing was not firmly in place because there was much less in the infrastructure to support it.

Here's the meaning of the other *S*'s in the following diagram:

Structure. The organization chart, job descriptions, and the like. Ways of showing who reports to whom and how tasks are divided and integrated.

Systems. The formal and informal processes and flows within an organization. How things get done from day to day. Everything from systems for service delivery to systems for manufacturing. Systems for accounting, for quality control, for performance measurement. The list goes on.

---

* Tony Athos and Richard Pascale used a similar framework in their book *The Art of Japanese Management.* That framework was developed by the four of us while Tom Peters and I were at McKinsey & Company, Inc., and Tony and Richard were working with us as consultants.

Symbolic Behavior. This used to be "style." It is the attention dimension. It is tangible evidence of what management considers important, especially as depicted by nonverbal communication, the way managers spend time, the results they reward, and the way they act in crises.

Staff. The people in an organization. Their demographic characteristics. Their experience, education, and training. The fit between the jobs that need to be done and the skills of the people who fill those jobs.

Shared Values. What the company stands for—stated and implied, good and bad. What a company is proud of or would like to be proud of. Shared values go beyond, but might well include, simple goal statements. How a company behaves in tough times is a good indicator of the value system.

Strategy. Narrowly defined, a company's plan for allocating resources and achieving sustainable competitive advantage. In what follows, this definition will be considerably elaborated. The strategic dimension will become a framework in its own right.

7-S FRAMEWORK

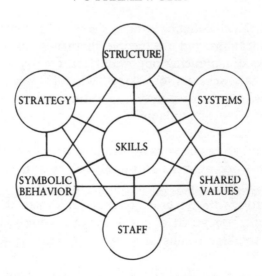

To get a feel for the usefulness of a framework like this, let's revisit Wells Fargo. Considered in terms of the 7-S framework, the *skill* the organization lacked was the kind of regular attention to operating detail that leads to cost containment. Fundamental problems existed in structure, systems, symbolic behavior, and staff. To illustrate, Wells restructured by closing more than ninety branches in two and a half years. They changed systems to reward people for expense control rather than volume growth. Reichardt and his team changed their own symbolic behavior. Reichardt says, "I harped on the subject all the time. I've been accused of managing by vignette." Reichardt would look for silly things done at low levels in the organization, then use them as illustration, always asking his people: "What else are we doing like this? What if this were multiplied a thousand times? Our costs would be astronomical." As a result, the mind-set of the whole staff changed. Says one observer, "Nobody from the tellers to the officers wastes anything in that bank."*

Another Happy Atom

Planning includes communication, elements of control, ways to keep organizations and the people in them from doing dumb things, ways of embracing opportunity on the fly, techniques for generating data, schemes for asking "What if?" and getting sensible answers, means for reinforcing cultural values, and a whole lot more. The last thing planning seems to do is cough out a plan that anyone takes seriously.

These differing purposes of planning don't fit neatly together. Often they work at cross-purposes. To the extent the process helps with control, it drives out opportunity, and vice versa. Too many controls with too little communication can straitjacket an organization. Too much opportunity generation with too little "What-if" thinking results in distastefully random corporate di-

---

* As Reichardt well knows, his zealous approach to cost control—taken to extreme—eventually lowers service, though in the early years of the program, quality and service often improved. He has been willing to take that risk, wisely it seems, to ensure cost competitiveness in the new deregulated environment.

rection. The renewers seem to understand the problem. They are continually testing the mix among the various purposes of planning, and correcting imbalances among them when they occur. They don't always get it right, of course. Most renewers probably do not give much conscious thought to the matter of managing the scrimmage among these purposes. But they do it well nonetheless.

Planning, as it is practiced by the renewers, *is* complex. One way we deal with complexity is to hunk it up into buckets or categories that seem more manageable than the totality. Maybe we're fooling ourselves, but the ruse seems to work. We can either chuck planning or chunk it. These days, the latter seems the way to go. With the chunking idea in mind, we can build a picture of planning that is similar to the 7-S framework. This time the alliteration is built around the letter C. While it seems a little cornball to do it this way, the alliteration does help people remember it, talk about it, use it.

7-C FRAMEWORK

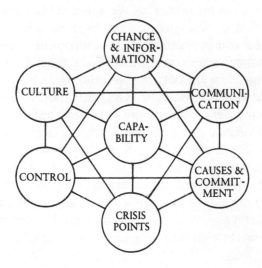

In the center of the new framework is the word *Capability*. The dependent variable, it means the same thing as *Skills* in the other framework. The purpose of planning, like the purpose of organization and of most managerial work, is to keep building capability. Build institutional skill. Build corporate capability. Create what the theorists call *distinctive competence* or *sustainable competitive advantage*. At the very minimum, fight organizational entropy and dry rot. Around *Capability* go the six chunks representing the multipurpose activity that we have come to call *planning* or *strategy*.

Communication. Life in organizations is all about dividing up tasks—remember Adam Smith's division of labor?—and then reintegrating. Planning as communication is a powerful force for integration. People can use plans to let one another know what they intend to do. Thus Mr. Right Hand knows what Mr. Left Hand has in mind. If potential problems exist, they can get to them sooner; if opportunity for useful coordination exists, they can get to that sooner. Planning as communication enables the large organization to deal with complicated issues of integration without resorting to nightmarish ways of structuring, like the matrix. For small organizations the value in planning as communication is that it forces people to be explicit; small organizations assume good communication because everyone knows everyone else, and managers see one another all the time. That helps, but it doesn't insure they are talking about the tough issues.

Chance and Information. While this hardly needs saying to grown-up managers, we live in an imperfect, unfair, unpredictable world. The *Chance and Information* chunk of the planning atom is the same idea in strategy as informed opportunism. Chance and information remind the manager that some of the biggest strategic decisions he makes will be unpredictable. Recognition of the prominent part played by chance makes managers rightfully suspicious of forecasts, keeps them from being blinded by their own plans, makes them more ready to snag opportunity as it passes by.

The manager cannot do much to control the random, the stochastic, the stray consequence of outrageous fortune. What the manager can do is be informed. Then he knows to duck or to seize the moment.

Causes, Commitment, and the Issues. Planning can be a barren, boring numbers exercise unless it is supported by a system that regularly surfaces big issues and puts priorities against them and transforms them to causes that people can commit to. Though the issues can and should be subject to analysis, their wellspring isn't usually rigorous analysis. Rather, they result from the subjective, esthetic, informed-but-seemingly-whimsical judgment of the company's leaders. An institutionalized, but *movable,* issues list becomes the source for one of the main instruments of renewal: the causes and commitments that transform companies. The list of issues and causes must stay "movable" because the environment changes. People responsible for planning should act as "issue brokers." Their role is to make sure the important issues get surfaced and that someone is working on them; it is seldom to take on an issue themselves. (More on this subject in Chapter 9.)

Crisis Points. Planning helps insure that the company will be economically healthy in the future. But it can do more; it can help anticipate crisis or unusual opportunity through the generation of "what-if" scenarios. Take existing trends in existing businesses and, using the computer as aid, project them forward three years, five years, ten years. Is the outcome acceptable? It almost never is. By playing around with the assumptions that go into the model, you can usually figure out why the outcome is unsatisfactory. You also find the crisis points—what could happen if something doesn't change. This enables companies to change course before crisis hits. Crisis does bring about revolutionary change, but it's unpleasant and usually too survival-oriented. (More on this subject in Chapter 4.)

Control. Like budgeting, a part of long-range planning is a congenial control process. Renewing executives ask managers to commit to a growth, earnings, or market-share target five years out. Given forecasting uncertainties, nobody knows for sure what will happen that far into the future. But both executives and managers need a way of saying to each other: "Here is what I think it will take to keep this business in good health five years from now. Do you agree? What will it take to get us there?" The renewing companies are looking at only a few numbers like this.

They maintain flexibility by reviewing the five-year targets every year and changing them if necessary. This part of planning is a form of congenial control. "Let's invest only in businesses that will nourish our future; let's do our best to ensure good returns on equity capital." (More on this subject in Chapter 4.)

Culture. This is the same as *Shared Values* in the 7-S framework. Many companies use planning as a way of reinforcing the aspects of their culture that they actively want to manage. The annual rite of long-range planning is a nice venue for restating shared values, vision, and overarching goals—what you stand for or would like to stand for.

Putting It Together

The 7-C framework helps make retrospective sense of the planning that we saw in the renewing companies. But it can do more. Think of the six C's surrounding *Capability* as a diagram of the cylinders and pistons in an engine. The engine works best, obviously, when all the pistons are working together. If one or two cylinders aren't firing, the engine runs, but at great loss of power. If the cylinders are all firing at the wrong time, the engine doesn't run at all. It's the same with the 7-S or 7-C framework. For an organization to have a well-developed skill or capability, all the parts of the framework need to support it. To build a new skill or capability, all parts of the framework need to be built.

This helps explain why renewal is such a complex set of processes. It also suggests a reality check for planning and organizing change. If the skill to be built is too different from the ones presently in place—if great change is needed in all the supporting variables in the framework—implementation is almost impossible.

The 7-S and 7-C frameworks can be linked. *Skills* in the first framework is the same as *Capability* in the second; *Shared Values* in the first framework is the same as *Culture* in the second. By putting these two frameworks together, we can draw the "renewal ring." It offers one view of how organization and planning processes can work in unison to build the unique skill, competence, and culture that make organizations strong.

THE RENEWAL RING

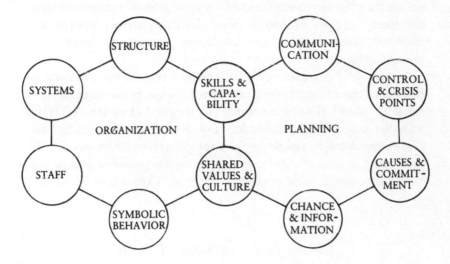

Usually gimmicks, fads, and simple prescriptions for success don't work. The trouble with putting forward something like the 7-S or 7-C framework, or the renewal ring, is that they look gimmicky. But their value is to help people look beyond expedients. The frameworks suggest that neither strategic planning nor organization is simple, that one doesn't necessarily follow the other, and that in managing change, all the factors are linked.

The 7-S diagram is an excellent framework for figuring out why organizations don't build the capability and the competence they aspire to. Sometimes they are structured wrong. In other cases—banks are a good example—the structure is okay, but the systems give them no reliable information on cost, profitability, or risk. In still other cases the structure and systems may be right, but the people in the organization—the *Staff* dimension of the framework—don't have the right background or training.

The combined framework works the same way. There are several companies that want to maintain division autonomy but also need to coordinate division activities; they could use their planning system for communication. Others rely too much on the control aspect of the planning framework but do not use planning to anticipate crisis points; they do little "what-if" analysis. For others the planning system could be a great information generator— the basis for the "informed" side of the informed opportunism equation. Instead, these companies use planning to develop detailed strategies.

Like the 7-S framework, the renewal ring keeps returning to the questions of capability and culture. What is the organization good at? Why? What does it need to be good at to renew? What will that take? The framework is not prescriptive. It does not tell a manager how to renew or in what dimensions renewal should take place. It does clarify how companies use planning and organizing processes in their pursuit of renewal. That is a good start.

Steps for Getting There

In summary, though renewal "ought" to start with a strategy for change, the reality of change defies our best attempts to plan it. Renewal requires continuing adaptation to an uncertain environment, and the reason we can't plan renewal carefully is that we cannot trust our forecasts. So what do you do when you *know* strategy is important, but you want to make it as forecast-proof as possible? What follows is a partial "to do" list that is meant to get you started. The complete list depends on your own situation; one of the "to do's," then, is to come up with a list like this that applies to you.

1. Treat strategy as a matter of informed opportunism, with equal emphasis on both words in that phrase. Being opportunistic alone only gets companies, divisions, departments, and individuals in trouble. On the other hand, gathering all the information you can before acting is a nice idea, but it's usually impossible. Often, getting more information is just an excuse for not acting if there's risk involved.

    Strategic events lie at the happy intersection of opportunity and information. This is as true for units within companies as it is for the companies themselves. As you move down the line, there are fewer degrees of freedom to act opportunistically, but the concept of informed opportunism remains just as important. Departments may not be able to make acquisitions, but they certainly can, and should, be both informed and opportunistic when they innovate.

2. Assume that opportunity knocks often, not just once. Further assume that the important strategic decisions of your company, career, and life will be inherently opportunistic. The best way to approach the future is with a general sense of direction, continuous learning, and a high degree of flexibility.

3. Set direction, not detailed strategy. As it is currently practiced, long-range planning assumes that given enough time, analysis, and brainpower your organization can get its strategy "right." This assumption is heroic but wrong. Too many major and minor shocks that influence strategic options can't possibly be anticipated.

4. Keep thinking of Simon's determined ant on the dunelet, with its general direction and haphazard path. "Management is an unstable technology," says Bernie O'Keefe of EG&G. "The only way you learn in unstable environments is through deviation. You set a course, observe the deviation, adjust. That's why we move between centralization and decentralization, entrepreneurialism and planning, line and staff." Unlike budgeting, strategic plans and goals are intended to produce a better understanding of deviations, rather than to set a standard that doesn't allow them.

5. Think and rethink basic direction, but keep the statement of it simple and general. Recognize that in doing so, you will frustrate people who are looking for "the strategy." Our idealized image of strategy as a complete game plan is so strong that general statements like Wells Fargo's emphasis on cost control and IBM's four goals seem unsatisfying. You may find that directional strategic statements stimulate internal disagreement over whether or not your company has a "strategy." The people look-

ing for specifics will argue you don't, and those who see the purpose of strategy as providing a few guiding principles will argue that you do.

6. Treat renewal and strategy as a series of successive approximations to the future. Inch into uncharted waters; don't test the water with both feet. Learn by experimenting. If possible, make several smaller opportunistic moves rather than one big one. This in essence is the game played by the venture capitalists with their investments, by the HPs and 3Ms through their multiplicity of divisions, and by IBM with its independent business units. Of any ten deals being made by a venture capitalist, he expects a few failures, several between okay and successful, and a couple of wild successes. He would never bet the whole portfolio on one or two big deals.

   Like the venture capitalist, you win on the averages over a period of time—not on any one hand. Don't make big, bet-the-organization decisions unless you have no other choice. Even when you are forced into this position, try to break the big program into many small ones. This principle holds even with companies like Bechtel or Boeing, where every transaction is of mega-deal proportions.

7. Keep repeating what essayist and ecologist Garrett Hardin calls The First Law of Ecology: We can never do merely one thing. This law, says Hardin, "warns us that any human intervention in the order of things will likely have unforeseen consequences; and that many, perhaps most— perhaps all—will be contrary to our expectations and desires." He gives as an example the building of the High Aswan Dam in Egypt, which produced electricity and water for year-round irrigation—and which also increased the incidence of disease-bearing parasites, decimated shrimp fisheries in the eastern Mediterranean, and disrupted the five-thousand-year flow of silt nutrients into delta farmland.

   Organizational theorist Karl Weick makes a similar point with an example of what he calls long-chain, casual, but unpredictable events. "If the National Hockey League has been wondering why it cannot keep expanding indiscriminately, the final round of the Stanley Cup playoffs between the Buffalo Sabers and the Philadelphia Flyers may have provided one big reason: Fog. Last night the temperature was about 76 degrees at game time, but near the 90 mark inside the rink. For the last 33 minutes . . . the contest was halted 12 times . . . when the clouds of steam made it impossible to see the puck. Rene Roberts of Buffalo burst out of one fogbank in sudden death to tally the game-winning goal." Expanding the number of teams—and hence the playoff schedule and the season— seems like a perfectly sensible, well-planned decision. But who would have planned on fog? A good plan with a perverse, self-defeating outcome.

8. Make it your business to get better at thinking in terms of probabilities, and encourage others to do the same. Most of us don't get any formal training in probability and statistics, except in graduate school or maybe poker. Kahneman and Tversky have done extensive research on why most of us make decisions that ignore or go against the probabilities. Their studies suggest that we tend to trust small samples more than large ones; we tend to make judgments on "fact bases" that have absolutely no informational content; we tend to associate events that are demonstrably unrelated; we cling to pet projects that should have been shut down years before; we are suckers for lottery tickets and Las Vegas. The list goes on, but what it adds up to is the need to get better informed about and more comfortable with probability.

9. Recognize that any business decision is inherently probabilistic. You stand a chance of being wrong no matter how carefully you analyze a decision. People don't like this conclusion. It means accepting a fair degree of uncertainty, and the human mind suppresses uncertainty. It means admitting that we don't know as much as we like to think we do about our jobs, our spouses, our kids, or ourselves.

10. Recognize also that forces that drive events in the environment are random—stochastic. One of the hot fields in physics right now is the study of chaos, based on the observation that even a few simple events can set off a chain of others that are both chaotic and random. Sometimes these stochastic shocks are the unanticipated consequences of your own actions; at other times they appear out of the blue, from outside, disrupting the best-laid plans.

11. Supplement the planning process by consciously looking for opportunity. Any formal management process—budgeting, long-range planning, calculating discounted cash flows—is inevitably conservative, because part of its purpose is to guard against downside risk. But this conservative bias chokes out opportunity. Keep an active planning process going; it serves many useful functions, including the generation of information. But keep your own antennae up for opportunity. Think Columbo: What doesn't fit? What doesn't make sense? Why? Celebrate the curiosity factor and encourage the people in your organization to be curious as well. "I have no particular talent," Albert Einstein once said. "I am merely extremely inquisitive."

    Peter Philip, head of gold operations for the exploration firm Newmont Mining, tells his geologists to be "Fred Astaires"—well-trained and fast on their feet. Warren Phillips, chairman of Dow Jones, observes of opportunity generation: "It's not so much originality as it is a mixture of luck and having something brought up and suggested, combined with the receptivity to get it started. It is certainly not somebody sitting in an office saying"—Phillips widens his eyes and makes an *aha* sound—" 'Hey, I have a brilliant idea.' It's a receptivity that pervades: 'Let's assume this guy has a good idea; let's go explore it and look for ways to make it work.' "

12. Treat information as the main strategic advantage. Assume that there is always more to know about your business. Invest heavily in building the fact base and in research—basic research, applied research, market re-

search, research on the competition. Research is cheap compared to the cost of development. Like Ore-Ida or James River, maintain an industry focus; it helps you know more than others about the business you're in. But also read widely outside your own field for parallels that might apply to what you're doing.

13. Go with your gut. The brain can process data in both straight rational form (the left brain) and in forms of overall patterns (the right brain). These two sides of the brain are complementary, not conflicting. Give them *both* room to maneuver. Get the facts, analyze them, and then do what *feels* right. Use your intuition and don't be embarrassed about it. Good decisions are neither all rational nor all intuitive.

Tony Athos refers to this as "what is tasteful and right for a situation at a given moment." No amount of purely left-brain analysis, even if skillfully done by human or simulated intelligence, can provide "fittedness." Whether you are functioning autonomously or on behalf of your company, you need that intuitive, pattern-recognizing, nonclassically rational, right-brain, aesthetic, fun-seeking side of the intellect. Only time can absolutely prove whether a decision is right or wrong, but we are much more apt to make decisions work *if we like them.*

14. Recognize the value of experience. Intuition is not as mysterious as it seems. It enables us to bring years of experience to bear without having to think about it consciously. A business school professor and consultant who specialized in strategy once put together some venture capital money and bought a set of companies that seemed to make good strategic sense, but the venture failed. He said, "I used to think strategy was everything. I still believe that strategy is crucial, but only if you have good operating people. Mine weren't. None of them had an instinct for the business." All the strategy and opportunity in the world would not make up for that lack of experience. It's simply another way of saying that intuition is not the soft side. At its best, it is the hard product of years of experience, years of collecting information.

15. Remember that planning serves multiple purposes. Use the 7-C framework, or something like it, to make sure that you and your troops understand the purposes of planning, to ensure that you're getting full benefit from the planning process, and to remind yourself not to take the plan itself too seriously.

16. Think of strategy, capability, and skill-building as much the same thing. Use the 7-S and 7-C frameworks separately or together to decide what will have to be changed as you build new skills. Use them as a check. Does a new strategy call for such dramatic changes in all the *S* and *C* categories as to be improbable? If new capabilities—innovation, marketing, service, or cost control—are central to the strategy and seem feasible, what do the frameworks say about priorities for change? Will you need to restructure? Find new ways to communicate? Use the framework to be specific about priorities for renewal. Use the framework to ensure that planning and organization help you move with the tides of change.

THREE

Direction and Empowerment

*We have 120,000 employees stashed in various
places around the world, and I frankly
have no idea what the hell they're doing.*

—ANDY PEARSON, FORMER PRESIDENT, PEPSICO INC.

*I think our business educational system has been
literally overwhelmed with ideas and concepts
that say to people, "Never mind your own beliefs. If you do these things you are going to succeed." I don't know that anyone has spent much
time trying to bring the sense of self out in
people.*

—JACK MACALLISTER, CHIEF EXECUTIVE OFFICER, US WEST

Look up the word *boss* in a book of synonyms. At the start of the
list you find *manage* and *direct*. Not bad. Then the list continues
with *control, order, command, take charge, preside over, oversee,
supervise, superintend, domineer, dominate, push around, ride
herd on, ride roughshod over, trample under foot,* and *shove
around.* The bulk of that list accurately reflects the way our

culture sees the manager, but it leaves little room for the brand of employee initiative that is central to the renewal of corporations.

In some very important sense, the boss is not really in control. An overseer for a ceramics operation tells a story that shows just how dependent the boss can be. One of his company's perpetual quality and yield problems had been teacups with handles that cracked off. A new plant manager, intent on solving this problem, assembled the workers for some brainstorming on the subject. He asked if anyone had any ideas. A tentative hand went up in the back of the room. "I think it's the slip [the clay mixture]." The fellow, who had been around awhile, explained that twenty-five years before, a plant manager who had experience in a German ceramics plant made them alter the slip formula. Ever since that time, the handles had been cracking off. "Is the old formula written down anywhere?" the new manager asked. Nobody could find it. Did anyone remember the old formula? The same employee said, "I think I do." They changed the slip. The handles stopped cracking.

Or another, more familiar illustration. A ubiquitous sight in American business offices is a copy of *The Wall Street Journal*. The paper's logo is an icon for capitalism; just look how often it shows up in "dress-for-success" clothing ads. Less well known is the management of Dow Jones & Company, the *Journal*'s owners, who took what was basically a newsletter for the New York financial community and transformed it into the largest-circulation newspaper in America.

Perhaps one reason for their success is that the people at Dow Jones are not trampled underfoot, domineered, or shoved around. An illustration: When Dow Jones bought a new printing press, the vendor estimated that installation would require closing the plant repeatedly over a six-week period—a major disruption. Management concurred. On their own initiative, a down-the-line operations team at Dow Jones did what they described as "back-of-the-envelope calculations" and figured out some shortcuts. They were able to install the machinery within six days, requiring only three days of downtime. In the process the team learned so much that they now have a tightly choreographed plan and can install new presses at other Dow Jones facilities over a weekend, with no lost time. When managers guide instead of control, the sky's the limit on what people can accomplish.

The empowerment idea goes back a ways in the Dow Jones culture. Ed Scharff, in his book *Worldly Power: The Making of The Wall Street Journal,* relates an incident that happened in 1956 involving the company's former chairman, the late Barney Kilgore and assistant production manager George Flynn. "Kilgore wandered through the plant one day while Flynn was wrestling with some nettlesome mechanical problem. 'I don't think we should do things this way at all,' said Flynn. . . . Kilgore shot back: 'Then why *do* you do things this way?' Flynn answered: 'Because New York does it this way'. . . . 'Well,' said Kilgore, 'not all of the brains are in the East.' " Flynn, later the company's general manager, recalls, "I worshiped him for that."

Dow Jones's story with the new press is similar to one we heard at Delta Airlines, a company that is doing one of the best jobs of navigating the not-so-friendly skies of deregulation. As part of their normal fleet modernization program, they were renewing fifteen DC-8s by putting on new engines that would be much quieter and more fuel-efficient. They subcontracted with McDonnell Douglas for the first one, but decided they should train some of their own people to make the same modifications on some of their other planes. Before the subcontractor finished the first aircraft, Delta's maintenance folks had completed the second. By the time Delta started on their fourth airplane, they had cut the turnaround time in half. "The program has been so successful," reports one Delta employee, "that the subcontractor has asked Delta to do the same modifications for three other airlines."

Stories like this—people down the line implementing imaginative programs for renewal—are legion. Procter & Gamble attributes $900 million in annualized cost savings to a collection of 25,000 such ideas from employees. Southern California Edison, widely regarded as one of the best-managed utilities and among the best-prepared for the wild swings in fuel prices and legislation that pummel the industry, tells a similar tale. They estimate that $100 million in savings over the past five years have come from the ideas of some 5,000 of their people. IBM says that its Suggestion Plan yielded ideas from 30,000 employees during 1985 which resulted in savings of more than $125 million; the company gladly paid these employees $18 million in cash awards for these suggestions.

Then there is John Psarouthakis, an immigrant from Crete with an MIT degree, who runs the eponymous JP Industries, Inc., in Ann Arbor, Michigan. He buys, at cheap prices, faltering manufacturing companies that make such mundane products as transmission bearings and toilet bowls. He then proceeds to turn them around; according to *Business Week,* he "counts heavily on the line workers for help in making plants more efficient. 'Just because they don't have a college education doesn't mean they don't have common sense,' " Psarouthakis says. Psarouthakis— known simply as "Dr. John"—bought one auto-parts maker that had an operating margin of less than 1.5 percent and boosted it within a year to 8.5 percent. His company has averaged a 30 percent return on equity since 1983.

There is nothing new about the basic idea of employee empowerment; the problem is getting non-Japanese managers to buy into it. In 1942, Allan H. Mogensen, or "Mogie" as his friends call him, published an article in *Fortune* called "65 Billion Man Hours." The article still makes for lively reading today. As a consultant in the 1930s with such clients as General Electric, where he and Thomas Edison were friends, Mogie found that it was possible to increase the output of a work force by as much as 50 percent. *Fortune*'s editors didn't believe him, sent reporters to companies using his methods, found out he was right, and printed the story.

An underlying tenet of his philosophy, then and now, is that "the person doing the job knows far better than anyone else the best way of doing that job and therefore is the one person best fitted to improve it." That's a comfortable and appealing idea. It's also a hard one to put into practice, for if it is true, then what's the boss for, except to get the hell out of the way?

Mogie and his contemporaries Joseph M. Juran and W. Edwards Deming are all now in their eighties. They have been right for a long time about how to improve productivity and quality. Some of the best American companies listened to them. But the culture that listened and took their message to heart was Japan. It is in Japan that the Deming Award for quality is given.

And it's in Japan that Deming, Juran, and Mogensen are cultural heroes. Even so, the typical American and European manager probably doesn't know much about Mogensen and friends. A philosophy like Mogensen's (the employee knows best) and the words we use to describe the boss (control, domineer) don't exactly jibe.

We have never come to grips with this question of management and control versus freedom and empowerment. Unless we do, our ability to restore high productivity and growth in this country is in doubt. Yet, in the renewing companies, especially in industries threatened by foreign competition where change has been successfully accomplished, there exists a balance between freedom and control that would make Mogie smile—a management style that combines the boss's need to be in command with the employee's need for individuality. A way of managing that keeps the leader in the position of directing, but recognizes that, at some level of detail, the employee *does* know the job better. The style is called "directed autonomy."

Directed Autonomy

In directed autonomy, people in every nook and cranny of the company are empowered—encouraged, in fact—to do things their way. Suggestions are actively sought. But this all takes place within a context of direction. People know what the boundaries are; they know where they should act on their own and where not. The boss knows that his or her job is to establish those boundaries, then truly get out of the way.

Nowhere did the concept seem more alive than at Steelcase. They are the folks, headquartered in Grand Rapids, who make office furniture and think of themselves as an office environment company. They say they are in the business of white-collar productivity. The market leader in office equipment since the mid-1960s, they continue to grow fast, edging out their closest competitor, Herman Miller, another great company.

Steelcase breaks all the rules. All of us "know" that nepotism is bad business practice. Steelcase makes it a point to hire relatives. One fellow we interviewed had more than a dozen brothers, sisters, uncles, aunts, cousins, and other assorted kin working at Steelcase. For most of their hiring, the company depends on recommendations from employees. They don't have to worry about finding applicants; there are so many people queued up to work for Steelcase that employees now have to have fifteen years' tenure in the organization before they can start sponsoring others. Steelcase knows there is a danger in becoming too inbred, so they require that 20 percent of their new employees come from other sources. Those other sources are minority groups, people laid off from other companies, and former Steelcase employees, especially ones who didn't work out previously and got fired.

What everyone also "knows" is that automation is anathema to the work force. But Steelcase gets the machine operator right into the decision to replace a machine. The company will not bend metal on a new piece of equipment until the operator has reviewed the design, suggested necessary engineering changes, and finally approved the machine that he or she will be running. When the equipment is delivered, it comes with a brass plate inscribed with the operator's name.

This process exemplifies directed autonomy. What stands out more than anything else at Steelcase is that although the basic decision to invest in new equipment or automate a line is management's (no question where the fundamental responsibility for productivity lies), the operator has a big say from then on. Nothing moves forward until the operator has been involved. At Steelcase, involvement does not mean cursory sign-off. The operator often makes suggestions that require substantial engineering changes.

Contrast that with the General Motors experience at Lordstown, Ohio, a little over a decade ago. The plant was built to be a paragon of modern work conditions and efficiency. Up and operating, it would turn out just about double the industry average of fifty-five cars per hour. Trouble was, it was slowed down by an almost endless stream of strikes and grievances. According to management professor James O'Toole, the people who designed and ran Lordstown never took advice from the union and the workers. Of the stories he tells about Lordstown, my favorite is the one about "doubling":

Under this system, four workers might agree among them-selves to become an informal team, and for a set period of time (say fifteen minutes to half an hour) two members of the team would work like the devil doing the work of all four, while the other two workers would rest, smoke, or chat. The workers claimed that this method improved the quality of their work by forcing them to concentrate on what would otherwise be a routine task, and improved their job satisfac-tion because it gave them a chance to schmooze with co-workers. . . . Doubling drove GM's efficiency experts up the wall. Nothing was more galling to them than to "have work-ers stand around chatting, while they are being paid to work!" The managers responded by disciplining workers (sending them home for a day or more without pay). In turn, the workers responded by filing more grievances.

The people who designed and ran Lordstown must not have been listening to Mogensen. Apparently their ideas on managing are straight from that book of synonyms for the boss: control, domi-nate, ride herd on. The Lordstown style was all direction, no autonomy, no empowerment. The investment in state-of-the-art technology was not paying off. As GM has since learned through its joint venture with Toyota in Fremont, California, even an ordinary plant can outperform highly automated plants elsewhere if the total workplace is better managed and the work force motivated.

Regarding American productivity, the reaction of many man-agers is resignation. They see the battle as already lost. It's not, but because they see it that way, their attitude could become self-fulfilling. Leaders who feel this sense of defeat and ennui are the real enemies of renewal. They see themselves as realistic, hard-nosed businessmen. What the people who work for them see is not the hard nose, but a hard head caused by being dead roughly from the neck up.

The fact is that American workers are still the most produc-tive in the world. According to *The Economist,* "Americans work every bit as hard as (and often a whole lot harder than) the

Japanese—and generate proportionately more wealth in the process. The average output of American workers last year [1985] was $36,800. The Japanese equivalent was $22,500 (at an average 1985 exchange rate of Y220 to the dollar)." But growth in America's productivity has been much slower than that of other nations. It *feels* as if we are falling behind, even though we haven't—yet. There is evidence that the situation is improving. Since the early 1980s' recession, something called "multifactor productivity," a measure that combines labor productivity with the productivity of the capital standing behind the worker, shot up in the United States at 5 percent per year. This compares with a 2 percent annual growth in the period from 1960 to the first oil shock in 1973, and a miniscule 0.1 percent annual growth between 1973 and 1981. Something is working, although there is no room for complacency. We are still at a disadvantage in labor cost and cost of capital.

The Economist puts forward the "kick in the backside" theory of American economics. Every now and then—Pearl Harbor, Sputnik, Vietnam, foreign competition—we get a massive boot in a very broad backside. There follows "an awesome display of industrial muscle coupled with unexpected consensus between old adversaries—most notably between Congress, business, and labor." Most American companies were severely taken aback by the double whammy of the recession in the early 1980s and Japanese competition. No question that this kick in the backside sparked renewal. Most of the renewers have sprung back with encouraging results. Some, like Maytag in white goods or Nucor in steel, were doing well all along. The question, as usual, is "What were they doing to generate productivity?" And the corollary: "What should the rest of us do?"

We can start by examining our own beliefs about what we *do* when we manage. How much does each of us resemble that second part of the list of synonyms: *control, dominate, push around*? Most of us are closer than we would like to think and most of us are uncomfortable with the ambiguity inherent in a leadership style that calls for both control and autonomy.

The most complete corporate model we have found of directed autonomy in action is at Super Valu, the nation's largest food wholesaler. Super Valu, based in suburban Minneapolis, distributes groceries to more than 3,000 independently owned food markets, many of them "Mom and Pop" stores in rural locations.

Fifteen years ago, we would have written off the independent grocery store as mortally wounded, if not already dead. Chains like A&P and Safeway would dominate; the little guy could not survive. But just the reverse has happened. The small grocery chains and independents have shown amazing growth and strength. A part of the reason is the ability of small organizations in general to innovate and adapt. Another part is the enormous support they get from grocery distributors like Super Valu (or Sysco, in Houston), who make it their business to keep the independents healthy. These companies are fascinating examples of how to combine the strength of a big corporation with the entrepreneurship that comes from smallness.

If Super Valu's customers functioned as a unit, they would comprise the country's fourth-largest chain. As you might expect, these grocers are proud of their independence, and are accustomed to competing in their towns over fractions of pennies against the big food chains. They aren't shy about speaking their minds. Says Tom Dekko, Super Valu's vice-president of sales: "You won't find a Kroger store manager giving his CEO hell. But if a meat program or an ad campaign turns out bad, you'll have an independent retailer walking into my office or getting [Super Value CEO] Mike Wright on the phone."

Super Valu also has a big central "staff" that offers the independents an array of support services: store location research, such as telephone surveys and focus groups; advisory services for labor relations, such as contract negotiations and grievance handling; architectural help, such as floor plan design; and even tax counseling and estate planning. That's the "directed" (or in this case "guided") dimension. But all services are on a take-it-or-leave-it basis. There are no contractual ties that obligate the independents to use these services. "You can't work that way [contracts] with entrepreneurs," says John Ferris, Super Valu's senior vice president of finance. That's the "autonomy" dimension. The dynamics of the balance are crucial. Most staffs the size of Super Valu's would collapse of their own inertia, taking the company with them. But at Super Valu the staff has little actual power over the independent retailers. Explains CEO Mike Wright: "We offer customers a support mechanism they never had before, but it is a matter of giving them more resources, not telling them what to do." Wright continues: "We don't try to tell them from here if they need more square footage in Cheyenne, Wyoming. They're likely to think, 'Why don't you just come out here and run the store for me?' "

The recent success of McKesson, now the leading distributor to independent pharmacists, has much to do with a structure that, like Super Valu, forces directed autonomy. Just like Super Valu, they support the independents; they do not control them. Their revenue is derived from distribution and supporting services. In effect, McKesson and the independents have the advantages of a chain operation without being a chain. You wonder whether it might work elsewhere. With all the turmoil in health care, many doctors talk as if loss of their independence is a certainty. Concurrently, the American Medical Association wonders whether it will have a role in the future. They both should take courage, though they wouldn't like the comparison, from the examples set by the independent grocers, independent druggists, Super Valu, Sysco, McKesson.

Implementation Starts
Day One

There is no simple, linear progression from decision to action. If some of the best ideas come from the folks down the line, then optimum efficiency results from involving them *before* a decision is made. Alternatives, decisions, and steps for implementation should spring up together. These aspects of a truly inspired program move together simultaneously or in parallel, rather than sequentially. They interact. In other words, implementation starts day one.

An organization that makes appropriate decisions adapts as it moves. Organizations are supposed to first study alternatives, then make recommendations, and *then* implement the decisions, but it doesn't always work that way. It sounds eminently logical.

It isn't. This kind of process is inefficient. Carrying out a decision doesn't start after the decision; it starts with the decision. Figuring out how to get something done is just as important as deciding what to do.

This principle captures much of Ford Motor Company's recent success, something that seemed clear to me during a trip to Chicago. Ford has one of its largest manufacturing facilities here—2.3 million square feet under one roof. The automobile continues to be, both emotionally and symbolically, the *lingua franca* of international competition. And Ford serves as an excellent example of renewal.

Ford and other American car companies used to build cars sequentially—one step at a time. First, the designers would determine what the car would look like. Then, when their plans were complete and clay models had been made, they would turn the car over to the engineering department. Engineering would make their changes and hand it off to the manufacturing people, who would figure out how to build the car. Sales and marketing would create ways to sell it. By the time the people on the production line who had to build the car, or the customers who were expected to buy it, got to cast their votes, it was too late to change anything.

This sequential process has turned out to be hopelessly flawed. People at Ford refer to it as "tossing it over the wall." Design works on a project, tosses it over the wall to engineering, which tosses it over the wall to production, and so on. But engineering might not like whatever design tossed; production might not like what engineering had done, and so on.

For two reasons those on the receiving end usually don't like what they are tossed. The first is simply the NIH factor—"not invented here." A fairly well-known phenomenon in the management of technology, NIH refers to the fact that most engineers are predisposed not to like things that other engineers have invented. The second reason goes beyond mere unwillingness to accept somebody else's ideas. Engineers might not be able to find an economic or safe way to do what the design guys came up with. Or the production people might not be able to find a good way to make the car that has come from engineering.

The over-the-wall syndrome means that considerable reinventing occurs. Thus, a process that looks simple and logical turns out to be costly and duplicative. Furthermore, nobody ultimately feels responsible for making the thing work. Either it wasn't his idea in the first place, or it was changed so many times as it moved down the stream, it no longer resembled his idea.

Ford decided to do things differently with the Taurus. Everything proceeded in parallel. A big task force was formed under the direction of Lew Veraldi, who was chosen to spearhead the Taurus effort. From the beginning, all the disciplines, from design through assembly to marketing, came on-stream in unison. In a company news release, Veraldi explains: "If you bring people from those disciplines into the act early, you can effect changes to make the inherent quality better." All of the relevant disciplines interact and contribute from the beginning. They participate together as the car develops. NIH is mitigated. Most important, quality goes up, and the customer voice is heard. Veraldi continues: "Four and a half years before job one ["job one" is the first car off the production line] we visited assembly plants, manufacturing facilities, major suppliers, the Service Managers Council, and insurance companies. We asked them: 'If you were doing this type of vehicle, what would you like to see in it?' "

John Risk, who worked right under Veraldi during the entire Taurus program, remembers his early days on Team Taurus: "I'd be down at the Atlanta assembly plant. I'd climb in the car as it went down the assembly line and introduce myself. Then I'd ask for ideas. In one case, I saw two people juggling an instrument panel, so I asked them what might make that job easier. They suggested a small locator pin that would secure the panel in the same place every time. The effect would be [and is] less juggling and only one person to do the job."

Team Taurus came up with a "want list" with no less than 1,401 items suggested by Ford employees. In Atlanta they put drawings on the wall. (What a contrast from the secrecy that characterized the industry before!) They asked the folks what they would like to see in a new car built in their plant. They wanted to know what would make their job easier or the quality higher. One line operator suggested a one-piece body side and doors, "so we have integrity in the door margins and a better overall fit." Risk added, "We couldn't get a press big enough for that, but we did get the design down to a two-piece assembly, instead of the twelve or fifteen that is typical for us."

John Risk estimates that the Taurus team was able to incorporate approximately 80 percent of the want list from the plant visits. Veraldi's estimate is a little more conservative: over half. In either case, it's a splendid example of the power of the Mogensen philosophy. It is also a vivid illustration of the way implementation should work. The people who had to carry out management decisions were involved in management decisions; the sources of the ideas were, as often as not, the implementers of the ideas.

Risk adds a nice postscript to the want list. During the process of collecting ideas, the Taurus team had a system of regular reviews and ideas logged on computer. In every case they got back to the people who had made the suggestion. Even—or maybe especially—when they didn't use an idea, they went back to the individual and told him or her why the idea didn't fly. The last thing Ford wanted to hear was "I gave you ten ideas and never heard from you, and you never incorporated anything I suggested."* The results: The Taurus won *Motor Trend*'s 1986 Car of the Year award.

In the newly deregulated banking industry, New York's Bankers Trust Company has made one of the more vigorous, and so far successful, efforts to renew. They saw themselves as having no special strengths in consumer banking, so they pulled out of that part of the business. Then Lynn Shostack was brought in from Citicorp to manage the division that caters to wealthy individuals. When she took over her part of the bank, it employed 325 people and was losing $7 million a year. Not long after, her division

---

* Employee relations are not picture-perfect throughout Ford. Jim Roti Roti, president of the UAW local at Ford's Green Island, New York, plant, told us about Ford's decision to close the plant in 1988 even though it has an exceptional employee involvement program. Thanks to a cooperative union and management, the plant has improved quality 60 percent, reduced grievances, and sponsored a joint fund-raising campaign to put up billboards urging people to buy Ford products. Union members even volunteer their time to send out letters about Ford vehicles and distribute brochures in Ford automobile showrooms. But in 1984, Ford decided to begin using aluminum instead of copper and brass for the radiators and heater coils they had been making in Green Island for the past six decades. Despite Green Island's super track record, its leaders couldn't convince headquarters to retool the plant for aluminum—or anything else, for that matter. The new aluminum radiators and heater coils will be made in Michigan. Undaunted, Roti Roti is still "fighting to keep the doors open." He concludes, "I won't quit until the door is shut and locked for the last time."

employed 1,000 people and was making $18 million in pretax income. She spent most of the time urging her view that figuring out what to do is not hard. It's making it happen that's difficult. Facing her desk was a sign that her husband made after she was quoted in a press interview: "The concept is easy; implementation is a bitch." She talked about what she called "peace on earth proposals": ideas that sound terrific, can't be quarreled with, and can't be implemented—like universal customer information systems. "When people present those," she says, "the sign comes in handy."

The reason implementation is so difficult is that we think of it as something managers do after they make a decision. What the Taurus example so *clearly* illustrates is the power of implementing in parallel.

The traditional management model demeans nonmanagers. It celebrates hierarchy. Bosses decide things and workers carry them out. It is what author Richard Pascale refers to as the big brain school of management. People at the top do the thinking. People down the line obey orders.

The Ford Taurus story is about the power of empowerment. Decisions made with the people are better decisions. First, the creative quotient is higher. At some level of detail, the people doing the work *do* know it better than those who are managing. They live with it every day and probably have wondered a hundred times: "Why do we do it that way?" or "Wouldn't it be better if? . . ." But they seldom ask these questions aloud. Often they have the impression it "isn't their place" to be making suggestions. Or they feel that all the smart thinking is done "in New York" or some other preordained place. "I don't make the rules; I just work here," goes the refrain. And often the reason they have that impression is that the boss lets them know, explicitly or implicitly, that he feels that way.

The other reason that implementation works best (or perhaps, only works at all) with day one empowerment is that all of us are most committed to our own ideas. If a decision has come from somewhere else, few of us can get very excited about making it work. If a decision arrives complete with detail on how to carry it out, we may even take perverse delight in screwing it up.

But if the idea (or a part of it) is ours in the first place . . . well, it's hard not to like that idea *and* its source.

The success of the Taurus might never have been possible without a Ford program for empowering people that started in 1978. The words are right out of the Mogensen philosophy: "If you want a job done better, listen to the people who actually do the work." Writing about it several years ago, then Ford Chief Executive Philip Caldwell stated:

*T*he magic of employee involvement [EI] is that it allows individuals to discover their own potential—and to put that potential to work in more creative ways. A survey last year of more than 750 EI participants at seven facilities found that a full 82 percent felt they now had a chance to accomplish something worthwhile, compared with only 27 percent before EI was initiated. . . . People develop in themselves pride in workmanship, self-respect, self-reliance, and a heightened sense of responsibility.

This has also contributed importantly to the significant improvements in product quality and productivity. . . . The quality of Ford cars and trucks on average has increased by more than 50 percent since 1980. Independent research shows that the quality of our 1983 models is 10 percent better than GM's and 36 percent better than Chrysler's. It is also better than many of the major Japanese and European imports. . . . There are more than 15,000 finished parts on each car, and when a car rolls off the assembly line, every nut, bolt, weld, and piece of trim must be in place—and it must be right. That is why individual employees have been given the authority to stop an assembly line if the quality is not right. That is also why, long before they are ready for production, prototypes of vehicles are brought into the plants that will make them, and employees are asked for their ideas on how they can be made better.

The way it works in Ford's Chicago plant is that the employee involvement program is strictly voluntary. People form six- to ten-person teams and tackle any problem they see. "Housekeeping" —the basic maintenance of the work site—is a typical first concern. That is probably because housekeeping is an easy place to start and the work area is usually more of a mess than people like. "Then," says Dick Ross, who heads up personnel at the plant, "they move on to other problems, and the first one they usually choose is the set of artificial and habitual boundaries that divide job responsibilities." Joe Bobnar, the plant manager and a veteran of the Ford system, told me emphatically: "If I had to manage a plant again without employee involvement, I wouldn't do it."

In one case, some Ford employees formed an interior-trim group to tackle a problem they had had for two years: No matter what they did to adjust the carpet properly on the car floor, there was a persistent bulge. Although the problem had been referred to engineering, there was still no solution. Within three months of working on the problem themselves, the trim group figured out that if they cut a notch in the carpet in just the right place, the bulge would go away. They did it. Solved a problem in three months that engineering hadn't solved in two years.

Giving Up Control to Get Control

Ford's Dick Ross thinks one of the most important ingredients in employee involvement is the manager's attitude. A continuing problem at Ford, and in the automobile industry in general, is the unwillingness of old-school managers to refrain from being secretive and directive. To them, employee involvement feels like loss of control. It is nothing like their understanding of what the boss is supposed to do.

The problem is especially severe at the level of first-line supervision. The old-line supervisors grew up in an environment of relentless head-to-head confrontation with the unions. For them the idea of directed autonomy is counter to everything they stand for. Asking them to change is asking them to deny their past. At one manufacturing company a manager confesses, "The directed autonomy idea is working great in our new plants." But it has been tough, if not impossible, to break down the existing cultural norms of conflict and contention between union, first-line supervision, and the work force. They see no solution short of massive retraining, and they wonder if even that will work.

Stanford professor David Bradford sees the problem as deeply embedded in the American culture. He cites all sorts of research suggesting that a leadership model involving directed autonomy can lead to higher productivity. Even so, he observes that "no widespread models yet exist for managers who might be tender *and* tough, team-minded *and* independent, development- *and* performance-oriented. The most telling commentary comes from a student at a top business school describing his image of managers, whom Bradford quotes:

> ... *My ideal of a leader is a person who would really be looked up to by those around him as a model for their lives and for help and guidance. Many people might even have kind of an awe or reverence for him. He would be much more concerned with being respected than liked. Close personal relationships would be somewhat incidental. The person would clearly be seen as in control of the organization and know everything that is going on and how to handle it. He would be viewed as infallible and unaffected by things going on around him, not very emotional and rarely, if ever, displaying emotions to others. He'd usually be perceived as the brightest person in the organization, able to solve things quickly and with a high degree of sophistication. The leader would be essential to the functioning of the organization; without him it would quickly fall apart. He is responsible for orchestrating the workings of the entire system.*

Good God! Who wants to work for a person like that? While many M.B.A.s don't talk the way Bradford's business school student does, plenty of others do. The antidote for the manager-as-hero syndrome is what Harry Quadracci at Quad/Graphics calls "management by walking away." The idea began when he was trying to get his managers away to do some strategic thinking during a retreat known as Spring Fling. They thought they would shut down the presses for a day, but "then some [printing] work came in, and rather than cancel Spring Fling, we decided to let the hourly employees run the presses." Now, leaving the hourly employees in charge of the plant during the annual Spring Fling has become a tradition at the company.

In other words, give up control in order to gain control. Ask for ideas. Widen the boundaries around the latitude people have for doing their jobs. Walk away from decisions where you aren't needed. It *does feel* like loss of control. You have made yourself less central to every decision (and in that narrow sense are less "in control"). But at the same time you are more in control of what counts: the results.

With more people truly involved in implementation, real implementation—not going through the motions—is what you get. Some consultants take pride in their ability as implementers, people who "effect change." And on a literal level, they do bring about changes. But their evidence of implementation rests on criteria such as structural reorganization or company-wide programs of goals and objectives. But often these "changes" don't get results.

To get results you loosen the reins. The first time you try it, it will scare the hell out of you.

That certainly was my reaction during one of my most profound lessons in management. In 1969, I was part of a team working with the Sanwa Bank in Japan, now one of the largest banks in the world. It's unusual for anyone from the outside, let alone a foreign consulting firm, to be working with a Japanese company. Fortunately the problem—a substantial market share loss—was fairly easy to solve intellectually. After a few months we were ready to go to the board to present our analysis and recommendations.

But a couple of strange things were going on at Sanwa. At the beginning of the project we had asked for a full-time Sanwa team to complement our own team. Joint consultant and client task forces are more effective than solo consultant teams. The client members know their way around the organization and where the facts are buried; and, too, they are there after the outside consultants have left. After a long negotiation in which we thought Sanwa management had agreed with us, we figured that two or three of their people would join forces with us the next day. Twenty showed up.

"What's this?" we wanted to know. "Your study team," they explained. We protested that what we had meant by a team was smaller—certainly not twenty people. They said we had done such a good job of explaining the need for a client team that they thought they would do it right. We couldn't understand why this otherwise bright group of executives insisted on such a large team when it was obvious that the problem-solving would have been more efficient with a smaller one. But they were paying the bills, so we lurched forward with our unwieldy gang of twenty.

After two months we presented our results. The team of twenty reacted with horror. They explained that before we talked to the *jomu*s, we should discuss our findings with a fairly large group of people around the bank. They started a list that grew to several hundred people. We told them that would take a few months, reminded them of the project's cost, and suggested again that we simply report our solution to the board and get on with restoring market share. They reminded us that they were paying the bills and suggested we do it their way.

Several months later we finally made the presentation to the *jomu-kai*. It lasted only an hour and was mainly ceremonial. By then all the *jomu*s were well acquainted with what we were going to say.

Then something amazing happened. About two days after the presentation their market share started to rise! We had never seen results that fast. (In fact, as anyone who has consulted will tell you, getting results at all is sometimes a surprise.)

Involving twenty people on the team had nothing to do with problem-solving "efficiency." Our talking to hundreds more after we had the "answer" to the market share problem had nothing to do with crisp decision-making. Both processes had everything to do with *getting something done*.

By the time we made the final presentation to the *jomu*s, a significant part of the entire Sanwa organization had already been involved in the project. All those study-team members, all their friends in the bank, and all the people we talked to subsequently understood that market share was of prime concern to top management. They knew what the study team thought was the root of the problem. But most important, they had the chance to engage in the problem themselves. They could, and did, vigorously express their own views on the cause of the problem and solutions to it. They could, and did, contribute to the team's thinking. There was deep wisdom in Sanwa's insistence that we conduct the project in a way that at the time appeared to me to be inefficient, burdensome, and more than a little foolish.

When Andy Pearson was still president of PepsiCo, he said, "We have 120,000 employees stashed in various places around the world, and I frankly have no idea what the hell they're doing." Throughout the Sanwa project, with hundreds of people involved, we had no idea what they were all doing. In any sense of the word *control,* the project seemed out of control. But in a broader sense the thing was under control. The market share went up. Give up control, in the narrow sense, to get control, in a broader sense.

Later, one of the members of the team of twenty commented about presenting the results to the board early. "Good show business, bad consulting," he said. It says a lot about why "implementation is a bitch" for so many American and European managers. We are so busy grandstanding with "crisp decisions" that we don't take time to involve those who have to make the decisions work.

Solution Space

A helpful way of thinking about directed autonomy is a metaphor straight from higher mathematics, where many problems do not have single, unique solutions of the kind that we used to find, or try to find, in high-school algebra. Instead, they have a host of feasible solutions contained inside a set of boundaries, which are defined by the sets of equations and inequalities that describe the problem. Business problems are like that. Lots of reasonable, good answers. The manager's job is to establish the boundaries around a fairly broad solution space. The individual's responsibility is to find the best way of doing things within that space.

To understand this idea, think of Steelcase or Ford. When production management decides on new equipment for a Steelcase factory, the boundaries around the solution space are defined by management. They include the decision to upgrade the equipment, the general design of the equipment, and the way the equipment fits into the general scheme for continuing automation. At the same time, however, the Steelcase employee is expected to contribute to the development of the exact solution within that space. He or she reviews the plans for the new machine, maybe decides that the buttons would be better if placed here rather than there. Or she suggests that a certain part of the machine might function more smoothly if designed in a different way. He points out that his job might be easier if the equipment were higher so he didn't have to bend over so far.

Or at Ford, the boundaries get defined when top management decides that employee involvement is going to be a way of life, that the styling and quality of cars they are producing must be improved, that they will try a project team approach to product development rather than a sequential one. But the folks at all levels in the organization come back with the specific solutions inside their own solution space, all of which contribute to the broader purpose described above. At one level, Jack Telnack and his team came back with their ideas on design—specifically, an aerodynamic look. At another level, and in response to a different solution space set out for them, employees in Atlanta told them how to make the car easier to manufacture, of higher quality, and less costly.

Dick Madden, the chief executive who over the last fifteen years turned Potlatch Corporation into a top performer within the wood-products and paper industry, suggests an analogy for solution space. Think of the boundaries within which your staff operates as you would the walls of a room. Make sure that the walls are far enough apart to give people maximum space, but never so far apart that management can't support people if they stumble. The walls are there to strengthen and guide; they aren't there to restrict or confine. As skills develop, the boundaries can be enlarged.

A classic case of boundaries drawn too tightly occurred on the Skylab 4 flight in December 1973. In an attempt to get the most information possible from this final mission, ground control in Houston had scheduled the astronauts' days so tightly that they were even forbidden to participate in their favorite pastime— watching the sun and the earth. Houston daily "sent up about six feet of instructions" to the astronauts' teleprinter. . . ." Commented the mission flight director: "We've learned how to maximize what you can get out of a man in one day." That was hardly the case. The civilian physicist on board begged ground control to "give the astronauts a bare framework of a schedule, together with a shopping list of things for them to do, *and then let the guys on board figure out the best way of doing them.*" (Emphasis added.) When Houston decided against letting the astronauts design their own calendar of activities, the crew protested with a daylong sit-down strike. The first one ever in space.

Another illustration of solution space came at Children's Television Workshop in New York City, whose main product— *Sesame Street*—is one of the best examples of continuing renewal in the not-for-profit sector. Each segment of *Sesame Street* is designed around its own solution space, defined in terms of educational content, entertainment value, and what's best for the development of preschoolers.

In the summer of 1981, Will Lee, the actor who played an adult character named Mr. Hooper on the show, died. This posed a difficult set of issues for CTW. Should they deal at all with the subject of death? If so, how would they explain it to their 10 million viewers, most of whom are under the age of six? *Sesame Street* writers usually approach tough judgment calls like this by defining a solution space. They draw the space with advice from their own research department, along with their sense of how television communicates with children.

A staff writer describes it this way: "We asked ourselves: 'What do we want the kids to know? What can they absorb? What might open up things we can't answer?' We try to create boundaries around what we can safely teach without doing any damage."

Child-development experts who specialize in loss and separation provided some specific don'ts for the solution space for dealing with death on the show: Don't say Mr. Hooper got sick and died, because you don't always die when you get sick. Don't say he was old, because children think their parents are old. Don't say he went to the hospital and died, because people go to the hospital all the time. The staff also decided to avoid religious issues, such as saying that Mr. Hooper had gone to heaven.

What about the do's? "Early on we decided we were going to say a few basic things. He's gone—acknowledge the reality. He won't be back. He'll be missed. We also wanted the cast to express how they felt about Will. And we wanted the kids to know that death stimulates a full range of emotions. You're sad, you're angry, you're frustrated—all at the same time."

The show that resulted aired on Thanksgiving, so that parents could watch with their children. In one segment, Big Bird walks on camera and says to the cast: "I just drew pictures of all my grown-up friends on Sesame Street and I'm going to give them to you." He passes out sketches and the cast members ooh and ahh over the likenesses. He's left with Mr. Hooper's picture. "I can't wait till he sees it," says Big Bird. "Say, where is he? I want to give it to him."

One cast member explains: "Big Bird, don't you remember? We told you . . . Mr. Hooper died. He's dead." Big Bird says, "Oh, yeah, I remember. Well . . . I'll give it to him when he comes back." Another cast member gets up from her chair and touches Big Bird, saying, "Big Bird, Mr. Hooper's not coming back."

"Why not?"

"Big Bird, when people die, they don't come back."

That scene reflects one of the best examples I have seen of change handled in a way that was sensitive to the needs of both the people in an organization and its market. Members of the cast recall the incident: "It was totally out of the question to have another actor replace Will. Most of us thought we really ought to deal directly with the subject of his death on the show. Though we were tempted, we didn't allow our emotional distress over Will's death to overtake what we should do on the show. At first I wanted a great eulogy—show all his best scenes—and suggested that to Dulcy [the executive producer]. She said, 'Well, that's our own thing. That wouldn't help the audience.'"

The heart of the solution space idea is that within the boundaries there is no "optimum" answer, other than what the employees suggest. If what the people come up with fits within the solution space and they like it, that is about as close to optimum as you can get. In fact, *that is the test of the optimum.*

For most management issues there are thousands of alternatives—most of them lousy. The job of the manager—that is to say, the boundary definer—is to toss out the bad ones. Those are the ones outside the boundaries of the solution space. But having done that, a company may still be left with dozens, maybe hundreds, of good answers. It is not—repeat, not—the job of the manager to figure out which of these acceptable answers is "the best." Most managers feel guilty when they can't do that. And if they don't feel guilty all by themselves, their subordinates or superiors will help by suggesting that they ought to know what's best. But they shouldn't. Once they have narrowed the space down to a set of good alternatives, the only ones who can select the best alternative are the people who will carry out the decision.

Potlatch's Madden refers to a related concept he calls *subsidiarity*: Never make a decision at a higher level that can be made at a lower level. A decision made at a higher level is an averaging decision and not necessarily the most appropriate one. To illustrate, he tells the story of two neighboring towns. One town had a young population; it needed two schools. The other had an old population; it needed two hospitals. When the regional planners met, they combined the information from both towns and decided that each one needed a hospital and a school—not exactly an optimal solution for either community but one that the "averages" on paper justified.

This is not to imply that boundary setting is easy. It's simply another way of deciding what to do, by pushing some of those decisions to lower levels in the organization. Another note of caution: The word *boundaries* makes the situation sound more static than it is. Management's job is to keep testing those boundaries to make sure they are appropriate. Maybe they need to be modified as circumstances change. Probably they need to be broadened as managers and subordinates gain experience. The critical image is one of boundaries around solution space. It makes for better management and better decisions.

Individual Renewal

Renewing the corporation, to the extent it was considered at all, used to be judged as mainly the job of top management. Individual renewal was something most of us dreamed of, but mainly off-line, off the job, on weekends, on vacation, or at home. Few made the connection between the corporation and the individual. But with the destaffing, delayering, and demanualization that is going on in the American economy, renewal isn't the frosting on a dull managerial or supervisory cake. It *is* the cake. If you're a manager at any level, it's your job.

In the mid-seventies, Dana had fourteen layers of management between the chief executive's office and the person on the factory floor. Today, Dana's president, Woody Morcott, takes extraordinary pride in the fact that there are only five layers. Their struggle to keep unnecessary bureaucracy out of the system is relentless. Gerry Mitchell, Dana's CEO, has a simple logic: "Five is better than six, and when we can get to four we will do it." At the extreme, the company has one plant in Nebraska that employs 120 people. The organization structure there is simple: 120 people, one plant manager, and nothing in between. When Dana moved into their headquarters building in Toledo, Ohio, they had 475 people on the corporate staff. Now they have about 75, including secretaries, though the company's total revenues have grown severalfold.

Dana was among the leaders in the movement to delayer and restructure corporate America. In human terms the transition costs are high. But the effect is more autonomy for each person. This points to the increasing importance of the individual. Leaner organizations set the stage for renewal.

In the steel industry, where you have to be lean and mean to survive these days, the pleasantly profitable Nucor Corporation rivals Dana for the prize for fewest layers, and beats them hands-down on size of corporate staff. Nucor is no small company, with sales quickly closing on the billion-dollar mark. Yet finding their corporate headquarters in Charlotte, North Carolina, isn't easy. Symbolic of their self-concept, mission control for this company resides in a small and nondescript, just-this-side-of-shabby building next to a shopping center. It doesn't even have a sign out front to let you know you have found the right building. They occupy only a part of one floor; in fact, their entire corporate staff totals seven people.

Dana, Nucor, and other renewing companies in corporate America herald a supremely positive message. Because of delayering, reduction in corporate staffs, and radical decentralization, people at almost every level are finding they have more freedom and more flexibility. But with the freedom comes the responsibility for choice. Like it or not, managers at all levels are becoming the renewers, the planners, the strategists. What they do collectively will affect the destiny of an organization almost as much as the decisions made by the top leadership.

As author and cardiologist George A. Sheehan writes:

Where have all the heroes gone? They've gone with the simplicities and the pieties and the easy answers of another era. Our lack of heroes is an indication of the maturity of our age. A realization that every man has come into his own and has the capability of making a success out of his life. But also that this success rests with having the courage and endurance and, above all, the will, to become the person you are, however peculiar that may be. Then you will be able to say, "I have found my hero and he is me."

Jack MacAllister, chief executive of US West, seems to share Sheehan's philosophy. Jack has the lean, spare look of a Midwestern minister with a good sense of theater, taking a phrase and a cadence and starting several consecutive sentences with it. He sees a part of his job as "deregulating the minds" of the people at US West, most of whom came from the highly layered, highly bureaucratic background of the old Ma Bell.

MacAllister is fully aware of the importance of the individual in renewing the various parts of the US West empire. Although he says he is dependent on his ability to develop the deregulated manager, he is adamantly reluctant to generalize about the characteristics of a successful manager in the new company. According to him, "The most important characteristic is understanding your own unique strengths and emphasizing them, not trying to remake yourself into somebody else. It's very difficult for people to come to that understanding. It's very personal, very private."

MacAllister believes that his first task is to try to help the staff recognize the importance of self-understanding. "If you stop to think about it, how many books, how many seminars, how many courses, how many successful people have for years talked about things people can do to make themselves successful? I don't know that anyone has spent much time trying to bring this sense of self out in people. I think our business educational system has been literally overwhelmed with ideas and concepts that say in effect to people: 'Never mind your own beliefs. If you do these things you are going to succeed.' "

He spends a lot of time talking to employee groups, urging individuals to be proud of what makes them unique. "I don't know how many people have come up to me and said, 'Even as far back as my parents, no one has ever suggested that I am unique, that there is something about me that is different from anyone else, and that I should be proud of that, I should understand what that is.' "

It seems clear that the energy for renewal comes from the actions of the individual. We used to look primarily to the top of the organization for both the energy and the leadership. The leadership still has to come from the top, but it's a kind of leadership that creates the environment for renewal. It's the kind of leadership that encourages, nurtures, nudges, supports, and inspires people everywhere in the organization. It's a leadership that offers direction, but doesn't pretend to know all the answers. At some very important level it is counting on the totality of individual initiative to be a lot smarter.

There is only one enemy of this kind of renewal in a free society like America. The enemy is you, me, all of us as individuals. This freedom is possible in many companies. Our obligation is to do something with it.

Several things stand in the way. The first is that the place where you happen to work may not allow much solution space. No real freedom. You can't vote for renewal except with your feet. A torpid environment will dispirit you; an apathetic employee will do the company no good.

The major barrier may be that people don't know themselves well enough to use the freedom they have (or, as MacAllister suggests, don't believe that understanding themselves is important to their company). Many companies consider this issue an important one. There are extensive training programs and a host of companies with physical wellness programs, drug programs, and programs to help those with mental problems.

But it is hard to find any companies with any systematic ways of helping people find the career path best suited to their own skills and temperament. This is an important unresolved barrier to renewal.

The power to be unleashed is enormous. Listen again to MacAllister. He talks about spending time with one group, a local service improvement team, that analyzes customer complaints and reactions. The team has been given more decision-making latitude and has been freed from the old A.T.&T. policies which had restricted every move. Now they are empowered to do whatever is necessary to improve customer service: "I met with those people not too long ago. The energy in that room almost blew me out. I literally could not sit in that chair. These people were excited. One person said, 'I'm doing things I didn't realize it was possible to do. I never thought I had it in me.' Here was a group of people who had been empowered to think. The atmosphere alone was bringing out the very best they had in them. They were so highly energized . . . it was just remarkable to see."

Steps for Getting There

One of the big reasons companies do not renew is that their people feel no responsibility for it. A major reason for *that* is the way we are inclined to think about the role of the boss. A partial list of steps toward improvement:

1. Start by examining your own attitudes about your role as boss, supervisor, chief executive, head honcho, or

whatever responsibility you have for directing people. How close is it to the cultural stereotype? Probably closer than you think.

As you examine your own beliefs, or make decisions from now on, ask yourself how much your managerial mind-set makes room for both giving direction *and* empowering people. The trade-off is constant, and it creates the kind of ambiguity that makes us all nervous. Push for empowerment, because that's the source of renewal and the area where most managers have trouble. Keep thinking in terms of the Steelcase example: Automation has to come, but the people operating those machines need a say in *how* it gets done. At the same time—and this is the hard part—remember that the final responsibility for results is yours. Directed autonomy is not democratic management, where everyone has an equal voice in everything. It's like being a parent. No rules and the kids rebel. Too many rules and the kids rebel.

2. Treat all your people as the main creative engine for your organization. When we think about the creative element of organizational change, we tend to look mainly to top management, the research department, marketing, a relatively few individuals. While it is true that some people seem naturally creative and others not, we are too prone to leap to the conclusion that creativity is the realm of a relative few. That belief is not only wrong but impractical. Look to each person as a wellspring of renewal.

3. Ask yourself, and your colleagues, why it has taken us Americans so long to take Mogensen, Deming, and Juran seriously. Ask yourself, and your colleagues, why it has taken your company so long to do the same (if that's the case). It's not that the message has changed. These people have been preaching the same gospel for forty years. Based on your answer, figure out what you can do to make it happen now . . . or if not now, what will it take? Remember that the combination of direction and empowerment is a moneymaker—P&G's $900 million, IBM's $125 million in cost savings from employee suggestions,

Maytag's ability to learn from its employees year after year with no change in the basic product.

4. Look for ways to speed up the process of getting things done by organizing projects in parallel, rather than in series, much as Ford did with the Taurus program. The risk is overlap, confusion, and duplication as the program lunges forward. The benefit is that the project in total moves faster and is less prone to mistakes. Organizational theorist Karl Weick helps explain this when he says that implementation clarifies design and design clarifies implementation. In other words, learn as you go with thousands of small and overlapping feedback loops. Learn as you go by bringing the whole project along at once from initial concept to manufacturing and marketing considerations.

5. Start thinking about the implementation of a decision at the moment the decision arises as an issue. Keep prominently in mind that in real life a decision and the ability to implement go hand in hand. What counts is results. To think about first getting the strategy right, then deciding, then implementing, is as flawed as Ford's old "over-the-wall" design process. Neat on paper; messy in action. Implementing from the outset is messy both on paper and in action. But it gets results.

6. Ask, explain, communicate. The way to empower people is to let them know what you are trying to accomplish. Ask for their ideas, reach mutual understanding. Consensus would be nice but probably is not possible; understanding is what you're looking for. You cannot force involvement, but you can get good ideas from everywhere on what would make implementation easier. The involvement process is slow, but remember the Sanwa Bank story; the results are fast.

7. Stop worrying about looking dumb, out of control, and "not really in charge" to those reporting to you. First of all, you probably already look that way. Second, your role is galvanizer and catalyst, not roadblock; managers who need to know, and thus control, everything strangle initiative. Citicorp's Tom Theobald: "I'm not the least

embarrassed not to know very much about our businesses in most places. In order not to be a barrier to change, I don't expect to always be consulted or asked to express an opinion. People from other financial service businesses are horrified at our lack of knowledge about what goes on in particular units. We aren't obliged to know about a whole variety of business transactions. We prevent ourselves from becoming a blockage."

8. Expect that backing away from tight control is a frightening experience. It feels like loss of control, which is just what it is in some narrow sense. But take heart. If one of *Fortune*'s "America's toughest bosses," Andy Pearson, doesn't mind admitting that he has no idea what all his people are up to, you don't need to be embarrassed about feeling slightly out of control either. By managing the boundaries, you maintain control over what matters most: the outcome.

9. Do give a lot of thought to the boundaries. Try them. When people get outside the boundaries, ask yourself whether the boundary was wrong. If so, modify it. If not, nudge them back into the solution space. Keep monitoring the process. Don't be afraid to step in and create a new boundary if something is not working. Look for ways to widen the boundaries for people who can operate effectively within those wider boundaries. Think in terms of Dick Madden's concept of subsidiarity: How close to the action can we push this decision? Fight the "averaging" effect that comes with making decisions at higher levels.

10. Recognize how unique each individual is. Design jobs and boundaries with that in mind. Everyone needs directed autonomy and solution space to work the best. But different jobs and different people mean different boundaries and smaller or larger solution spaces.

11. Remember that most business problems have no one best solution. There is an infinity of bad ones; it's your responsibility to keep them out of the solution space. There are also, usually, a host of potentially good solutions. Out of that group, the optimal solution is the one an individual

chooses to do within the solution space. He or she knows the details of the job better; therefore, the solution is apt to be more appropriate and more creative. He or she sees the idea as his or her own; therefore, implementation is pretty much assured.

12. Keep pushing for lean organization structures in terms both of smaller staffs and fewer layers. But think about the implications for the people; more responsibility, less direction. Think of MacAllister's advice: Understand your own unique strengths and build on those. Get yourself into jobs that are the most natural fit with your own strengths, skills, and inclinations. Find the job—the solution space—that best plays to your strengths. Help others do the same.

MacAllister could easily be speaking for more than the Baby Bells when he says: "Where we came from was pretty safe. If you followed the rules and lived within the measurement systems, there wasn't much risk. Now we're asking people to operate with practices designed by themselves that pertain to the market they're dealing with. We've had to stimulate our people to think in terms of risk-taking, entrepreneurship, independent action, as opposed to following rules and regulations and practices. The hallmark is flexibility instead of predictability."

As Ford's former CEO Philip Caldwell observed, in a keynote address to management: "The real 'bottom line' is the sense of pride and personal satisfaction that comes to people who know they've done a good job." He continued: "We launched Employee Involvement so that all our people—in white collars and blue collars and T-shirts—could bring their own inventiveness, their own experience and knowledge, and their own enthusiasm to the task. People were—and are—the key to all the things that we had to accomplish."

FOUR

Friendly Facts, Congenial Controls

Facts are friendly.

—J. IRWIN MILLER, RETIRED CHAIRMAN,
CUMMINS ENGINE COMPANY

Shoot the guy who shoots the messenger.

—RYDER EXECUTIVES

The house of delusion is cheap to build but draughty to live in.

—A.E. HOUSMAN

Ryder System Inc., whose yellow vans are a familiar highway sight, is one of the distinguished survivors of the shakeout in the trucking business. They have stressed, in recent years, the importance of financial controls and of meticulously keeping commitments to their lenders and fully informing Wall Street analysts about their every move. The reason? The company almost went belly up in 1974. While their basic rental truck business was sound and threw off lots of cash, management attention back then was fixed on making highly leveraged acquisitions and taking on lots of debt. When the prime rate doubled, the debt burden became crushing and the company lost credibility with the financial community. Tony Burns, who now leads Ryder, was one of the small team that stopped the financial not-so-free fall and put the company back on the road to fiscal health. In retrospect, Ryder's management lost control, and today they are determined not to let it happen again.

Unfortunately, it often takes a crisis such as Ryder's to get people thinking seriously about controls, in part because the word *control* carries such negative connotations. In fact, while the control issue is important, it's not always central to renewal unless the company really is in deep yogurt. Still, there are exceptions. One example: Cummins Engine.

Cummins is not a household name, unless your household takes an interest in the manufacture and sale of heavy diesel truck engines. Cummins Engine, however, is an interesting company. Its top managers are Ivy League graduates who came out to the Cummins headquarters in Columbus, Indiana, during the early 1970s to try their hands at running a basic manufacturing firm. Their mentor was J. Irwin Miller, now retired but still a Cummins director. Miller is an unconventional businessman, a Republican liberal enough to have gotten himself on the infamous Nixon "enemies list," and who has been active for years in causes that he considers socially important. Author and corporate observer Milton Moskowitz calls Cummins "a company with a conscience." Russell Train, first head of the Environmental Protection Agency and now president of World Wildlife Fund, says Cummins senior managers are among the most socially responsive and responsible executives he knows. Others laud Miller and Henry B. Schacht, the current chairman and CEO, for their passion for racial equality and the example of it that they set in their own company.

But focused as it is on social issues, Cummins is as hard as the steel in their engines when it comes to business competition. What makes Cummins especially interesting, from a renewal perspective, is that they have successfully defended their position in heavy- and medium-truck engines against determined Japanese competitors, who cut prices by as much as 40 percent—no misprint, 40 percent—in order to gain a foothold in the U.S. market. They are one of a small, but growing, number of American manufacturers that have reduced their costs and matched or beaten the Japanese on price and value.

Henry Schacht explains what Cummins has done by referring to something he learned from his mentor, Irwin Miller: "Facts are friendly. Facts that tend to reinforce what you are doing and give you a warm glow are nice, because they help in terms of psychic reward. Facts that raise alarms are equally friendly, because they give you clues about how to respond, how to change, how to deal, where to spend the resources.

"We have to look at the world the way it is," Schacht emphasizes, "not the way we wish it were. If news is threatening to our current way of life, we *absolutely* want to know it. Events aren't going to go away; you ignore them at your peril." He continues to say that the only way you can respond and renew before real crisis strikes is to welcome the facts, seek them out, treat them as the kind of best friends who *will* tell you what you need to know.

That open attitude toward both good news and bad provided the edge in 1984 when long-time customers told Cummins they were testing Japanese medium-truck engines. Komatsu and Nissan were getting ready to move next into Cummins's core market—heavy-duty diesel truck engines—where Cummins holds close to 60 percent of the U.S. market. This news wasn't pleasant, but it was what Schacht thinks of as a friendly fact. That and some analysis made plain that Cummins had to cut costs—not by a little bit, but by one-third—in order to prevent the Japanese from getting this penetration. Although Cummins president James A. Henderson said the problem "honestly looked insurmountable" at first, Cummins tightened controls, bettered its cost position, and defended its market share. "If you don't give the Japanese a major price advantage, they can't get in," Schacht maintains.

Henderson elaborates: "One of the things that nobody's cost system tracks very well in this country is overhead. A lot of production costs, like producing for inventory or just the cost of moving a product around unnecessarily, end up being buried in 'overhead.' " That fact, plus other facts on overhead, led Cummins toward the kind of cost position they needed to survive.

Meanwhile, senior management at Cummins worked hard to make sure that the friendly facts were understood by everyone in the organization and in the extended Cummins network, including suppliers and customers. "Knowledge is liberating," Schacht says. "We spend a lot of time communicating the absolute facts of our business to all our folks, right down to the most recently hired person in the office or on the shop floor." Jim Henderson makes hourlong tapes four times a year that are followed by question-and-answer sessions with groups of employees, fifty at a time, until the whole work force is briefed. "We found out that hierarchical information passing is impossible," Schacht said. "By the time the message gets passed down from the person who attended the staff meetings to the people who need to know, it is so diluted and different it is worthless."

There were layoffs at Cummins, whose labor force is unionized. There was enormous pain, although the pain was shared by work-force reductions across the entire organization, from management to shop floor. Schacht calls it "a slice off the side of the pyramid." He explains that, faced with the sad necessity of, say, a 20 percent layoff, "Everyone from top management to shop floor is reduced 20 percent."

Schacht says that friendly facts plus communication build support for what you have to do, even when it hits everyone right in the wallet. "We had a fantastic year two years ago, and everyone shared in our profits. We are in a break-even position now and there isn't any profit sharing. The shop floor guys are saying, 'What do we need to do?' Most of our people read the newspapers, watch television. They understand what's happened to Detroit. They look and see all the Japanese cars, Japanese TVs. They are bright and intelligent people and when treated as if they are, it brings important sets of commonality to the system." Cummins executives explain that if everybody has a common grounding in the facts of the competitive situation, of the economic environment, of the wage scale differential, of the productivity environment, of the quality differential, then you have a shared understanding of the need to change behavior. Everyone also understands the penalties likely to be imposed for lack of the will to change.

Cummins has lowered materials costs by 18 percent in the past three years by working more closely with a smaller number of suppliers. It has cut inventory supplies from sixty days to three or four days. It successfully dropped prices on medium engines to offset the Japanese discount. Cummins isn't out of the woods yet; Schacht estimates that the Japanese still have an overall advantage on costs of between 10 percent and 15 percent. But Cummins, armed with an array of friendly facts, has defended its market share in heavy-duty engines, and its offshore competitors must realize that they have engaged a tough and resilient adversary.

Schacht concludes that change itself is friendly and something that ought to be exciting and renewing and invigorating. But fear of change is the relevant dynamic. "Change brings institutional fear to the front, and that is the base case," he says. He argues that the company's philosophical approach to change is the thing that makes one organization lively and another moribund. The constant urging that facts are friendly that goes on around Cummins is the basis for their amazing responsiveness.

Ryder executives put it more succinctly: "Shoot the guy who shoots the messenger."

Congenial Controls

Controls are congenial. Internal financial controls such as budgeting, cost controls, inventory management, auditing procedures, cash flow reports, and the like, lead managers to the facts they need to renew their organizations. Ideally, friendly facts and congenial controls should have a circular, symbiotic relationship. Good controls generate the facts that management needs to keep costs down, improve product quality, and offer better value to customers. The fact base, in turn, tells management how it can design even better controls, for any measurement system will outlive its usefulness as conditions change.

Abraham Maslow's hierarchy of needs, from his 1954 book *Motivation and Personality*, urges that before a person can even consider moving toward his own vision of excellence—something Maslow calls "self-actualization"—he first has to be assured of the physical needs for survival: food, air, sleep, water, shelter. Then he has to feel secure from illness and danger. Next he needs a sense of "belongingness": acceptance, affection, understanding.

Next a sense of esteem, pride, self-respect, status. And having assured all those needs, he can then move toward achieving his full potential.

The Maslow parallel to business is that when *the life of a unit is threatened,* no one can think about much of anything else. The only way leaders can make it worse is by not being straight about the trouble (even pretending things are all right in a hollow effort to protect morale). Then all sorts of dysfunctional behavior occur, as people try to get management's attention to ensure that someone in charge knows what is going on.

In Search of Excellence argued that companies were collapsing because of their bias for numeracy over action. Analysis paralysis. An extreme example of this is represented by ITT under the reign of Harold Geneen, where operating managers were held to a thick set of nonnegotiable financial controls established by the corporate center. The point is a subtle but important one. At GE's Appliance Park in Louisville, Roger Schipke recalls how they became so mired in complexity that refrigeration alone was broken down into five different businesses. "It was mind-boggling. We made two billion dollars' worth of white boxes and no profit. I came close to leaving. We were General Electric's two-billion-dollar albatros. Even when we started to recover, we called ourselves Jonathan Livingston Albatross." The control system had become so complex that nobody could make any sense of it. People weren't sure Schipke could ever make it work. "There was talk that some people wanted to send in the GE Air Force and strafe the place," Schipke says. The turnaround began by throwing out the monstrous controls process and simplifying the matrix organization it fed upon. Even though in Schipke's case the story has a happy ending, experiences like those of ITT and GE Appliance Park have caused controls to become associated with a strictly by-the-numbers, inflexible, discredited style of management.

That is where congenial controls come in. These are controls that don't strangle or choke, but instead reflect the realities of running a business and serve—not entangle—the people doing the job.

James River's Terry Brubaker learned the importance, and subtlety, of controls early in his career, as manager of one of the company's paper mills in New Hampshire. Brubaker, now a group vice-president, said that when he took over the mill, "You would hear adjectives to describe the mill that I seldom heard in my days as a navy fighter pilot. Their whole approach to making money while making paper was to run the mill flat-out, twenty-four hours a day with as close to a ninety-four percent utilization as possible. The people hated it."

Brubaker believed the only way to change the attitudes of the work force, and improve the results from the mill, was to focus on customer service and quality instead of capacity utilization. That's what he did, and the employee attitudes changed. Quality improved. Customer service improved too. Brubaker's division could charge more for the product. Profits went up, or so it looked, and just when everything seemed to be going right, the mill damn near crashed. Inventory records and real inventory were way out of whack. The accounting people who should have been on top of the problem were hiding it, and Brubaker had to take a *big* write-off, one that wiped out the year's profits and then some, and almost destroyed his credibility.

Brubaker's near miss was in the paper business, but it could have been anywhere. Few corporate stories looked to have a sadder end than 140-year-old Brunswick Corporation in Skokie, Illinois. In the late 1950s and '60s, Brunswick rode the recreational boom in bowling, buying everything in sight that was related to bowling, which they liberally defined as "wood technology." At one point the wood technology argument even had them in the school furniture business. A little later Brunswick's aim was to be "the General Motors of the leisure business." Then, when the conglomerate movement was all the rage, they shifted their emphasis to defense, education, and health care. But the strategy wasn't working, and in 1982, Brunswick was forced to sell its most profitable division, which made medical products, to fend off a hostile takeover by Whittaker Corporation, a health care conglomerate. Brunswick was left with an unprofitable collection of cats and dogs.

Among the melange was Mercury Marine, a division that built outboard motors. The situation was so desperate that Brunswick's chief executive, Jack Reichert, told Mercury Marine's top manager, Dick Jordan, that the corporate parent could no longer afford to finance Mercury: "Starting today you'll have no more capital." Jordan's first thought was to resist the directive, but then he rolled up his sleeves, put in some cash controls, and almost immediately pulled $50 million in working capital out of the division. With a lot of hard work, another $50 million followed.

In the next three years Mercury Marine went from negative cash flow to $150 million in profit, all the while competing against less expensive Japanese products. It seems that a few friendly facts told Jordan that overhead and quality, not material costs and direct labor costs, were the places to start constructing congenial controls.

His reasoning went like this: First, Mercury's most important single material was aluminum, and there wasn't much difference in aluminum costs for Brunswick or its foreign competitors. It's a world market, so unless there was some big difference in the cost to transport aluminum, materials costs had to be the same for the Japanese. Direct labor costs, surprisingly enough, were also about the same. "We pay twelve dollars an hour and they pay eight dollars, but when you adjust for the labor content [productivity per worker], you come out about the same," Jordan says. Therefore, the critical cost factors had to be quality (the cost of reworking the product) and factory indirect cost (overhead, buildings, electricity). Jordan focused on rapid inventory turnover, cutting fixed assets, and making a perfect product every time. On the subject of overhead, Jordan sounds like the people at Cummins. "America has a 'just in case' and not a 'just in time' mentality," he says. "We keep lots of inventory around just in case something doesn't work or flow smoothly, whereas in Japan they have 'just in case' people—extra engineers who can descend on a problem when they are needed."

Jordan's concentration on friendly facts and controlling the costs proved congenial for Mercury's (and Brunswick's) health, but he remembers it as tough, often discouraging, exhausting work: "People would rather go off and talk about acquisitions. That's more fun. Every time I hear a manager talk about acquisitions, I know he's tired."

Turnarounds

When a company's inability to renew has reached such a state that survival is at stake, it's a pretty sure bet that facts and controls are the place to start the turnaround. In his autobiography Lee Iacocca refers to the phenomenon, with some astonishment, in a chapter he calls "Aboard a Sinking Ship": "Gradually I was finding that Chrysler had no overall system of financial controls . . . even the most rudimentary [financial] questions were impossible for them to answer. But never mind the answers; these guys didn't even know the questions!" Iacocca recalls how he asked in vain for a list of Chrysler plants ranked by their rate of return on investment. "I couldn't find out *anything*. This was probably the greatest jolt I've ever had in my business career."

Most successful turnarounds, it seems, begin with a search for the friendly facts and the imposition of some controls—tough controls, but congenial to the situation at hand. The crux of a turnaround is not financial wizardry, strategic brilliance, or managerial sleight-of-hand, but the willingness to find, accept, and act on the facts—facts that are generated by simple but effective controls. Carlo De Benedetti has pulled off a near-miraculous change in the fortunes of Olivetti, the Italian office-equipment company. He not only saved Olivetti from almost certain bankruptcy but made it the second largest microcomputer manufacturer in the world and a symbol of entrepreneurial success for Italian society. Asked about the achievement, he says, "Frankly, the magnitude of our success has been a surprise to me, too. When I came here, we had no money. We were full of debt—we were losing something like ten million dollars a month."

In a situation so desperate, he explains, "The real problem is in defining reality. In my mind, reality is the market, the numbers, the comparisons with others. The first two or three months, I had many, many meetings—probably fifteen *a day*—where we discussed facts. Not opinions, just facts. This was a company used to discussing ideas and opinions. My contribution was to transform this thinking and way of behaving from concepts to numbers. I'm a great believer in the power of numbers. Of course you have to understand and interpret them. They are a good starting point for any plan, any action."

De Benedetti goes on to explain that to save Olivetti, he and his top management team had to lay off 20,000 people in a period of less than a year and a half. Olivetti has always been known for its particularly humane approach to management, and even in this situation, De Benedetti made sure that everyone laid off had another job, or could retire comfortably. But had the facts and controls been better at Olivetti all along, the layoffs probably would never have been necessary.

Bob Conrads, who headed McKinsey's electronics consulting practice, tells similar stories in an article in *Electronic Business*. Conrads recalls an acquaintance who had just been brought in as chief executive to turn around a formerly fast-growth, now struggling electronics outfit.

"He is an industry veteran, a seasoned corporate manager, so I was a little surprised by how shaken he looked. 'I can't believe what I'm finding,' he [the acquaintance] said. 'Or rather, what I'm not finding. A total lack of systems and controls. People seem shocked when I ask for them.' At the end of his first week at work, he called the personnel office and ordered a hiring freeze. It was the only action he could take to stem losses without information on what was causing the problem."

Conrads continues: "One company was so choked with inventory that it rented parking lots and trucks in order to stash the excess during the recent downturn." In yet another case, a newly recruited president spent his weekends and evenings going through invoices, order entries, and service records after asking for customer purchase information—and being told that there were no records available and that there weren't any prospect lists, either. "It is difficult for managers from mature industries to grasp how thin many electronics firms are on internal operational controls and systems," Conrads observes.

The need for facts and controls as the starting point for turnaround is not confined to mercurial high-tech companies. San Francisco's McKesson Corporation is the foremost distributor of the products that fill the shelves of America's independent drugstores. Over the last decade the company's performance has moved from the south side of lackluster to the north side of impressive, and the stock market has recognized it. A prime mover in

McKesson's rejuvenation was the assimilation of a fact base—and it took a mini-crisis for the fact base to come about.

Neil Harlan, McKesson's chairman and former CEO, explains it this way: He joined the company in 1974 to assume the role of chief financial officer under CEO Rudy Drews. Drews was the mastermind behind the 1967 merger of his company, Foremost Dairies, and McKesson & Robbins, a drug wholesaling company. Harlan has obvious respect for Drews, and explains that his predecessor's main talent, interest, and obsession was making deals: "He loved to make deals for the sake of making deals." In those days there was no particular strategy other than to make more and more acquisitions. Harlan says, "Nobody was sitting back and asking, 'With all this deal activity, why has there been a five-year picture of flat-to-down earnings?' "

In fact, the company at that time was nearly out of control. Two weeks after Harlan arrived, Drews left. Bill Morison, an operating Frick to Drews's deal-making Frack, was made CEO. Morison told Harlan that he was uncomfortable with Harlan's brief corporate experience and explained that, as the new CEO, he needed some time to figure out just whom he wanted on his team. Harlan, a former professor of finance at Harvard, decided he might as well try to make himself useful during that time. He and his staff pulled the records on all of McKesson's 200 profit centers and started to construct a five-year history. "We used every parameter we could think of—cash flow, sales, profit, investment, return rates, and a lot more—and ended up with three piles of paper," he recalls. "Some centers were doing great; they went in pile one. Some were performing miserably; pile three. Some fell in between; pile two."

Harlan then went to each operating company with his compilation of figures. In the centers that weren't doing so well, he gave a challenge: "Give Bill Morison an operating plan within the next three months that will convince us to continue with the center. If that can't be done, then let's try to get our money out." At this point, he'd gotten Morison's attention and complete support. Over the next couple of years McKesson started to shed its unprofitable and unrelated businesses. Profits began to increase.

The story of McKesson is one of metamorphosis from the food company that it was to the distribution company that it is.

They never would have planned it that way—informed opportunism again—but the steadily improving fact base was crucial to their ability to move at all. A lot of the power in the company and on the board of directors was with people who had come up in the food and dairy business or had been on the board when the company was in that business. Their instinct was to stay in that business. Harlan recalls one board meeting where he and Tom Drohan, Morison's successor as CEO, presented a list of food companies they felt would eventually have to be sold or closed. There was quite a commotion. Though the returns in each business were not satisfactory, the totality of what they were proposing to sell *was* the company's history. "We turned the question around," said Harlan. "As a board member, looking at the investment we have in each of these businesses, and seeing the returns we are getting, which would you recommend we buy?" The board was convinced, and voted with management's proposal to sell.

This story brings up an interesting aside. The facts and controls are crucial. Without the fact base Harlan and Drohan would not have known what to suggest. What convinced the board were the facts *and* the way they were presented. As Ampex executive Ridley Rhind says, "If truth were self-evident, eloquence would not be necessary."

Using the fact base and control system as starting points for action is just as important in the nonprofit sector as it is in the corporate world—maybe more so. My personal insight into this came as head of a task force to "get long-range planning started" at the San Francisco Symphony. Everyone involved was of like mind; the goal of the symphony and the purpose of the so-called long-range planning activity was to move the orchestra from a not-bad-but-second-tier orchestra to greatness. We wanted to be world class, to join the ranks of a Boston, Cleveland, New York, Chicago, or Philadelphia.

Such noble aspirations aside, our first problem was strictly short-range. We had a huge "accumulated deficit," and it was continuing to accumulate at a frightening rate. Moreover, we found that at board or committee meetings, there was little shared understanding of what it took to be great or even to be recognized as world class.

Although the long-range planning committee was supposed to be planning for the future, what we actually did was put together a massive fact pack. Like Neil Harlan at McKesson, we gathered information on everything we could think of, measured by as many parameters as we could find. First we tackled the financial state of the orchestra, then our own past and that of some of the world's "great" orchestras. We looked at things like the long tenure of great conductors with the great orchestras: Koussevitsky's twenty-five years with Boston, Ormandy's four decades with Philadelphia, Szell's twenty-six-year tenure with Cleveland, and Bernstein's fourteen years with New York. We compared the average weekly salary of our musicians with that of the great orchestras. We contrasted the utilization of our symphony hall (83 percent at the time) with that of the others (all running in excess of 90 percent). We measured our subscription ticket sales (70 percent) against those of the others (most running over 85 percent). We evaluated factors like average ticket revenues and income from broadcasting and recording. We looked at the catalog of current recordings. The London Symphony topped the list with 436. Most of the great orchestras had well over 100. We had 9.

The first presentation to the board of governors consisted of facts and figures organized around the issues raised by our own aspirations to greatness. The report had two effects. First, it focused everyone's attention on the alarming state of our financial condition. We could easily have been forced to shut our doors. Second, it brought the board together on common ground. Committee and board meetings can be chaotic when everything is treated as value judgment and therefore subject to debate. With the friendly facts in hand, we could contain debate to things that *really were* questions of value, such as what we really meant by "greatness." On other questions we could, and did, move quickly through the agenda. We were in agreement, not only on common purpose but also on the underlying facts and the ever-present necessity to keep our financial house in order. Within a year we had erased the financial deficit.

David Britt, chief financial officer at Children's Television Workshop, tells of a similar experience when CTW decided to go into product-licensing to stabilize its financial base. The problem was "to bring the two cultures together—the production/research types and the business types. At first, conversations were going by each other. The for-profit business people we brought in talked about 'the bottom line,' which meant 'no quality' to the production staff." How did CTW open communication between the "flaky artists" and "grubby businessmen"? "We started by familiarizing them with the same fact base," Britt says. "We had a brainstorming meeting and weekly show-and-tell sessions. That resulted in understanding and empathy; both groups were dealing with the same problems similarly." Looked at another way, both groups shared a common language—the growing fact base.

As Herbert Simon wrote in his classic *Administrative Behavior*, a fundamental management discipline is separating fact from opinion—distinguishing between which issues are subject to factual analysis and which remain in the domain of value judgment. "Unfortunately," Simon wrote, "problems do not come to the administrator carefully wrapped in bundles with the value elements and the factual elements neatly sorted." How does a manager distinguish between facts and values, especially when the differences between them tend to blur? Values, Simon concludes, refer to what *ought* to be, while facts refer to what *is*.

"It's Just Something That Happened"

The importance of friendly facts and congenial controls is obvious in troubled or turnaround situations. But the need to keep the factual armor bright and the controls polished is fundamental to renewal, even when the straits are not dire. Like the renewal issue itself, the problem seems always with us, never quite solved. *The Economist* editorializes that "Americans believe that problems generally have solutions, while Europeans sigh, tinker at the margin, take the long view." But, says the magazine, "it also makes Americans confident—overconfident, probably." Some problems are for solving, and others are for living with, as former Harvard professor Tony Athos reminds us. Keeping up with the facts and keeping the control system helpful and nonbureaucratic are problems that fall into the second category—the kind that must be lived with. Dick Jordan speaks of how tough the controls were to build and maintain at Brunswick; Larry Small at Citicorp calls expense control "generally unpleasant, very demanding detail work."

Controls lapse when things are going well, long before things start going wrong. For example, there was a plaintive little news story that ran one day deep inside *The Wall Street Journal*. Daisy Systems Corporation, once Silicon Valley's most dazzling start-up but now just another struggling high-tech company, pleaded guilty to tax evasion in Massachusetts, one of its major markets. The company hadn't paid state tax on $2.3 million in sales from 1982 to 1985. A Daisy spokesman said, "It's just something that happened. Most of the sales took place in 1984, a year in which the company's sales quadrupled, and we simply didn't have the systems in place to take care of it."

From Boise, Idaho, one Richard J. Petso writes *The Wall Street Journal*:

*A*nd we wonder why American business is not competitive! On Nov. 7 [1986] you reported that the SEC had quietly buried a proposal that would require public companies to provide a quarterly breakdown by business segment of their sales, operating earnings, and assets . . . you quoted a representative of the Financial Executives Institute as saying, "We're strongly against it because it would be burdensome for companies, and there aren't any reporting systems in place at most companies to provide such data." The SEC should require public companies that don't furnish this information to issue a warning on their quarterly reports going something like: "WARNING. Investing in this company could be hazardous to your financial health. Your management is not competent enough to have installed basic financial reporting systems. We have no idea what our sales and profits are in each of our business segments. We just muddle along and hope things come out OK at the end of the year."

Right on, Petso. Though his statement exaggerates the situation a little, too many organizations don't know their friendly facts at a level where it counts. At a meeting of senior executives and customers of one of the nation's large, troubled banks, the executives saw themselves as having seen the worst. They knew, for example, that their operating costs were 30 basis points (0.3 percentage points, a big difference for a bank) above comparable banks, and that they were taking steps to reduce the gap. Were they serious? Operating costs are a fundamentally important number in banking (as in any business)! Why hadn't they had this fact—*and acted on it*—years before? Even more dismaying was that while they felt they had contained the losses in the major parts of their loan portfolio, they still weren't entirely sure. The trouble was they couldn't *identify* the total commitments, loans outstanding, and probable risk in the various elements of their loan portfolio. Their information systems, they informed us, had not kept pace with their growth. They couldn't trust the numbers. This bank's management, which was honestly trying to set things right before things got completely out of control, would have eagerly embraced a friendly fact base.

Contrast that with Wells Fargo Bank's recognition that the banking environment was changing and that the control Wells imposed—one that said "no expense growth"—didn't seem so congenial at the time. Carl Reichardt, Wells Fargo's CEO, today calls their attitude toward life in the new world of banking "genteel poverty." He hastens to explain that, although everyone misses the good old days, they also take pride in how well they've done. They all understand the need for cost controls. In explaining this mentality, one of their people sniffed at the way other banks use automatic teller machines. "You can get money out of those things in increments of $10," he chuckled. That means they have to stock the machines with both ten-and twenty-dollar bills. That's expensive and requires a more sophisticated system. At Wells you can get cash only in $20 increments; it seems to satisfy the customers. It's a big cash saver for Wells.

Reichardt says that the bank reexamined every product in order to figure out what to keep and what to discontinue. "We have thousands [of products]. Did you know we had something called a 'burial plan'? You could go into a branch, buy a coupon book, and make payments just like a Christmas Club. The kids in the branches called it the 'layaway plan.' In a big branch, in a good year, we may sell five of those. But the sale of one of those brings our system to its knees. Chances are that the person who gets asked about a burial plan will never have sold one before. Complicated or unusual transactions like this bring the whole [teller] line down. It's costly, and service for the rest of the customers in the branch goes to hell." Friendly facts. Cost control. High performance for Wells Fargo.

The Unfriendly Service Sector

As the banking stories suggest, controls are worse in the service sector of the economy than on the manufacturing side. Service companies, such as advertising agencies, banks, and insurance companies, have not had the same natural stimuli to understand their costs. The typical service firm is less likely to have cost information that can be broken down by product line or customer segment. They can't tell where they make their money or where they lose it.

Manufacturers, on the other hand, have had to know their costs because they've had to value inventory. In addition, they've been pushed hard by foreign competition to get their costs into line or go out of business. Companies like Cummins and Brunswick looked at Japanese production technology, found that their own controls concealed instead of revealed costs, and introduced new systems that did the job better.

The paucity of congenial controls in the service industry will prove to be a critical weakness for those that don't change. A difference between the service and the make-and-sell company is that in service, the product is delivered and consumed all at once. You don't buy a product that has been carefully inspected before it gets out the factory door. You buy a hamburger, life insurance, a bank loan, a local phone connection, health care. The only way McDonald's, State Farm, J.P. Morgan, US West, or Humana can reliably meet their customers' expectations is through a system of unobtrusive, yet real, standards that let all who deliver the service know what is expected. The trick is the congeniality of the control system, as illustrated by one of the country's premier banks, J.P. Morgan, whose best-known operating unit is Morgan Guaranty.

One of the reasons a bank like Morgan not only survives but prospers, despite massive change in the market segment in which it competes, is that its financial controls work. Jack Ruffle, Morgan's vice-chairman, says that the bank realized in the mid-1970s that changing market conditions and technology were forcing a need for information on a common worldwide basis. So Morgan started building a single chart of accounts to be used by all its units. (This sounds simple, even obvious; however, few banks even come close.) General ledgers in every Morgan office, domestic and international, had to be modified. Local managers cried, "You're just raising my costs; there's no benefit to this."

Ruffle explains the benefit. "We have a seventy-billion-dollar balance sheet, and we add in all the off-balance sheet items." In doing so they know exactly where they stand. "If you ask me what our exposure in the steel industry is in southern Europe, you'd get it within seconds. Other banks do not have a way to tie this information into the underlying financials; the people don't trust the numbers."

Ruffle pauses for a moment, then shakes his head. "We never could understand why [he mentioned a major competitor] prices services the way they do. Absolutely ludicrous. No way on earth could they be making money. Then I found out. Their cost system is in total disrepute in their organization; the numbers it kicks out aren't believed by anyone."

Like Morgan, Citicorp takes justifiable pride in its controls. You would be hard-pressed to find a collection of more free-wheeling entrepreneurs, in or out of banking, than the set who populate Citicorp. But the reason they can operate that way is that they have a very tight system of credit checks and financial measures. You would expect that of a bank, but Citicorp's system is tight, even by the standards of the better players in the banking industry.

Citicorp is similarly proud of its ability to measure profitability by product line, by market segment, or by individual customer. The fact that a relationship exists within a given geographic area is not enough. As Larry Small puts it: "Stop counting 'connections' and start figuring out whether you're making any money." As simple as this sounds, most service companies have a tough time doing it and end up in double jeopardy. First, competitors who *do* know their costs take away the profitable business segments and stick you with less profitable segments *and* higher average costs. This creates a nasty spiral: Your average costs keep going up as competition takes away the most profitable pieces of your product line or customer group. Second, people in service companies who don't understand their costs and profitability are lousy negotiators. They don't know when they can afford to give ground to a customer or when to stand firm. They either get beaten by a competitor who understands the trade-offs better, or else they "win" the contract under conditions that will prove ruinous.

Citicorp's Larry Small has the final word on control:

There isn't a company in the world that is really a good one that isn't excellent at cost control. IBM can tell you down to hundredths of a cent what each piece of wire costs in every single piece of machinery they make. A call on the chairman of McDonald's inevitably ends up in a discussion about some infinite detail of managing costs in the hamburger business, such as the number of washes you can get before a plastic tray loses its luster and has to be discarded. When our people visit Milliken and Company, the largest private textile company in the world, they are always surprised to see that whether it's the personnel specialist or financial controller taking them on the factory floor, they all know the operation inside out and can talk about nothing other than how to increase productivity.

Why are control systems like this congenial? They keep the business healthy so that the business and the people in it have the financial wherewithal to invest in exciting future projects. Control the financials; controls are liberating.

It's Always There

During my years at McKinsey, we did a prodigious amount of work that we liked to call "strategy." I once analyzed the content of much of that work. A typical strategy presentation might contain fifty to a hundred pages of charts, graphs, and exhibits, and ten or so pages of recommendations. Most of our recommendations were essentially the same: Raise prices; lower costs; find out what's profitable and what is not; do more of the former and less of the latter. My first reaction was to be amazed that clients would pay us for advice like that. Either they were foolish or we had them fooled. Then it dawned on me that the "strategy" wasn't what they were buying. It was the set of facts, intelligently analyzed. This seems too simple to be useful. It's not that simple and is almost always useful. There are not many things in this world I'm sure of, but this is one of them. The approach almost always pays off. The question is, how do you go about it?

The trick is to start simple. When we talk controls and facts, we're not advocating big corporate staffs and complicated computer models. The fact base is a never-ending quest; you never quite know enough. But one of the best ways of putting off decisions is to say, "Let's study it further." The resolution, as in most things, is to start with the simple, basic things and work toward the more elaborate ones. At Citicorp the system that tracks profits by product line, by customer, and by customer segment is highly sophisticated. But the premise behind it is simple. If you are pricing a product or service, pushing more of it, or cutting it back, it's a good idea to know what it costs.

A good place to start simple is with cash position. The problem is that the standard accounting reports, income statements, and balance sheets, because of the way things are capitalized, depreciated, and inventoried, don't always tell you where the cash is. Furthermore, as typically presented by the accountants, the reports jump to a level of complexity so fast they blow right by the simple question: Are you in financial control?

As Robert Townsend, author of *Further Up the Organization*, says: "No accounting system is very good and all of them are infinitely variable. . . . The easiest way to do a snow job on investors (or on yourself) is to change . . . one factor in the accounting system every month. Then you can say, 'It's not comparable with last month or last year. And we can't really draw any conclusion from the figures.' "

So start with good data on cash flows. Where next? Peter Drucker answered the question in his book *Managing for Results*. He showed how to first break a business into components, then figure out what to do with each piece. The major proponents of strategy urged a grander version of the same thing in the 1970s. Break a diversified business down into its various parts, analyze the dickens out of each, decide which ones are working for you, which are not, and what to do about it.

Whether the business is broken down by product line, as Drucker originally prescribed, by market, by strategic business unit, or by geography, the underlying principles go roughly as follows:

1. Recognize that even in businesses that are doing well and are profitable, you are probably only looking at an aggregate. Within that totality some parts are better than others.
2. Even if you understood which parts were which a few years ago, the situation has probably changed. Some things you thought were doing nicely are headed for the boneyard. Some things you've not been paying much attention to are good, and with a little investment and management attention would be a lot better.
3. Your cost information isn't as good as it should be. It doesn't go down to a low enough level of detail. It responds to the wrong questions. It will not allow you to cut the business both by products and markets. Or it is based on standards, and the standards no longer relate to reality.
4. Because you aren't trying as hard as you should, or you are not keeping at it, you are probably falling victim to the average-cost syndrome. Costs are aggregated more than they should be. High-margin stuff is carrying low-margin stuff. Competition picks off the high-margin stuff because you've overpriced it to carry the low-margin stuff. As you lose the better business to competition, the lower-

margin items have to carry more overhead. Your average costs go up. You become less competitive.

From Facts to Information

Most of us have seen companies that are data-rich and information-poor. Wells Fargo's Carl Reichardt characterizes most of the banking industry that way. Lots of data; no information. Ecologist and philosopher Gregory Bateson, in his book *Steps to an Ecology of Mind,* captures the idea when he points out, quite reasonably, that *the map is not the territory.* He says, "What gets onto the map, in fact, is *difference,* be it a difference in altitude, a difference in vegetation, a difference in population structure, a difference in surface, or whatever." His point is that the way we humans make sense out of raw data—in other words, translate friendly fact into amiable information—is by communicating *difference.* We compare and contrast. At its best, what we ought to mean by *information,* says Bateson, is "a difference that makes a difference."

On Bateson's "difference that makes a difference" point, I'm reminded of comments made by Ian Mitroff, USC professor of business policy, on a paper originally published by sociologist Murray Davis:

*H*e *[Davis] contended that the great social scientists were great because they produced theories that were "interesting." But what makes a theory interesting? According to Davis, an interesting theory is one that first raises to the surface an assumption that a significant body of people take as valid without question. Second, the theory mounts a very strong challenge to the assumption. And third, it replaces the initial assumption with a counterassumption that is the complete opposite of the initial one.*

Stated in a lighter vein, it's Sherlock Holmes answering a constable's question in Arthur Conan Doyle's story *Silver Blaze,* where a dog that usually barks doesn't:

> *"Is there any point to which you would wish to draw my attention?"*
> *"To the curious incident of the dog in the night-time."*
> *"The dog did nothing in the night-time."*
> *"That was the curious incident," remarked Sherlock Holmes.*

Congenial controls should have the comparative factor built in: Here's what is expected; here's how we are tracking. At Nucor, the mini-mill steel company, Ken Iverson's division managers file a monthly operations statement that is compared against the annual plan. It is only four pages long and is uniform for each division. A cash flow problem is transparently obvious. To lend a light touch to the process, Iverson puts a little face opposite some line items on the managers' reports. A woeful countenance says the manager isn't doing so well on, say, cash management. A happy face indicates on-target performance. If a division manager does really well, Nucor has a smiling face with a halo, and Iverson buys that manager a case of his favorite libation. Very congenial, convivial, and comparative controls.

Most of the truly interesting business problem-solving work has that difference-that-makes-a-difference quality. At Nucor it was an important decision about how to price their product. Like the rest of the steel industry, Nucor had routinely given a price break of $20 per ton to anyone who ordered more than six hundred tons. They also used to equalize freight, a tradition in the industry, so someone a distance from the mill would not be penalized in buying their steel. But their cost figures told them that the *real* difference for them between producing twenty tons and six hundred tons was only 35 cents per ton. Furthermore, they didn't see why they should have to subsidize either their railroads or their customers by equalizing freight. The result was a restructured pricing schedule called "Nucor HOPS," which stood for "Nucor Has One-Price Steel." Nucor built market share among customers who were profitable for them; they willingly lost the customers who were not. What made it possible was a reliable fact base about their costs and the curiosity to question conventional industry thinking in a way that made a big difference to their profits.

Consumer marketers regularly look for differences that will make a difference. A standard practice, when a product is not selling up to anticipated results, is to ask whether the problem lies in awareness (people don't know about the product), initial trial (people know about it but aren't buying), or repeat purchase (people tried it and didn't like it). When Ore-Ida bought Foodways National, the company that makes the frozen dinners under the Weight Watchers brand, their original strategy was simply to use their own marketing muscle to build the brand and volume as quickly as possible. But careful study of the market facts told them that while awareness and initial trial were strong, repeat purchase was dismal. This usually indicates quality problems and can be disastrous; an aware market that has tried the product and been disappointed is very hard to recapture. Ore-Ida and Foodways looked at quality, found it sadly wanting in many respects, and immediately went to work on a complete reformulation of the whole product line that, in the end, was a rousing success. Ore-Ida's zest for facts, and their natural proclivity toward looking for differences, uncovered *this* difference—strong sales, weak repurchase—that changed their strategy. (Another good example of strategy as informed opportunism.)

The point is not only to illustrate the data-to-information phenomenon, but to stress that it is not at all unusual to be able to dig out gems. In any business that hasn't been intensely studied for a while, it's a next-to-sure bet that there is money to be made by methodically reviewing the pieces. At some level of detail, you never know enough.

Feedforward

One way to make the control system especially congenial is to build it into the way you go about planning. People like HP's executive vice-president, John Doyle, and James River's president,

Bob Williams, use the word *feedforward,* drawing a contrast with that overused word *feedback.* Traditional control is a feedback system. Something goes wrong, you pick up the signal that all's not well, and you do something about it (yell, shout, punish the "guilty"). The problem with this kind of control, they point out, is that it's always after the fact. Why not try to *anticipate,* as the top athletes and sportsmen do?

Watch a fast-moving tennis match. The best players can't afford to wait until their opponent hits the ball to decide where they should be on the court. They have to anticipate where the ball will probably be hit, commit themselves to that part of the court, and be there. Or talk to an experienced fisherman; he'll tell you that chances of hooking a trout are far better if you see the fish coming at the dry fly, rather than waiting for the splash when the fish does hit it. Feedforward. Anticipation. Not always possible in tennis, trout fishing, or business, but better than feedback when you can do it.

In his book *The Intuitive Manager,* Roy Rowan says that *feedforward* is used by Stanford neurophysiologist Karl Pribram to describe "those images of achievement that spur us on to creative action." Apparently a mental image of some future event will trigger connections in the nervous system that resemble actual experience. Research suggests that the body can't distinguish between the imagined event and the actual event. Rowan says, "That's why a vivid mental picture of ultimate success helps steer an individual intuitively to a desired objective." The reverse is probably true also. A vivid mental picture of disaster steers the individual toward disaster.

At Citicorp, Larry Small calls their version of this idea "selling forward" and explains it with an anecdote about the late Charles de Gaulle. According to this story, which Larry confesses may be apocryphal, *le grand Charles* decided to quit smoking. He marched out of his office and into his anteroom, where he announced to his surprised staff: "I, Charles de Gaulle, will no longer smoke." Having made that public commitment, a person of de Gaulle's pride and stature could hardly go back on his word.

Small says that Citicorp does the same thing. He illustrated by talking about the bank's four priorities over the next ten years: financial stability (in reaction to the public's loss of confidence in banks in general); earning power; external image (because as aggressive as they've been, they have a tendency toward arrogance); and internal climate (to ensure that the high-talent people whom they take pride in attracting consider Citicorp a fun place to work).

Will they achieve those aspirations? Who knows? But Small says, having formulated those general goals, they talk about them so much, internally and publicly, that they are de facto committed. He says, "It's like selling commodities on the futures market. You commit to sell so many bushels of wheat on an agreed date sometime in the future. You don't have the wheat when you do that but you sure have to come up with the wheat when the date arrives. We use the same process to make sure Citicorp changes along the lines we want." Although something like this emanates from the planning process at Citicorp, this outcropping of the plan is really control—feedforward control.

Humana's Hank Werronen described his own version of feedforward, which he calls "planning from right to left." He explains that most scheduling processes, like Gantt charts, start on the left-hand side of a piece of paper and work their way to the right, the way you'd read a sentence. "Ours is the other way around," he says. "We start with the answer out there on the right-hand side and work our way backward. *Put the stake in the ground*—get the answer first. Now figure out how to get there."

What If . . .

A feedforward system by itself can be unstable. People get locked into plans that turn out to be constraining rather than liberating. Whole industries plan on the same set of events and commit to massive overcapacity. Everyone anticipated a bigger growth in home computers than occurred, although attention to some friendly facts would have told them to back off. Nonetheless, the antidote to the instability in feedforward systems is the simple question "What if?"

The setting is IBM, in an uncharacteristically plush office building in Purchase, New York, that IBMers—longtime masters of Reichardt's "genteel poverty"—hasten to explain they bought from somebody else. They never would build anything *that* elegant for themselves. Dean Phypers, senior vice-president and director, who has long made it his business to think deeply about how IBM manages itself, jumps up to illustrate a point at the flip chart that is always ready in his office, always in use. He draws a pyramid. He says the top represents IBM generating revenue from the sale and lease of a few thousand computers. The old days. Big boxes. A high price for each. As time goes by, he explains, they move down that pyramid, now selling millions of boxes, smaller ones, lower prices. In the future the boxes will be even smaller, and the sales will be in the tens of millions. "These products [at the projected prices] can't support the kind of marketing and distribution costs IBM is used to. What do you do? You either change something or you go broke."

He illustrates with another example. The huge success of the PC proved to IBM how quickly they could launch a new product and turn it into a major success using parts made on the outside. But when you do it that way, the value IBM adds to the product by doing only the assembly will not support the kind of margins IBM needs. What happens if more IBM products can't be manufactured as inexpensively as foreign competition, and IBM has to assemble more computers the way it did the PC? "Unacceptable," says Dean.

The pattern that emerges here is a very strong sense of the "what-if" mentality that keeps IBM vital. Take a trend in part of your business. Project its implications. Match the implications with your aspirations. If the match is acceptable, fine. If not, change something.

Innovations in computer software during the last few years have made "what-if" analyses possible for all organizations. Author Bill Davidow, who writes about marketing in high-tech industries, calls them video games for executives. Dow Jones's Bill Dunn says, "They will be the death of us all." Both men are talking about electronic spreadsheets, like Lotus 1-2-3 or its predecessor, VisiCalc. Dunn, who is president of Dow Jones's Information Services Group, likes to be provocative, but he's making a serious point that is closely related to the analysis paralysis syndrome that affects so many companies. "The planners wear such beautiful suits and ties," he says. "The spreadsheets look so good. They give the appearance of having meaning. What result would you like? What assumption do you want me to prove?"

Dunn and Davidow are skeptics. They are also experienced managers of people who have seen enough of spreadsheets to know their limitations as well as their enormous potential. But the emergence of microcomputer and spreadsheet technology may prove to be the most important development in the field of congenial controls that most of us will see in our lifetimes.

Feedforward is not forecasting. *The renewing companies try to make plans as forecast-proof as possible.* They analyze not just one but multiple scenarios, asking the celebrated "what-if" question. While the notions of scenarios and "what-if" planning have been around for a while, only recently have these techniques been widely available or practical. You could ask the questions all right, but the multiplicity of calculations required to tell you "what if" were so burdensome that all the energy and attention were on the numbers.

With personal computers and spreadsheet software, time and focus shift from the numbers themselves to the issues, to assumptions and outcomes. If the San Francisco Symphony raises ticket prices, tours more often, records more, invites more guest artists, and performs more choral works, what happens to the bottom line? Ten years ago we had no friendly facts on issues like that, and things were not-so-congenially out of control.

What is so interesting and encouraging about the technology of "what if" is that it makes a pretty sophisticated control system both available and convivial to the small firms and the nonprofits. These organizations seem, at one and the same time, to be the most important sources of job creation in the economy and the most notoriously out-of-control.

The Control Imperative

Control systems aren't talked about much during the current wave of mergers and takeovers in the United States. When billions of dollars change hands, and household names like TWA and

Revlon change ownership, something plain and ordinary like a control system gets overlooked.

But controls become even more important after a big merger or takeover. Many of these merger deals are financed on extremely high levels of debt, helped by a financial creation that goes by the unlovely name of *junk bonds*. The junk bond—a high-risk, high-yield IOU—has been around for a while, but it lingered on the dusty back shelves of corporate finance until its potential was recognized by Mike Milken, a financial whiz at the investment bank Drexel Burnham Lambert. Milken reasoned that a company that otherwise could not get the credit rating needed to issue bonds might be able to issue them anyway if the interest rate was high enough. The high rate is supposed to compensate for the extra degree of risk, and it might. It might, that is, if we really understood how risky these things are.

But nobody understands the risk completely, or that the risks are higher than most of us think because of the collective lack of experience with this form of finance. Because of their high debt structure, leveraged buyouts require extremely tight controls, and too few managements treat facts as friends and control as congenial. Difficult as it is to build effective controls within a single organization, it is more than twice as hard to build them within two. As Ryder System discovered when it nearly went under in the 1970s, leverage works both ways: It compounds your growth when things are going well, and it compounds your decline when things are going poorly. Ultimately, the question is not whether takeovers are good, bad, or neutral for society, nor whether the likes of T. Boone Pickens and Carl Icahn are heroes or scoundrels. The question is whether anyone knows how to manage these new corporate entities, which have the debt of an elephant perched on the legs of an ostrich. Some raiders get around this question by shrinking the new corporation down and selling off units so that they can both raise cash to service the debt and avoid worrying about getting the disposed unit under control. But that only passes the problem on to somebody else, and the thought of so many uncontrolled businesses ricocheting through the economy like errant billiard balls is not a comforting one.

To find a situation like this in a bank, for example, is not surprising; as we've seen, banks tend to be data-rich and fact-poor. The same is true for the savings and loan industry. Both banking and the thrift institutions operate on a relatively small capital base; they are highly leveraged, and cannot afford to treat facts or controls as strangers.* Otherwise, as in the recent cases of Continental Illinois and Bank of America, problems that have been developing for a long time suddenly surface with devastating impact. To summarize, America's merger mania and takeover boom have made the control imperative for management in all industries more urgent than ever.

Steps for Getting There

As with so many other aspects of renewal, the starting place for all of us is attitude. An attitude that mistrusts the facts, that doesn't desire their presence, that doesn't treat them as friends, is one that leads to trouble and eventual crisis. An attitude that treats controls as constraining rather than liberating leads to complexity and paralysis. Conversely, a starting point for renewal can be the collection of a fact base and the institution of simple controls. A way to ensure continuing renewal is to keep the fact base and the controls fresh, up to date, expanding.

1. Figure out where you can cut costs without lowering quality. Use your fact base to point you in the right direction. Is there room for improvement in overhead, inventory turnover, making (or doing) it right the first time? Can your suppliers, dealers, or distributors suggest ways you can make your operation leaner? Have you even asked them? When you've identified how and where to get rid of the excess, mobilize your system of controls to make it happen. Doing this has other benefits, as Maytag's Dan Krumm reminds us: "It's funny. When-

---

*In years past they could. National policy, following the Depression, was to keep banks in business. This meant that even the weakest competitors survived, that the industry was, in a very important sense, protected and subsidized. Any situation that protects the weakest competitors in the system makes it easy for the rest to do just fine without taut management systems—in other words, while they can still stay in business without them.

ever we do something to save money—to simplify—we get a more reliable product. We're surprised every time."

2. Reward the messenger. Make it a point to let people in your organization know that you welcome new information, even when it tells you that all is not copacetic. There is a fine balance here. As a manager you need support and you need teamwork; you don't need continual carping from those around you and you don't need doomsayers. But you do need the facts; when the messenger brings the bad news, thank him and ask for the facts that support it.

3. Once again, communicate. Let everyone know the facts so that they understand better what you are trying to do, and contribute to that purpose yourself. When you can, be personally available, but when that's not possible, make use of video technology. One thing we noticed on this round of research was how many companies have invested heavily in their own studios and videotape equipment for all the field locations. Chances are you will be just as uncomfortable in front of the camera as you were when you first heard a tape recording of your own voice. Go for it anyway. Nobody expects you to be a star; almost everyone has a seemingly insatiable appetite for information.

4. Use the fact base as common language for communication. This is especially helpful when groups from different backgrounds, different parts of the company, or different companies are meeting. Use of a fact pack can be especially helpful in times like those mentioned by CTW's David Britt to "bring two cultures together." The idea extends to any meeting of multiple corporate cultures—different functions in a company, different levels in a company, management and union, directors and top officers, people from a newly formed unit, or board members of a community organization.

5. Treat financial control as liberating. The difference is between controlling others, which no one likes, and controlling the health of the business, which people may grumble about but which most appreciate. If your orga-

nization is out of control, everyone is trapped on a fairly low rung of Maslow's hierarchy. Survival is at issue; there are few options except further cutbacks and retrenchment.

As Iacocca or De Benedetti would urge, when the business is in a tailspin, most people, including the top executives, do not know what is going on in enough detail to pull it out. In this state nobody will think of the facts as very friendly or the controls as congenial. But compared with the failure alternative they are amicable.

6. Go for simplicity in what is admittedly a complex world. Ask the naïve question: "Where's the cash?" Fight clutter in the control systems and in the fact base. This is no easy task. The source of the data that lead to the friendly facts and congenial controls is very complicated. But struggle out of that swamp. Remember Morgan Bank and Jack Ruffle. The key to it all was a single, uniform chart of accounts. A simple idea that took years to make work. Remember Ken Iverson at Nucor and his comprehensive reports on cash position from all operating units— and the happy faces he bestows when things look right.

7. Push for better and better cost information. Compare your costs with those of the competition. Make sure you're working with data broken down by product line, service area, or market. Watch out for the assumptions that underlie the cost figures. Averaged data are dangerous; they don't provide specific information about where you're making money and where you're losing it.

Those of you in service businesses should read this chapter twice, since you are less likely to have your profitability broken down by type of services and customer segment. Admittedly, cost information is harder to pin down for services than it is for products. But it *is* possible, and if you're not doing it, you should be.

8. Assume that no matter how good the fact base and control system are, they could be better. Things are changing. At some level of business detail, you never know enough. Remember Cummins's and Brunswick's finding about how little they actually knew about overhead. You can

always put a different twist on the data and learn some new and friendly fact that might well result in genial gain.

9. Insist on comparisons. Remember the difference between data and information. Don't let yourself or your people off the hook by looking at data only. Information is contained in comparisons and should be presented as difference—difference from what is expected, from history, from competitors, from similar institutions, from customer needs. The best information is the difference that makes a difference; it's always there. Keep digging.

10. Make friends with your electronic spreadsheets (or the people who know them well). You don't have to be an accountant or have a doctorate in high finance to use and understand them. The managers of the San Francisco Symphony and the Children's Television Workshop run sophisticated "what-if" planning scenarios as part of their day-to-day procedure. Neither of these institutions was predisposed to controls, financial facts, or microcomputers. If they can use electronic spreadsheets effectively, so can the rest of us. Maybe electronic spreadsheets really *are* executive video games. Who says managers shouldn't have a little fun?

FIVE

A Different Mirror

Everyone, when they are young, has a little bit of genius; that is, they really do listen. . . . Then they grow a little older and many of them get tired and listen less and less. But some, a very few, continue to listen. And finally they get very old and they do not listen anymore. That is very sad; let us not talk about it.

—GERTRUDE STEIN, AS REPORTED BY THORNTON WILDER

A desk is a dangerous place from which to view the world.

—JOHN LE CARRÉ

My first message is: Listen, listen, listen to the people who do the work.

—H. ROSS PEROT

Nothing creates momentum for change like crisis. A close brush with bankruptcy, an unfriendly takeover attempt, a flood tide of red ink—all these are the corporate equivalent of the heart attack that puts an overweight executive suddenly on the scales, off cigarettes, and in the health club. But crisis-generated change, though easy to lead, is very hard on everyone affected by it. Still, it is common; many renewing organizations, such as Ford, GE's Major Appliance Business Group, Olivetti, and Jaguar, trace the seeds of their renewal to crisis.

The reason is a deadly combination of habit and management isolation. Both cloud the organization's vision of external events and dull the sense of urgency. The antidote would seem easy: walk around, listen, stay in touch. But the forces of habit and isolation are so strong that listening, really listening, is the quintessential case of Lynn Shostack's quip: "The concept is easy; implementation is a bitch." For some, the solution is management by wandering around (MBWA). For others it's staying close to the customer. Or both. But as important as these tools are, they aren't the right starting points, or even the right techniques, for everyone. They are part of a large repertoire of listening skills.

The pleasant surprise of this research was how the renewing organizations *have made curiosity an institutional attribute.* They listen to their customers, of course. They also listen to competitors, first-line employees, suppliers, consultants, outside directors, politicians, and just about anyone else who can reflect a different view of who they are than the one held inside. Their bouquet of listening techniques is rich and colorful. They seek *a different mirror,* something that tells them that the world has changed and that, in the harsh light of the new reality, they aren't as beautiful as they once were. The mirror also tells them that unless they change, they're in for a crisis.

William Colby, former director of the CIA, was speaking to a group of American businessmen, and his remarks were on the listening theme. "The trouble with the way you run your businesses," he said, "is that you don't listen. Looked at one way, American business has one of the most wonderful intelligence-gathering networks in the world. Branches, divisions, and subsidiaries everywhere. But the communication goes one way. You talk to them, tell them what to do. You don't listen."

On the face of it, what's the big deal? Listening? Of course leaders would listen. But do they really? Not too long ago, General Motors paid Ross Perot $700 million—twice the market value of his GM stock—so they wouldn't have to listen to him and, apparently, to keep him quiet so that we wouldn't get the chance to listen to him either. I *can* appreciate how the GM board of directors feels. Teamwork is vital to organizational success; Perot wasn't part of the team—he was a troublemaker. But renewal is not a pacific activity. The trick is in the equilibration: enough support from the inside to get things done while *seeking* discomfort from elsewhere. The courage to welcome this kind of discomfort is what keeps you fresh.

Crisis

Many executives would sigh and reluctantly conclude that crisis is the only thing that could bring about fundamental change. Renewal, if it happens at all, is more like the phoenix—a rebirth from the fire of destruction—than the zephyr, the gentle, refreshing west wind. That was certainly the case at Ford Motor Company, where the early 1980s combination of recession, loss of market share, and huge losses had management reeling.

From that crisis, Ford changed. Their rebirth is best symbolized by the Ford Taurus and Mercury Sable, a pair of autos that finally—finally—gives the American public reason to renew their pride in Detroit. Employees who build the cars love them. The union supports them. Dealers didn't have to offer discounts to sell them. After they came out, customers waited patiently two months or more for delivery, and back orders approach 100,000 cars. The company had to cut back on advertising because the plants couldn't churn the cars out fast enough. *Car and Driver* magazine enthused: "We were starting to wonder if America would ever get up the gumption to build cars like the Taurus and the Sable: friendly to look at, functional to use, and full of the world's best technology. Not only did Ford take the risk, it also spent the time and trouble to make its pair of breakthrough sedans roadworthy and fun to drive." *Business Week* was equally effusive about the Taurus: "A beautifully designed, well-engineered auto—made in Detroit!"

Only five years ago, few people inside Ford would have believed it possible to make a product this successful. American car makers were so deep in a depression that they seemed unable to lace up their sneakers, never mind outrun foreign rivals. When Don Petersen, Ford's current chairman, describes a particularly bleak moment from that period, it sounds likes one of those "good news/bad news" jokes. The company commissioned a study, Petersen says, to find out why customers were turned off on Ford. One place of particular interest was Marin County. Located just over the Golden Gate Bridge from San Francisco, affluent Marin had the lowest Ford market share in the country. A market research firm from Toronto assembled a cross-section of Marin residents to probe the mystery of this unseemly aversion to Ford products which, even by standards of Californian behavior, seemed odd to the Detroit car makers.

The good news was that no one had anything bad to say about Ford. No harangues against inferior quality, no complaints about fast-talking dealers, no horror stories about ghosts of lemons past. The bad news was that *no one had anything to say about Ford automobiles, period.* When researchers asked the big question "Have you driven a Ford lately?" the Marinites were at a loss for words. The question provoked a lot of head scratching, chair shuffling, and awkward glances around the room. Finally one young woman, her face a picture of intense concentration, came close. She remembered riding in her grandfather's 1968 Ford station wagon.

"The awareness of their complete turning off was manifest," Petersen recalls drily. "It was clear our advertising was absolutely fruitless; they weren't going to listen to an ad, because it didn't mean anything to them. They were saying that we just didn't offer the kind of car they were interested in. Even if we did have something that might be of appeal, they were afraid to buy it. What we *had* been doing had been against their interest for so long that we actually let a decade go by during which they didn't buy Fords."

The memory of the Marin debacle, and other sessions like it—which Petersen describes as "eye-opening and shocking"—will stay with Ford people for a long time. It helped trigger the events that led to the Taurus and the Sable. Ford's triumph with these cars crystalized a permanent change in the way the company sees itself, treats customers, deals with suppliers, motivates employees, designs cars, builds them, and sells them. More than anything, the events symbolized by the shock of that meeting in Marin were an overdue but constructive lesson—a lesson in the calamities that befall a company whose management gets isolated and out of touch.

A Passport to Reality

Management isolation is remarkably common. Sir Michael Edwardes led the dramatic turnaround at British Leyland, the proud British institution that spawned the Jaguar and Rover but almost failed a few years ago. In his book, *Back from the Brink,* he says: "The first priority was to *come to grips with reality*—as opposed to the images, politics, postures, and all the stage managing that goes on within a company that is in deep trouble." Lee Iacocca echoes Edwardes. "One of Chrysler's biggest problems, as I soon learned, was that even its top management didn't have a very good idea of what was going on." And Iacocca says the problem was not unique to Chrysler. Speaking of his old employer he exclaims, "When I worked at Ford, I barely knew that Chrysler existed. It was GM that we followed and nobody else."

Such isolation is not confined to turnaround situations like British Leyland and Chrysler. On precisely the same subject, listen to IBM's chief executive, John Akers: "It's *very* easy to get isolated. You have to work like hell not to!" He recalls a comment from former IBM CEO Vincent Learson, who was deeply involved in the highly successful 700 and 360 series and less so with the 370: "If I had been in the group and could have participated in the debates and discussions, I would have been better informed and perhaps we would have had a different system." Akers continues: "You have to force yourself to get involved in the debates and discussion. You can't just sit around and let the solution come to you."

IBM's Allen Krowe echoes Akers's point. "There's a tendency—I call it the 'holding-company syndrome'—for managements to remove themselves, to be concerned about the big picture, about financial structure, about redeploying assets. That's anathema to the team I work with here. We feel we better darned well understand those matters, but we *will not let go* of the business. When we all feel that we're getting a little out of touch on something, you'll find some of us on a field trip out to the Rochester lab, or on trips to a branch office to meet with customers, salesmen, and systems engineers, or perhaps on a trip down to Raleigh to get a briefing on our connectivity strategy."

He's quick to add the importance of balance: Don't kid yourself into imagining, or give the field the impression, that you're making decisions for them. "But, gosh, there's a great strength in every one of us trying with every ounce of energy we have to stay in touch with the customer and stay in touch with the business. There's not a single person that I know of on the executive team who would be comfortable with the statement"— Krowe deepens and slows his voice in mock imitation of the cigar-chomping executive in a William Hamilton cartoon—" 'My role now is to deal with the big issues, and I leave the details to the operating people.' "

Isolation of top management is accepted in some quarters as a regrettable but inevitable result of doing business on a large scale. Not so at the better companies. They are grimly determined to avoid isolation, and fight against it in seemingly perpetual pursuit of the truth about themselves. The fear of losing touch, of making important decisions in a vacuum, is like a continual, organization-wide anxiety attack. They keep inventing new ways to listen and, just as important, to sort out and utilize what they hear. They reexamine the old staying-in-touch methods to see whether they are still valid, or whether they have outlived their usefulness and are themselves inhibitors of reality. They tear apart the layout of their offices and put them back together so that people can better listen to one another. At times the determination to stay in touch verges on the comic. At Quad/Graphics, Harry Quadracci intentionally put the visitor waiting area between his office and his washroom. He'd be forced to mingle with whoever was out there: salesmen, customers, employees' relatives, Xerox repairmen. The intent was dead serious: Avoid that loss of touch with reality; try to ensure that the habitat of the manager's office is infused with the real world.

The starting point for change and renewal *is* staying in touch. It sounds simple; it is not. A host of forces conspire to keep managers at all levels away from reality, unable to use that different mirror. The combined effect is to choke out renewal as surely as weeds crowd out the flowers. The problem starts with the habit trap that I talked about in the first chapter, but goes far deeper.

The notion of organizations as creatures of habit is reflected in Graham Allison's classic *Essence of Decision*. Allison writes about the Cuban missile crisis and does it using several different models of what happens inside organizations. The first is a fairly standard, rational, deterministic point of view: Array the alternatives in light of your goals; decide which has the most benefit at least cost; pursue that one. But Allison's most interesting model is the organizational one in which he suggests that organizations are fairly predictable despite all the rational analysis, evaluating of alternatives, and strategizing that they do. If you know how they've behaved in the past in response to events, you have a fair guide to how they'll behave in the future. In short, their behavior is habitual. If this habit metaphor is even close to right, it suggests that the real problem in renewal is breaking old habits and forming new ones. As we all know from our own experience, few things are harder. We don't just change habits all that easily.

A closely related problem to the habit trap is that most companies have limited imaginations when it comes to thinking up fresh problem-solving alternatives. Theorists refer to this as "phenomenon-limited repertoires." In plain language, it means that an organization has only a smallish set of solutions that have worked in the past and *are culturally acceptable*. Even though people in organizations have great ability to think creatively about problems, the new ideas that get honestly tried are few and constrained by cultural norms.

Habits are comfortable, and so, probably, is your office. It's cozy there, behind your desk, in your niche on the organization ladder, in meeting with a group of like-minded, congenial colleagues. It's a support base, and we all need that, not only to get things done but in some larger sense to keep us sane. Add to that comfort your internal duties. There are all those people reporting to you; they need a piece of your time. The boss (you hope) needs a piece of your time. Then, there are papers to process, memos to read, forms to fill out, meetings to attend, and so it goes. Without ever intending it, your preoccupation with internal affairs—whether you're a branch manager or the president—can take your whole day, every day, and still leave you feeling that the day's work is never done. What it does is keep you isolated. But it's tougher than that. There are several deeper, and more subtle, problems behind isolation, as researchers in a variety of fields have shown. The first is denial.

In his accounts of the Kennedy administration, historian Arthur Schlesinger, Jr., talks about the isolation of the Chief Executive and the need for what he calls "passports to reality." Others talk about isolation as a way of coping with anxiety; it takes the form of denial and repression. Writes University of Toronto psychologist Jonathan Freedman, "Denial consists of pretending that the source of anxiety does not exist. . . . If you were anxious about getting cancer, you might deny any symptoms that appeared. Instead of going to a doctor when you felt a lump, you would ignore it. . . . This makes you less anxious . . . but it is obviously foolish and dangerous." But denial will persist, for like habit, it's a coping mechanism; it is related to hope. Physician Elisabeth Kübler-Ross writes, "Among the over two hundred dying patients we have interviewed, most reacted to the awareness of a terminal illness at first with the statement, 'No, not me, it cannot be true.' Denial functions as a buffer after unexpected, shocking news, allows the patient to collect himself and, with time, mobilize other, less radical defenses."

Walter Laqueur of Georgetown University, in his analysis of the world's intelligence communities, elaborates:

Denial of reality is a phenomenon well known to psychologists, similiar to repression but not identical with it. Denial is usually a defense against an outside danger. Extreme cases of denial of reality manifest themselves in psychoses. . . . Neurologists have coined the term anosognosia for a condition in which people who are obviously very ill, suffer from pain, or recently underwent an operation, deny any of these things.

There are countless cases, Laqueur continues, where denial occurred "because people were wedded to concepts and ideas that they found painful to give up even in the face of overwhelming counterevidence. They will rationalize their wish not to admit error, just as a neurotic will ignore the id and think of various explanations, sometimes ingenious, not to have to change his or her views and admit defeat."

In *The British Disease*, University of London professor G. C. Allen writes about denial:

> *Just after the Second World War groups of manufacturers and workers [from England] again went to America under the Anglo-American Productivity Scheme. Lately, a group of trade unionists from the iron and steel industry was given an opportunity of examining the highly efficient Japanese steel plants. In the course of official inquiries into [various] industries the members of the investigating body have often been taken to countries where the corresponding industry is supposed to be well conducted. But the industrial tourists, while admiring the methods of their foreign hosts, usually, on their return, bend their minds to finding reasons why foreign ways would not succeed here.**

A Brunswick Corporation planner recalls his company's version of denial and repression during its journey through a recreational bowling boom and bust, an ill-fated diversification binge, and a hostile takeover attempt: "We had seven years' warning, more or less, that our strategy was wrong. It had been at least that long, for example, that our market-to-book value was underwater." He went on to make the point that the signals were there, easy to read for anyone willing to look, but at Brunswick it took the crisis generated by the takeover attempt and the loss of its best division in the fight to defend itself and to galvanize renewal. Contrast this with Cummins Engine's immediate response to the Japanese price cutting.

---

*The reverse is a major competitive advantage for the Japanese. Listening to the outside has been part of their culture for centuries. For example, the written language in Japan comes from the Chinese, and a part of their industrial success is due to the fact that they were the first to research excellent companies in the United States.

Groupthink

The organizational cousin of denial is a phenomenon that Yale psychology professor Irving Janis labeled "groupthink." He quotes John F. Kennedy on the Bay of Pigs disaster: "How could we have been so stupid?"

If we look at recent business tragedies, we may ask the same question: How could this happen? In American banking, how did so many banks lend billions of dollars to Third World nations on the assumption that oil prices would stay high and that governments, as sovereign powers, were minimal credit risks? I've consulted with many of these bankers, and as Janis says, the problem is not lack of intellect. These bankers were victims of groupthink—as were most American steelmakers, car manufacturers, airlines, textile manufacturers, and so forth.

The groupthink process goes like this: When a board, committee, task force, cabinet, or Kiwanis Club meets to make decisions, its members are at conflict with themselves. They must make a constant trade-off between whether to voice objections, thereby risking the irritation and resentment of the group, or to bow to powerful pressures to comply with what seems to be the group consensus. Sometimes this pressure is articulated; often, it lies in the unspoken undercurrents.

Groupthink is not a condemnation of groups per se. Research has shown that groups potentially can solve new, unstructured problems better than individuals. The issue becomes how tolerant and flexible the group is in response to dissent. Janis writes, "Victims of groupthink avoid deviating from what appears to be group consensus; they keep silent about their misgivings and even minimize to themselves the importance of their doubts."

Janis quotes Arthur Schlesinger, Jr., in *A Thousand Days*: "I bitterly reproached myself for having kept so silent during those crucial discussions in the cabinet room. . . . I can only explain my failure to do more than raise a few timid questions by reporting that one's impulse to blow the whistle on this nonsense was simply undone by the circumstances of the discussion."

Terry Brubaker, a vice-president at James River, is wary of groupthink when his general managers meet at corporate headquarters: "I'll rabble-rouse when they get too polite. I think they are too courteous. I can't believe we all agree so much. Because of our politeness, we haven't forced each other to really back up our ideas." Says Jack MacAllister at US West: "I go bananas if I come up with an idea and everyone says, 'That's great.' I'm sitting there and I'm thinking, 'It can't be *that* great.' I try to find somebody who doesn't like it so we can talk about it." As MacAllister sees it, a lot of people confuse teamwork, a healthy idea, with group-think, an unhealthy one. "If it's a team that's based on agreement, covering up, not creating any waves, that kind of 'teamwork' leads to bankruptcy."

The crucial lesson is that dissent does not mean dislike. Disagreement does not mean disrespect. Every year Maytag holds a "Service Conference" in their Newton, Iowa, headquarters, bringing in service supervisors—yes, the godfathers to that lonely group of repairmen—from across the United States and Canada to meet with manufacturing personnel. At stake is Maytag's enviable reputation for product quality. As marketing vice-president Ralph Nunn tells it, things can get pretty brutal. "They have knockdown, drag-out sessions about problems identified by the field service people. The engineers are sitting there taking all that flak. It's a good reality check for them. They're inclined to say, 'Well, that's an isolated complaint.' Engineers get defensive, so you've got to hit them over the head sometimes."

To counter groupthink, Janis suggests that groups explicitly assign the role of "critical evaluator" to each member of the group and that the group be encouraged to air doubts and objections openly. At Morgan, a bank that puts top priority on teamwork, what Janis suggests seems to happen automatically, even when things give the outward appearance of going just fine. Maureen Hendricks, a Morgan Bank vice-president who heads their U.S. Banking Department, describes a typical post-mortem session after a successful client call. "We play devil's advocate. Why did we win the business? Were we too cheap on price? People at other banks tell me they never question their success. Here we do. We judge it by four criteria: Is it what the customer wants, is it a valuable service, do we make a profit on it, and is it a manageable risk?" She says that when things are *really* going well, Morgan's tendency is to say, "Something must be wrong."

At Steelcase, Howard Cooper, vice-president for marketing and product development, describes their way of piercing the groupthink fog as a management climate he calls "a milieu of information sharing."* Others describe it as a combination of beliefs that encourage everyone to "do it right," foster an environment of constant chatter and communication, and treat policy decisions "that we made last week" as just that—a week old and maybe out of date.

Cooper illustrates the company's willingness to put the kibosh on a project of the kind that usually rolls forward on the momentum of ego and wheels of groupthink. Steelcase had planned to build a new corporate marketing and development center in time for its seventy-fifth anniversary celebration in 1987. The original plans were for a 250,000-square-foot, state-of-the-art research center. Then the plans changed to a two-story, laboratory-type building with 510,000 square feet that would house research, product development, and marketing. After the foundation for the building had already been poured, Cooper and the architect had second thoughts. As they reviewed their original premise for the building, which was to bring people together, they started wondering whether a building this big could serve that purpose. At Cooper's urging, management decided they should halt construction and start over. The centerpiece of the anniversary will probably not be completed in time for the celebration. But, as Cooper recalls, "We weren't doing it right."

Double Loops and Single Loops

Harvard's Chris Argyris has studied behavioral change in organizations and uses the phrase *single- and double-loop learning* to describe one particularly nettlesome challenge to renewal. The phrase is borrowed from cybernetics, the science of control processes. To understand it, imagine a room with a thermostat ad-

---

*Note the interesting combination of responsibilities implicit in Cooper's job title. He has a line—not a coordinating—position and it automatically integrates the needs of the market with what gets developed in the labs (and vice versa).

justed for seventy degrees. When the room temperature drops a little below seventy, the thermostat says to the furnace, "Do something," and the furnace warms the room. That's a single-loop system.

Single loops are simple, feedback-based learning systems. But the single loop doesn't consider whether the thermostat should have been set at seventy degrees in the first place. Single-loop systems can't ask the kind of questions that are essential to renewal, questions like: "Do we still want our thermostat set at seventy degrees? Do we need a different kind of thermostat that saves energy at night?" Questions about the thermostat itself are double-loop questions. Just as the thermostat needs a system outside itself—the double loop—so do people and organizations.

In one set of experiments, for example, Argyris had a group of local and state government officials read through, then critique, both the content and the form of an interaction between boss and subordinate. In this particular case, the boss was being very ... well, bossy—lots of top-down instruction, very little listening to the subordinate, a fair amount of criticism. The students were able quickly to see why the "communication" was mainly one-way and why the session was likely to break the subordinate's morale.

The group was then asked to talk to the boss on how he could do a better job of coaching, not bossing, the underling. In doing so, the students, to a person, committed all the errors they had found in the boss's behavior. They were overly directive; they didn't listen; they were bossy themselves. Their working model for providing feedback—the person giving it is directive; the one receiving it is submissive—was so deeply programmed that their actions betrayed their single-loop thinking. No double-loop learning had occurred; participants were unable to produce the actions they had themselves recommended.

Organizations are pretty good at single-loop learning. Budgets are set, based largely on past experience, and when the numbers start to come in off-budget, the department, division, or company adjusts. It's like the thermostat—if the room is too cold, the furnace kicks in. If the numbers are below budget, cut costs, sell harder, or raise prices. That's just straight feedback—single-loop adjustment, and there is nothing wrong with it unless the environment changes.

But when something substantially different is going on in the environment which requires a radical shift in strategy, organizations have trouble. They need the outside influence for their double-loop learning. The best and most objective influences are the groups we've been talking about: customers, front-line employees, suppliers, competition, and the marketplace.

Bill Coors, chairman of the Coors beer company, talks about the single- and double-loop idea in terms of cooked frogs. He says there's a psychology experiment—which, he hastens to add, isn't done anymore because it isn't very nice. You start with a frog and two buckets of water. One bucket contains cold water, the other hot. Put the frog in the cold water and it doesn't do much. Put the frog in the hot water and it jumps around, makes quite a fuss.

Then put the frog in the cold water, and put the water over a low flame. The frog sits there. Eventually you have a cooked frog. The change happens gradually, the frog doesn't sense it, and the frog dies. Coors says too many managers are like that frog: They simply do not sense change in the environment until it is too late.

Bruce Enders, of General Electric's Appliance Park group, remembers how GE missed a fundamental change and almost ended up in frog soup. "We knew that builders were downsizing homes and that people were buying compact cars, so we assumed they'd also want smaller refrigerators," Bruce recalls. The planning appeared sound and the prototypes tested okay, so GE started building the downsized refrigerators. Fortunately, GE included some double-loop thinking when they started evaluating customer response. "We were heading one hundred and eighty degrees away from what the customers wanted. People want *larger* refrigerators so they can store more in them and don't have to go to the grocery stores as often. Twenty-five percent of the market *bought the biggest refrigerator that would fit in the kitchen.*" Sure, builders were making homes smaller—except, as Enders found out from customers, for the master bathrooms and the kitchens, which were getting larger.

Some senior managers refute the charge that they are isolated by gesturing to their jammed appointment calendars and reciting their exhaustive travel schedules. They have a point. If sheer physical motion alone could counteract isolation, and effect wisdom, then surely we would have the wisest generation of managers in history. On any working day thousands of them can be seen vaulting from West Coast briefings to East Coast meetings to European presentations. How could such a peripatetic crowd—who calibrate their Frequent Flyer mileage in six-digit increments—be isolated? Occasionally you hear workers commenting: "It's a great job—I never see my boss," hastening to explain that their chief travels so much that he is rarely in his office. Sadly, too much of this travel tends to worsen, not alleviate, isolation. A punishing travel schedule spent talking to people who are predisposed to think the same way you do and who are disinclined to express their dissent—since you are, after all, the boss or the client—is likely to drive you deeper and more stubbornly into your single loop. Clearheaded thinking gives way to jet-lag judgment. Nevertheless, we Americans, as the world's most mobile society, do deserve some credit for inventing a way of being isolated even while in motion, a kind of insularity-in-transit: mobilisolation.

With all the forces at work to induce management isolation, you have to wonder whether renewal can happen without crisis. It may be that in the life of every organization, some changes are so severe that only crisis will trigger renewal. But the hope is that there's a better way. Our tutors for one impressive model of what that better way may be are represented by Big Bird and his friends at Children's Television Workshop.

Different Mirrors

CWT's *Sesame Street* was built on listening to the outside. Perhaps it stays fresh because this dimension of renewal has been built in from the outset. Founder and chief executive Joan Ganz Cooney relates the story:

In the sixties I was at Channel 13 [the public television station in New York] doing a debate program on public affairs, education, foreign policy, and social issues. My boss, Lewis Freedman, and I did a documentary called A Chance at the Beginning *that focused on an education program that was teaching four-year-old kids in Harlem what middle-class kids could learn. That triggered my fascination with the problem.*

One night at dinner Lloyd Morrisett [then vice-president of the Carnegie Foundation] and I were talking about the project in Harlem, and he offered me a Carnegie grant to take a three-month leave of absence from my job at Channel 13 to study the issue further. I went all over the country talking to educators and researchers. I found out that most preschool programs did nothing to close the gap between middle-class and lower-class children.

That kind of listening revealed that there were 12 million American children between the ages of three and five, most of whom had had no systematic exposure to intellectual stimulation. Yet many experts believe that by the time a child reaches four, half of his or her potential growth in intelligence will already have occurred.

More listening told Cooney and the Carnegie Foundation that 97 percent of American homes had at least one television set; 90 percent of families with incomes under $5,000 had a set. Armed with the findings, she and Carnegie enlisted the help of the Ford Foundation and the U.S. Office of Education to support an experiment in educational television aimed squarely at preschoolers.

Dr. Edward Palmer, vice-president and senior research fellow at CTW, talks about how their listening focus changed from the characteristics of the audience to how they would reach them. "We began by holding a series of seminars involving the nucleus of the Workshop staff and some hundred advisers from every field we felt was relevant to our aim—psychologists, teachers, sociologists, filmmakers, writers of children's books, advertising personnel, and experts on television production. We pretty much started out with a premise—which I must say is a rather fresh one for a social scientist—that we knew little or nothing about our intended audience, especially that part living in the inner cities."

From the seminars emerged a set of goals which were incorporated into writers' workbooks. Meanwhile, CTW retained the Educational Testing Service to develop tests to measure achievement against the various goal categories and to give them a report card on the first broadcast season. More listening.

The main worry all along was getting and holding the attention of this eminently distractible segment of the market. How to listen to that market, let alone do market research? After a few false starts they settled on a technique that puts children in day-care centers in front of both a television monitor and a screen for carousel slide projection. As various segments of proposed *Sesame Street* programming are shown, slides designed to distract attention are shown alongside. Any time the child's attention shifts from the program to the slides, CTW knows it has a problem. They found, for example, that segments showing adults talking usually score low. As a result, a very creative idea, "The Man From Alphabet," which showed a bumbling kind of hero struggling with the alphabet, was dropped. He talked too much. Think about how gutsy this form of research is. By the time something like "The Man From Alphabet" is fully enough developed to be produced and tested, it's a sure bet some egos are tied to it. By then it's not just somebody's pet idea; by the time it's ready for testing with the children, the idea itself is like a child to a lot of people.

Other ideas were tested and survive to this day: Big Bird, a child surrogate who is clumsy, misunderstands, makes mistakes, and is incredibly naïve; Bert, who plays straight man to Ernie, whose childlike behavior is always bugging him.

Cooney, who had been watching children's reactions to "regular" television, noticed that the commercials were generally more exciting to the kids than the shows. Preschoolers seemed to perk up during commercial time. Thus, the heavy educational parts of *Sesame Street* are presented as short-burst commercials, rather than as part of the "normal" programming: "We'll be right back after this message about the letter 'A.' "

Study after study attests to *Sesame Street*'s success in achieving its aims. One compared a set of disadvantaged children who regularly watched the series with a set of advantaged children who didn't. You can guess the result. "Disadvantaged children who regularly watched the series showed greater gains in learning than advantaged children who watched only infrequently."

The listening ability that got *Sesame Street* off to such a good start has become an in-built part of the organization, a source of automatic renewal. Not only does it keep *Sesame Street* fresh as the times change, but it also leads to success in other programming, such as *Electric Company,* the reading program for seven- to ten-year-olds. Perhaps of utmost importance, it leads CTW to drop programs that aren't working, like *Feeling Good,* the adult health show it took off the air in 1980.

Joan Ganz Cooney listens carefully to the political winds in Washington. Despite massive cutbacks in CTW's federal funding base, the company still depends on federal monies to support a part of its programming. So Cooney routinely stays in touch with policy people on the Hill; she has learned never to take a penny of federal help for granted. "Preprogramming is a matter of politics," she observes. "The big issue now in education is the lack of good science and math instruction in our schools. You can never be too far ahead of public opinion of what's needed."

Best of Class, Best of Breed

Ralph E. Gomory, IBM senior vice-president and chief scientist, remarks on IBM's ability to stay in touch with the environment: "If you're a company of four hundred thousand people, your normal life is that you are surrounded by other members of the company. You have no natural stimulus from the outside. But, somehow or other, we are very conscious of the outside world. We look and we worry all the time. That's the basic thing."

Because of their historic belief in the dignity of the individual, and their longstanding no-layoff policy, the IBMers (as they call themselves) are a relatively secure bunch. But they worry. As a culture they fret.

At one level, they don't need to—they've got it made. At another level, it is precisely because they *do* fret that a company employing almost half a million people stays light on its feet. "You have to constantly sow the seeds of discontent, in your own mind and in other people's minds," says John Akers.

IBM tries to create crisis before real crisis occurs. It starts with the fret factor. IBM is willing to see futures it doesn't like when it looks in that different mirror. For most companies the deadly combination of habit, denial, comfort, and groupthink would prevent their looking in the first place, seeing something they don't like when they look, raising alarms when they see something they don't like. At IBM, disquiet is institutionalized, in a healthy sort of way.

Jacques Maisonrouge, who recently retired after years of leading IBM's extensive European operations, drives the point home. In the 1985 *Fortune* survey of most admired companies, IBM ranked number one, scoring within the top five in five of its eight measures.* "Any other company," said Maisonrouge, "would have broken out the Dom Perignon. John Akers immediately commissioned task forces to find out how we could do better on the other factors."

Despite the task forces, the company has been having its troubles lately. It slipped from number one in 1985 to number seven on *Fortune*'s 1986 list. Part, but not all, of Big Blue's blues is industry slowdown. A survey they took recently showed that salespeople slacked off and have been spending only 30 percent of their time with customers lately. And near (or at) the top of their list of strategic issues is their current lack of true market orientation—selling products instead of solutions like integrated systems. Still, they know these things; they worry about them internally and in public. With profits of nearly $5 billion they make more money than any company in the world. We have much to learn from them, including how tough the renewal challenge is.

---

* IBM ranked high in these categories: ability to attract, develop, and keep talented people; quality of management; long-term investment value; financial soundness; and use of corporate assets. The other three categories were innovativeness, community and environmental responsibility; and quality of products and services. (*Fortune*, January 6, 1985)

Productive worry about the environment seemed to start with a look at competition in many of the companies we interviewed. "We wanted to determine why our profitability had fallen off, so we decided to do a study comparing GE with our competitors," says Bruce Enders at General Electric's Appliance Park. "First we found out that GE had twice as many factories as our leading competitors. We had huge fixed costs tied to our overhead structure and underutilized factories. We also took a look at customer satisfaction and our quality relative to competitors." The results of this comparison with the competition further encouraged GE to reduce overhead, increase quality, and improve customer service in their Major Appliance Business Group.

Shift the scene to Citicorp headquarters in Manhattan, where Dick Huber gestures to a prospectus on his desk from Morgan Stanley, a leading investment banking house. "I just sent a copy of this to one of our staff and said, 'What are these guys doing?' I want their numbers compared to mine. This is a much more revealing look than I get from an annual report. What do they do that we don't do? What do they do better than we do? No one competitor is a direct mirror across all markets or across all products, but hey, these guys [Morgan Stanley] are pretty good in some. This sort of process is more than useful—it's necessary."

Huber adds that Citicorp people are a self-confident bunch; they don't get bent with awe or scared to death when they study competitors. Different firms excel in different areas: In leveraged buyouts the leader is Kohlberg, Kravis & Roberts; in mergers and acquisitions it's the likes of Morgan Stanley, First Boston, Salomon Brothers. There is a sharp, thoughtful focus to their competitive analysis.

Harvard Business School professor Andy Pearson says that when he was president of PepsiCo, looking at the competition was the company's best form of market research. "The majority of our strategic successes were ideas that we borrowed from the marketplace, usually from a small regional or local competitor. These include Doritos, Tostitos, and Sobritos, with combined sales of over a billion dollars. Each of these was developed by a different West Coast snack company. Pan pizza, a five-hundred-million-dollar business for us, was an idea that originated with several local pizzerias in the Chicago market. Pepsi Free, one of the biggest new brands in soft drink history, is an idea that we borrowed from a medium-size soft drink competitor, Royal Crown."

Pearson continues: "In each case what we did was spot a promising new idea, improve on it, and then outexecute our competitor. To some I'm sure that sounds like copying competition. To me it amounts to finding out what's already working in the marketplace and improving on it."

Sometimes the toughest barriers to executing an idea from a competitor are psychological. Getting ideas from the outside can carry the stigma of being sneaky or appear to be an admission of weakness. Ever since there have been research labs and test tubes, scientists and engineers have fought against the NIH ("not invented here") syndrome. Carlo De Benedetti remembers what happened when he first tried to get Olivetti managers to pay attention to—even *invest* in—good ideas from other sources, like Silicon Valley. "Everyone fought me. [There were] comments like 'Olivetti is another thing. How can you compare us with a garage in Cupertino?' "

Looking to competition is not a new idea to the academics or the consultants. Much has been written about competitive analysis in recent years, most notably and successfully by Harvard's Michael Porter. Porter presents three basic strategies for achieving competitive advantage: "cost leadership, differentiation, and focus." But my experience is that people get stuck in trying to carry out his ideas.

The problems are threefold:

1. Most of our ideas about strategy and competition come from warfare or sports, where there are clearly defined adversaries. In business, however, apart from a few prominent exceptions like Coke and Pepsi, there is usually no single, easily identifiable competitor. Executives like the idea of analyzing competition, but as they set about to do it, they find the task overwhelming. For example, who competes with American Express? The answer is just about everyone, in any corner of the world, from the credit card giants like Visa and MasterCard to the pawnbroker in the Bowery. No analysis, no matter how rigorous or determined, can account for such a varied universe.

2. Business, again unlike sports or war, is a positive sum game. Just because one competitor out there is winning big doesn't necessarily mean you are losing. Business can mean multiple winners. The best simple example of this is the neighborhood shopping center. Put a big Macy's in that shopping center, and the shopping center will do well. Macy's will do well, too, because they're good. But add another big department store to the complex, an Emporium-Capwell, and maybe a Saks, a Sears, a Nordstroms, and a Mervyns for good measure. The result is that they will *all do better* than any one of them would have done individually. The reason is that the collection of stores so greatly enhances the appeal of the center, its drawing power is greater by a factor that exceeds the simple multiple of the stores. At one level, they compete—fiercely. At another level, they help each other. Though they are loath to admit it, Apple Computer does better in personal computers because IBM is in there leading the market, making the personal computer a serious business tool instead of a toy.

3. You can easily forget that your competitors are human, too. Viewed from afar, competitors either look like damn fools—"They can't possibly be making money with a discount structure like *that*"—or they look superhuman. In a market where your managers are getting beaten up regularly by the competition, the other guys look as if they can do no wrong. Your guys start feeling like the team that gets asked to play the Harlem Globetrotters. Fear and trembling set in—How can we possibly beat them?—closely followed by paralysis and surrender. That misperception won't go away until you engage in some thoughtful, well-focused competitor analysis. Ford and IBM have something to teach us here.

When Ford Motor Company set out to design the Taurus, it looked hard at the competition, the way PepsiCo does: Let's see what we can learn from those guys. But the way they went about it was different, intriguing, and a focus-forcer.

Under Lou Veraldi's direction, Team Taurus identified

some forty cars in the rough class category they were talking about (midsize, four door). The idea was to pick the best cars they thought they could learn from—the "best of class"—and see what rival companies and vehicles from all over the world had to teach the Ford Motor Company.

Of the forty, they selected about a dozen cars (most of them foreign) which were then subjected to the indignity of what John Risk calls a "layered strip-down." They took them apart, piece by piece, to see what they could learn about how the cars were made.

And they learned a lot. The strip-down helped them identify 400 features that went on their Taurus wish list—items that, in the ideal world, they thought they might be able to beat, or at least emulate. The feature might be something as visible to the customer as a better lumbar support system in the seats, or as innocent and invisible as an engine part designed to be more accessible to the mechanic.

Of the 400 features on the wish list, Ford reckons that they either met or bettered the competition on 360 of them. In isolation, like Andy Pearson's PepsiCo example, it sounds like copycat stuff. Maybe that's why companies don't look at competition in this way more often. But Ford people will tell you that this is the first time in a long while that they *haven't* felt like imitators following a me-too strategy. It's a paradox—by taking little pieces of others, you become a better version of yourself.

Like Pearson, the Ford managers believe they can not only learn from the competition, but do better. The lessons are an amalgam from all over—not just a copy of whatever General Motors was up to (as Iacocca attests was the Ford tradition). Moreover, the ideas scrounged together from all the different cars were incorporated into a radically new design concept. Ford calls this new design "the aero look," while competitors call it "the jelly bean look." This styling is so much better aerodynamically that Ford believes the aero look alone adds a half mile per gallon to fuel economy.

IBM routinely calibrates itself against competition through a device they call "best of breed." Although on the surface IBM seems to be in only one business, it competes across a multiplicity of businesses all over the world. According to IBM executives, managers at every level are asked to figure out which competitor is best in the world at what they do. Who is best on quality, on manufacturing, on distribution, on research and development, and so on?

The key planning question, then is: "Why can't we do that?" What a marvelous way of keeping the attention of the whole organization focused on the outside. John Akers portrays the soul and spirit of an IBM planning session in a Gatling-gun series of interrogatives: "Who's your best of breed? What are the ingredients of his success? What's his rate, how come he can grow at forty percent? Why don't we do that?" Akers recalled an auto executive saying that the biggest mistake of the U.S. automobile industry was that the minute the first Japanese car hit the California beaches, American auto makers didn't put their own model side by side and *demand* cost and quality and price equity from their people.

Outsiders sniff that IBM can't help winning with the kind of market dominance they've had for years. Inside IBM it doesn't feel that way, which probably goes a long way toward explaining why they keep their share. Allen Krowe says, "We have a tremendous amount of competition. We react to that with just as much concern as any young, entrepreneurial company. They [the competitors] are *really good.* So there is no complacency, no feeling of having it made, no egocentric view that the market owes us something."

At IBM, the best of breed analysis can be—usually is—a very fine-grained look at the world. Four or five competitors may show up consistently on their list, but in any specific category, a major competitor might be only third or fourth. A Japanese company, for example, might be best on cost but weak in distribution. Moreover, the best come and go. Krowe says, "As you talk to some of our more thoughtful competitive analysis folks, they'll say so-and-so is best today, based on what's being shipped, but in six months, XYZ will be shipping a product they've announced. Then they'll be the best."

Tom Liptak, vice-president of management systems, describes the linkage between IBM's best of breed and their focus on cost: "We require the product managers to understand the best of breed competition at a cost level: our best estimate of their manufacturing cost, their administrative costs, their distribution costs. As they bring their plans forward, they better be ready to prove that they can be equal or superior to worldwide competition."

A Little Help from Your Friends

Smart companies are intent on getting lots of help from their friends: front-line employees, customers, suppliers, dealers, any others who know their business but are not in the immediate vicinity of their office. There are a great *variety* of listening techniques and a *rich array* of groups outside the normal hierarchy that are being heard. Listening to customers and wandering about remain important, but there is much more.

Dana Corporation Chairman Gerry Mitchell states bluntly, "In general, American management is no goddam good at talking to people and listening." So Mitchell keeps finding ways to listen. Walk into a factory of Dana Corporation, the $3.7 billion manufacturer of auto parts and industrial products, and you notice big blue posters all over the place bearing Mitchell's likeness. The caption on the poster says: WRITE A LETTER TO YOUR CHAIRMAN. On the bottom left-hand corner of the poster is a thick pad of tear-sheets, already stamped and addressed to Gerry Mitchell at Dana headquarters in Toledo, Ohio. Across the top of the card is printed: A LETTER TO THE CHAIRMAN, and below that the words *Dear Gerry:*

Mitchell says he gets 3,000 of these letters every year. He replies to every one.* It's one of the ways he stays in touch with a work force that numbers more than 36,000 people worldwide. He figures about 60 percent of the letters are routine gripes and bitches; the rest contain information about people, products, and processes that Gerry wants to know about. In addition, he makes fifty scheduled and one hundred unscheduled visits to plants each year.

Listening, really listening, is tough and grinding work, often

*He has staff help, but he reads all the letters and signs all the replies.

humbling, sometimes distasteful. It's a fairly sure bet that you won't like the lion's share of what you hear. Besides, it's not a passive activity; to do it well, your brain needs to be engaged every bit as much as it should be when you talk. Little wonder that many senior executives avoid doing it (or expect the marketing department to do it all for them). It's like the king in the cartoon strip who says in the first panel, standing atop the castle keep: "I think I'll put on a disguise and wander amongst my people and see what they really think." In the next panel he says, "On the other hand, the hell with it."

Steelcase President Frank Merlotti and Chairman Bob Pew have publicly listed home phone numbers and encourage employees to call. It is a fundamental part of the Steelcase culture that employees can call the top men at home or come by their offices without an appointment. It's no coincidence that Steelcase has a phenomenal record of labor productivity. "People will call if there's something wrong. They'll telephone and say, 'I don't think you know about this, and I know you don't want this going on,' " Merlotti says. "For an employee to come to the president or chairman of the company, he's got to feel he has a problem. It probably took him three days to get the nerve to do it. You may be busy; you may not think it's a very important problem. But you'd *better* listen. You *have* to listen."

Harry Quadracci, founder of the printing company Quad/ Graphics, has a bagful of tricks when it comes to staying in touch. In addition to his bathroom off the visitors' area, he's clustered all the top executive officers around the reception lobby on the first floor, where everyone crosses paths, rather than on the third floor, where the view is better. The employee services department— pointedly called this rather than the standard "personnel department"—is situated in the middle of an accounting area, just past the computers and engineering, so that an employee seeking an insurance form has to walk through all the other offices to get there.

Quadracci is just as interested in maintaining frequent contact with customers. He comments, "We want to get to know the customer's business as well as we know our own. We try to anticipate what customers will want before they are even aware of it themselves." To do this Quadracci stages "Quad Camp" for customers and Quad employees in Pewaukee, the Milwaukee suburb where Quad/Graphics is headquartered. Visitors typically arrive in the early evening, have dinner with Quad officers, and stay in the homes of Quad staff. Even Harry's family houses guests. Employees from all levels attend, from shipping clerks on up. Guests spend a day in the Quad plant, working through the production process and meeting the printers, whom they later join for dinner. Harry's reasoning: "It's putting our guys in the trenches in touch with their counterparts in the client companies, so they don't have to go up and down the hierarchy to solve problems."

When Quad/Graphics acquired another company that was encrusted with bureaucracy and formalized communications, Harry eliminated their interoffice mail system and organized "a symbolic bra-burning"—everyone tossed his in/out baskets into the garbage. "I said, 'Take the memo in your hands, bring it to the other person, put it in her hands, and while you are there, ask how her weekend was. While you're at it, think how silly it was to write her a memo in the first place. Why didn't you just call her up on the phone?' "

On the sophisticated side of customer listening is the Ore-Ida division of Heinz. The company had sales of $31 million when Heinz bought it in 1965; that same division alone has sales of close to $1 billion today. Their main product is frozen potatoes, where they command more than 50 percent of the market even though they charge a substantial premium over other brands. Their brand recognition factor went from 20 percent in the early 1970s to over 80 percent today.

Deitmar Kluth, vice-president of marketing, estimates that Ore-Ida commissions two market research studies a week. (Many companies are lucky if they do two a year.) Brand awareness checks, blind taste tests, price testing models and labs, measurement of advertising effectiveness, are only a few of the studies performed regularly against Ore-Ida's competition. Paul Corddry, former CEO of Ore-Ida and current president of Heinz USA, used to pore over the market studies. When most managers talk "management information systems" they mean the budgets and the controls. Not Corddry. Ore-Ida's elaborate system of market intelligence *was* his management information system.

On the listening to customers end is a story told by Mac Merrell, from the advertising agency Howard, Merrell, & Partners, who numbered the tiny company that makes the Boker knife among his clients. Few have ever heard of the Boker knife, and that, in fact, was the problem. Boker described their own situation as "stagnant growth." But looking at the market share figures, it was the *stagnant* and not the *growth* part of that mind-bending phrase that applied. Unsure what to do, management was ready to drop the brand. But they decided to give it one last shot, and a few people from Boker and the agency went to the field to listen to existing and would-be customers—people who hunt and fish.

According to Mac Merrell, "When we got back together to compare notes, the one common finding was that anyone who's been at his sport awhile tends to develop an almost mystical attachment to some piece of his gear." Apparently the attachment these people feel toward their equipment, and the natural tendencies of sportsmen everywhere, has them stretching the truth a little. "In fact," concludes Merrell, "we found that most of our potential customers are"—he pauses—"liars."

They knew they were onto something when they ran into a longtime Boker customer who told them what he liked about the knife. He said that whenever he wants to make French fries, he just opens his Boker, puts it in the glove box of his four-by-four pickup with a bunch of potatoes, and drives over a rocky road in second gear. He added, "Of course, for hash browns, I use third gear."

As they began to collect stories like this, others poured in. The agency ran a print campaign featuring fanciful pictures of old-timer Boker users. The title of the ad ran: IN EVERY LIE ABOUT THE BOKER THERE'S A LITTLE BIT OF TRUTH. The ads recounted the tall tales, which guaranteed high readership. Then the ads told the serious part of the Boker message. Within a year, both market share and profits had doubled. The Boker story has an outrageous, Paul Bunyan-esque quality. But the point behind it is fundamental and plain: Listen with your mind engaged.

Much of Humana's success is based on the premise that health care is, above all, a *service*, and that most health care providers don't listen to their customers. Humana says it has *three* sets of customers: the patients, the physicians who usually choose which hospital their patients use, and the corporations who pay for employee health care benefits. Humana listens carefully to all of these customers. "Our ability is to hear all the chatter out there and come up with a clear focus," says Chief Executive and co-founder David Jones.

Everyone who uses a Humana hospital gets a mailer asking for an evaluation of the service. About one third of the 300,000 surveys Humana sends out monthly are returned. Measures of customer satisfaction influence individual employee compensation and are used to identify areas for organization-wide improvement. In the early 1980s a patient care survey showed that while the company was perceived as being highly professional and efficient, it got low marks on the way employees interacted with patients. They needed to be more empathetic and personal. Humana responded with a special employee training program called Humana Care. Its basis is a series of films that portray the hospital experience from the patient's point of view. The theme is: "Treat each patient as you would a member of your own family." We watched it; it's very moving. It would be hard *not* to treat patients with care having gone through the Humana Care program.

In another example, Humana planners observed that one out of ten women will experience breast cancer. Early detection is crucial in these cases, but Humana's surveys showed that many women delay the examination because they fear both the possible results and the indignity of the examination itself. So Humana built special centers with pleasant, warm surroundings, an all-female staff, and terry-cloth robes instead of the usual paper "gowns." As a result of this bit of listening, they do everything they can to make a frightening experience more bearable.

Steelcase has myriad ways of keeping its reality passport in order. Most striking is the way they use their two corporate jets—not to cart around company honchos, but to fly customers and dealers into Grand Rapids, where they can negotiate surrounded by Steelcase products in the company's sumptuous headquarters. It's a point of pride for executives to say how little they use the jet; instead, they talk about how fantastic their closing ratio is once they can get a customer up to Grand Rapids for a visit. The people at Steelcase believe that "the customer wants to know as much about the company as the furniture."

Architects and designers are also a major influence on new product development at Steelcase; one of the most successful items in the line, the Snodgrass chair, was developed by Warren Snodgrass, an independent designer in San Francisco. The company pays particular attention to the independent dealers who sell its products. A primary source of market information, the dealers who carry multiple lines are vocal about their needs in a way no dependent group of employees could be. The dealers were the ones who pushed Steelcase into building more computer work stations. Recently the company launched a program that brings a half dozen dealers at a time to Grand Rapids to spend two days discussing issues with top management; the dealers—not management—set the agenda.

But the top executives don't just expect the dealers to come to them. They attend open houses given by the dealers to publicize a new showroom or display, some of which end up lasting an exhausting—albeit informative—three days. Merlotti makes sales calls on dealers, getting the nitty-gritty feel for the market that no report can capture. Even the accountants are expected to visit Steelcase plants and dealers, "so that they can do their job in the context of the whole organization."

When Bernie O'Keefe was CEO at EG&G he listened by spending about one day a week serving on outside boards—a bank, an insurance company, the National Association of Manufacturers. "Being on outside boards is a much better way to learn than going to business school. You get market feedback there. Then you can translate it into what you do with your own company."

Maytag stays current through a multiplicity of listening channels. They've had an employee suggestion system for decades. Year in and year out, they estimate that this system yields 20 percent of the company's accumulated productivity improvement. An impressive number in itself. But Maytag people argue that if you're only looking at the 20 percent figure, you're missing the point. More importantly, the suggestion system enables management and employees to work together on the same side of the productivity issue.

Maytag's internal listening has built-in checks and balances in the form of three test laboratories instead of just one. Ralph Nunn, vice-president of marketing, explains their different functions: "The marketing lab does performance testing with Maytag and its competitors. It compares how clean the laundry is, how well the clothes dry. The manufacturing lab does life-testing of parts and machine durability. And R&D's test lab does both performance and life tests. So we don't have to believe what [Maytag's] manufacturing and R&D tell us; we can judge our own results against theirs."

Maytag found an ingenious way to get customer feedback on prototypes of a potential new product—the stacked washer/dryer—before they entered the market. They had long been aware of the need for this product, since the space for utilities in new condominiums and homes was shrinking. Competition's answer was to build miniappliances, but Maytag didn't see how they could do that without compromising their quality standards. Someone in R&D came up with the idea of a full-sized "stacked pair," but it was a radical departure from their familiar side-by-side models. What to do?

"We brought Ralph Nunn over here right away," says John Mellinger, Maytag's director of research. "Then we took a wooden prototype to some shopping malls in Chicago and displayed it along with two other versions of our competitors' stacked pairs. None had brand names on them. We invited people who came by to open them, load them, use them the same way they would at home. Then we asked a lot of questions about what they liked and didn't like. It became clear that two criteria were key: The washer had to be top-loading (don't ask me why; American consumers like them that way), and the appliance had to be full-sized.

"So we made some working prototypes of a full-sized pair with a sloped front to permit top-loading and tested them in homes all over Newton [Iowa, where Maytag headquarters is located]. We also brought some contractors in—field people who might be putting them in condos they were building. They told us, 'It'll never sell; it's thirty-two inches deep. You'll have to take four inches off to meet our specs.' " Back to the drawing boards, and finally to the market with a stacked pair that has been extravagantly successful. Even so, Maytag sent follow-up surveys to the first 1,000 people who bought a stacked pair. Mellinger explains: "I'm interested in what the product is being used for, and why people selected it over other alternatives. And is that twenty-eight inches really a critical dimension?"

At the Hawaiian resort Kona Village, tracking the guests' needs and tastes is ingeniously built into the tender loving care of guests. Every Thursday night Kona sponsors a manager's cocktail party, where most of the guests gather for free drinks, hors d'oeuvres, and friendly conversation. General Manager Fred Duerr and Alex Smith, assistant general manager, host the party, then rush back to their offices to compare notes on the feedback from guests. "Sure we do other forms of market research," says Alex, "but our fundamental source is that cocktail party."

Kona Village is a spread-out place with no phones in the rooms, which are located in separate grass huts. Employees use portable two-way radios to communicate with one another. Smith said, "Most of the staff have these, and we leave ours on all the time. That way everyone, even—or maybe especially—the housekeepers, keeps in touch with the rhythm of the place." Another unobtrusive yet effective way to listen to what's happening daily.

Swissair is a master of the suggestion system. Flight attendants at Swissair, in constant contact with customers and therefore possessing the best information about them, can fill out forms reporting any problem relating to the flight, the service, a customer complaint. They can, and often do, check a box on the form that obligates top management to respond to the employee with a description of what is being done about the problem. On a recent flight, one flight attendant was apologetic about serving overly browned toast, and filled out a form to report the problem. It's the little things. Passengers are bound to reason that if Swissair has a system that responds to overcooked toast, then maintenance, training, and all the rest must be in excellent shape.

At General Electric's Appliance Park, Roger Schipke discovered the power of the postcard for soliciting customer suggestions. "We had to establish a new mind-set, one of providing service in the home—not fixing appliances. We began sending out a postcard to everyone who had a GE service call, asking for a satisfaction rating. We mail seven hundred thousand postcards a year and have hit the ninety-three percent satisfied customer level.

Then we get back to the 7 percent who are dissatisfied and ask them what they would like us to do differently."

But the most remarkable example of listening was GE's Answer Center. In 1980, GE studied changing consumer attitudes and expectations. What they found was that today's customer wants: 1) more information about product quality and price—consumers expect fewer breakdowns and are more discriminating; 2) help in repairing broken-down GE products; 3) rapid response to their request for assistance; and 4) personalized treatment—consumers demand it, even from a huge conglomerate like GE. This bit of listening led to GE's decision to pilot-test, then go national with, a toll-free telephone information center.

Housed in Louisville, Kentucky, the GE Answer Center is equipped with a computer that has 750,000 answers on file for 1,100 procedures and 8,500 models of 120 GE product lines.* Every hour more than a thousand phone calls are logged, averaging about five minutes apiece; 85 percent of the calls get through immediately, while the rest are answered within fifteen seconds. And 90 percent of the questions are answered while the customer is on the line; GE gets back to the other 10 percent within forty-eight hours.

The Center provides both an impeccably decorated work environment and a superb information storage and retrieval system. N. Powell Taylor, who directs the Center, explains: "From the beginning we defined our job as *seeing people over the phone.* We're trying to put a face on the company." An operator drove this idea home: "When the refrigerator breaks down and the ice cream is melting, the person at the other end of the line needs help. To the caller, I am GE." Operators have the latitude to do whatever is necessary to help the caller. They are encouraged to take as much time as they need to answer each question completely, all the while communicating in a warm, friendly way. The more technical questions can be referred to an available staff specialist. This ability to balance professionalism with a personal touch has chalked up a 91 percent satisfaction rate—unprecedented for telephone services of this type.

---

* The Answer Center is not directly linked to Appliance Park. It serves major appliance, lighting, and consumer electronics customers.

But fielding consumer questions is only one purpose of the Answer Center. In addition, it serves as a means of listening to the marketplace twenty-four hours a day. The subject of every call is recorded on computer and analyzed. From that data the marketing departments in the three groups that support the Center—major appliances, lighting, and consumer electronics—receive regular feedback about everything from consistent customer complaints to new product ideas. This is one of the most effective means of listening to the marketplace we've seen yet—all in the name of customer service.

Gerard Trigano, Club Med's CEO, says he is able to stay in touch because he doesn't sleep much. In the wee hours of the morning, when most of the guests are catching their last twenty winks, Trigano is up reading books on societal trends. What's going on out there that will (or should) change the Club Med format? He drives his staff a little crazy by taking all his own phone calls. Nine out of ten, he says, could be delegated, but that tenth call usually contains a seed of an idea that's too important to get lost in the shuffle.

Recently, when Trigano attended the birth of his first grandchild, he noted that while childbirth should be a joyous occasion, the surroundings didn't contribute to the mood. In fact, he says, much of the experience was unpleasant. He's now experimenting with a facility where couples can go to have babies, with equivalent or better professional care than they would get in a hospital, but with an environment that suits the celebration and caring inherent in the occasion.

In the news business, suppliers and customers are the same. Dow Jones's chairman and CEO Warren Phillips remarked, "It's difficult for us to get out of touch with our readers, because the people we deal with as makers of news, and the people we deal with as advertisers, are also our readers." The company supplements this built-in mandate to listen with readership surveys and focus groups. For example, at Dow Jones the personal finance columns have been beefed up in response to current reader interest in how to find mortgages and invest money. Nonetheless, Dow Jones is mindful not to disturb their *Wall Street Journal* following. "They're very comfortable with the paper they know,"

Larry Armour, head of public relations, cautioned. "More is not necessarily better."

Important as listening is, managers still have to overlay their own judgment. Although consumers did not like the look of the Taurus in initial focus group sessions, Ford management decided to use that information to build a program to accustom the consumer to the look rather than drop what they knew was a good design. In a similar vein, Dow Jones decided to expand its international section despite the fact that focus groups consistently ranked it as one of the least-read parts of the paper. Dow Jones is aware that American managers continue to show little interest in the international business scene, but the company deems it such a crucial area of concern, it now pays more—not less—attention to matters outside the United States.

Nucor has built its success on introducing a continuing stream of new steelmaking technologies. Track the schedule of many of their executives and you will find them often in Europe, Korea, or Japan, "listening to the technology" as it evolves around the world. It starts with chief executive Ken Iverson, who is quite simply hooked on steel technology. At the high-tech end of the spectrum, you might observe IBM's Gomory doing the same thing.

One characteristic of conscientious companies was the extensive use of outside consultants who were either specialists in their field, people with an international reputation, or both. Peter Drucker has influenced Humana, Ryder, Nucor, and many others, both through his books and through personal involvement. Quality gurus like Demming, Juran, and Crosby were mentioned everywhere. Ore-Ida uses Glendening, MCA, and Yankelovich (among others) for market research and testing. IBM seems willing to listen to just about anyone who may have something useful to say to them somewhere.

One of the most interesting groups of outsiders who act as different mirrors are the design firms. Among the most prominent is Landor Associates, a firm that makes its headquarters on a ferryboat converted to office space and docked off Pier 5 in San Francisco. Landor designers create the packaging, environmental design, and strategic images familiar to us all, for clients ranging from Pacific Bell to Mercedes Benz. Philip Durbrow, who heads

Landor's corporate identity group, told us, "Many strategic opportunities are related to a change in identity. Yet often managers are uncomfortable redefining their corporate image. The whole problem with most management thinking is too much logic. We bring an emotionality to the process. To change yourself into something that is *without character* is a loss of opportunity."

The importance of the kind of mirror Landor holds up is that it generates renewal without having to threaten clients with an impending crisis. After British Airways was returned to the private sector, for example, its executives launched many efforts to turn around the ailing carrier. They turned to Landor for help in developing a new identity. As Durbrow describes it: "Their planes looked worn out and so did their staff." The airline wanted something new and shocking. Landor's research, however, showed that the customer wanted a true reflection of England at its best: understated elegance, courtesy, class, a sense of the royal. Landor suggested a theme that reflected all this. Planes were repainted gray, navy-blue, and maroon with a "royal" crest on the tail. An information program was built to communicate to all employees what the airline should stand for. As the turnaround progressed, Durbrow notes, "For the first time in a long while people started taking pride in their work." He adds, "When you're in the service business, the most effective road to renewal is to enhance the sense of self-worth of the staff." The interest in that story is not just the listening-to-the-customer dimension, or even listening to an outsider. It's the use of the different mirror to reflect a sense of what could be.

Another different mirror for most organizations can be the board of directors. In theory it should be one of the primary sources of reflection of outside reality. Too often it is not. Several executives we interviewed, none of whom wanted to name the examples, talked of companies they knew well that were not renewing. They believed a main reason was the interaction between the board and the CEO. In theory the board is responsible for selecting other directors. In practice they are not going to pick someone the CEO doesn't approve; more likely it is the CEO who recommends new directors the board then approves.

"The trouble comes," as one executive told us, "when the CEO is not comfortable with controversy, debate, fresh ideas, and the occasional dissenting vote. Too often you find people on the board who are 'me too' people or the chairman's golfing buddies, social acquaintances, and the like."

Potlatch's Dick Madden recalled that one of the problems he faced in 1971 was what he and others assessed to be a board lacking experience in a number of specific fields. "We decided we were not necessarily going to pick people we knew, that we wanted people who embodied personal strength, general management experience, and who collectively represented different functional, industry, and geographic experience." Madden used their selection of James Affleck, at the time CEO of American Cyanamid, as an example. Research was an area that Madden and his colleagues were convinced had to be strengthened at Potlatch. Madden says, "Only a few of the top executives in the Fortune 500 have deep research expertise." Affleck was one of them. "None of us knew him well," says Madden, "but we went to see him, talked with him about what we were trying to do, and he joined our board."

Madden brings up an interesting slant in which the mirror itself sharpens the image. "If the management team, including the CEO, know they have to present something to a board that is smart, prominent, and inquisitive, the whole management is toned up."

Madden and others who talked with us on this subject are right. The renewing companies fashion a board for themselves that is worth listening to and then use that board actively. This is such an obvious step toward renewal, it should not have to be talked about. With all that has been written about director liability, you would think companies would not pick rubber-stamp boards, and directors wouldn't join boards like that. But the problems of groupthink seem to be just as pervasive at board level as elsewhere in the organization. Too few leaders are acting as Madden did to change this predicament.

Steps for Getting There

The fundamental issue here is that keeping a business's reality passport in order seems at first to be easier than it actually is. What follows is a modest set of suggestions on what to do.

1. Make a sign, framed or on a Post-it note, that says: THERE MUST BE A BETTER WAY. You can apply it to most aspects of the business, as Bob Williams does at James River. Wherever you go, ask "How can we do this better?" Then get accustomed to hearing people tell you things that make you uncomfortable. It's far better to hear the tough stuff now and do something about it than to be caught unaware later.

2. Make a second sign that lists all the isolation traps: force of past habit, the comfort of your office, the pressure of internal events, denial of unpleasant news, groupthink, inability to differentiate dissent from dislike, the difficulty of double-loop learning. Meet with others in your organization to go over that list, add other forces that keep you isolated, and share ideas about what each of you can do to combat each of those forces.

3. Remember that listening is not a passive activity. It's work, and it's central to renewal. You don't just wait for information to come to you whenever there's something you ought to know. And you can't depend on a small circle of peers to provide you with a current or complete account of what's happening. Instead you should listen around the hierarchy, and you need to do it yourself.

   At the next meeting, when you and others gather to talk about issues, ask yourselves why Americans in particular seem to be such poor listeners. Arrogance—the hubris that followed our impressive accomplishments in the twentieth century? Relative innocence about foreign trade? (We haven't been at it very long.) Does your company have a tin ear? What are its manifestations? What are the probable causes? How much of that problem is shared by you and your department or division?

   Recognize that listening is a high-leverage use of your time. For one thing, listening helps you ward off crisis by recognizing early warning signals from the environment, whether they relate to new technologies or tacos. You may have enough lead time to make the necessary adjustments and then go on about your business. Or you may want to follow IBM's lead and "create a crisis" for those you lead, to focus attention on the need to act swiftly and decisively. Either way, listening helps you anticipate changes and avoid debilitating crises.

4. Resist pressure from others to go along with the group for the sake of superficial politeness. Keeping silent about your own misgivings and doubts undermines teamwork and group success. Ask yourself this: When you run meetings or wander about, what are your ways of encouraging people to express dissenting opinions?

   In a recent graduation speech, Stanford's President Donald Kennedy told the graduates to "challenge authority." Will bright people, the kind you need for the continued renewal of your company, be able to challenge authority in your organization? As author Albert O. Hirschman points out, in *Exit, Voice and Loyalty*, people in your organization are empowered to express their dissatisfaction with the status quo in only two ways: exit (they leave) or voice (they make themselves heard). If they leave, the cause of renewal isn't served. If they stay but have no voice, renewal isn't served, either. While you're at it, figure out what kinds of voice are culturally acceptable in your company. How do new employees learn about them?

5. Play devil's advocate. Instead of discounting whatever threatens your comfortable view of the world, challenge your assumptions—especially the ones that seem to have taken on lives of their own. Get your brain out of its habit-lined ruts. Supplement single-loop questions ("How can we do this better?") with double-loop ones ("Should we be doing this at all?). Beyond that, find ways to make curiosity an institutional attribute.

6. Ask if your company has a sense of humor. Even the best-run companies cannot avoid stressful situations. One of the most effective ways we humans have of relieving stress is humor. In fact, the outwardly stuffy Morgan Bank seemed to practice it best of all. One of the most

dismaying moments in my career was when a company I was close to decided that its main problem was that it did not "take itself seriously enough." There may be organizations where that is true, but this particular company certainly wasn't one of them. If Ford's leadership had taken themselves too seriously, they never would have survived those focus group meetings in California.

7. Do your own version of learning from the best. The ability to look at the best-managed and learn from them ought not to be limited to business authors and the Japanese. Work out your own version of Ford's "best of class" or IBM's "best of breed." Competitive analysis helps you learn from your competitors—not just defend against them. Use the market's reaction to competitive offerings as one of the best ways to do market research.

8. Don't assume that listening is one of the things you do best. Your calendars, with all those meetings, conference calls, red-eye plane flights, and office visitors, offer no proof that there's any listening going on at all. How much time do you spend during the day actually *listening* (mouth shut, eyes and ears open) instead of talking? My guess is, not much. Or not as much as you should.

9. Keep looking for the different mirrors that others use to perceive reality. Landor's Philip Durbrow explains it this way: "I use a series of slides to help clients understand the difference between reality and customer perception of it. I have a slide of a red candle, which represents reality, and another one with a mirror reflecting it accurately. Then I project three slides distorting the candle. The point is you have to be aware of how others reflect reality back to you. Their perceptions, accurate or inaccurate, are reality to them."

10. Find listening techniques that work for you. The sheer variety in ways of listening was what was so astonishing in this round of research. From the simple to the sophisticated; from wandering around to letters to the chairman; from published home phone numbers to formal market research and attitude surveys.

11. Identify all the constituent groups important to your business. Are you listening to them? Which ones are being overlooked? The market is *still* primary, but for most companies there are a variety of customers and market segments. Beyond the market, there are the people on the front line, the suppliers, the board, the regulators, and the unions. They all have perceptions that at one time or another are likely to influence the fortunes of your business. Above all, remember that sometimes all it takes is asking the question. Cummins Engine asked its suppliers for cost-cutting ideas and got tremendous results from their responses. Why hadn't the suppliers communicated their ideas before? "No one ever asked us."

12. Let people know you are listening so they will take the trouble to talk. Recently a friend stayed in a Marriott hotel. The shower head wasn't working right and it sprayed too much water over the shower curtain and too little on him. Since he had heard good things about Marriott, he took the trouble to do something he normally would not do: He filled out one of those "please rate us" cards. Within ten days he received a two-paragraph letter, signed by Bill Marriott, referring to the incident of the misbehaving shower head, apologizing for it, and thanking him for his comments. Most of us don't fill out those cards, or respond to questionnaires, because we never hear back. He and many others will continue to talk to Marriott.

SIX

Teamwork, Trust, Politics, and Power

*Power has two aspects. . . . It is a social
necessity. . . . It is also a social
menace.*

—BERTRAND DE JOUVENEL

*The tendency to deplore profits stems from the
medieval idea that one person's profit is
another person's loss.*

—WALTER WRISTON

Citicorp's Dick Huber greets the subject with enthusiasm: "Thank
the Lord for corporate politics. How boring life would be without
it. I love it. It's wonderful!" He explains that much of his daily
job is persuasion—finding ways to persuade other people to do
what he thinks is important. "Is that politics? I don't know, but
by my definition it is. It's an essential part of the reality of what
we do."

But others disagree. In many conversations at the renewing
companies, executives were emphatic about the absence of political behavior in their organizations. A frequent comment: "What
makes this place work is that we have no politics."

Who's right? Both are. Nothing so clouds the renewal issue,

or our understanding of management itself, than our collective innocence about politics and power in organizations. When are these qualities bad? When are they beneficial? Few people get ahead who are not good politically. Few things get done without a power base. The answer, of course, is that politics can be bad, or good. As a culture, we Americans have been raised to be so suspicious of power and politics—while privately coveting what these forces can bring us—that we deny their very existence.

Eventually the good managers figure it out. That's one of the reasons they *are* good. They're good politically, but few would say so. (Dick Huber's honesty is refreshing.) For most, even talking about power and politics is political suicide. Many of our finest managers are closet politicians.

The importance of the politics issue is explained by McKinsey partner P. C. Chatterjee: "What bars renewal—makes change for the better virtually impossible in most companies I see," he says, "is the very high level of politics, low level of teamwork, and no general sense of direction." Chatterjee says that his greatest disappointment, as he moved up in the business world and spent increasing amounts of time inside the inner sanctums of corporate America, was how difficult it was to do the obvious. He attributes that to the leaders' simply not getting along with one another.

One well-meaning, honest, energetic manager cannot afford to trust a well-meaning, honest, energetic counterpart. Their company furnishes no basis for teamwork. Their environment fosters political shenanigans. If you get anything done, it is in spite of the organization. If you get too much done, it makes the others look bad; while your colleagues can't agree on much else, they can agree that you are a threat, and they see to it that your next effort is thwarted.

The companies we interviewed recognize the harm that lies in the backbiting behavior usually associated with "politics." They are clearly determined to make politics a positive by emphasizing teamwork.

Calm at the Top

From Morgan Bank, Super Valu, Bankers Trust, IBM, and Nucor, to Olivetti's headquarters in Italy, calm is the pervasive theme. Where is the frenzy? The fervor? The *angst?* Don't these people watch television and know that life is supposed to be frantic—that there should be more gesticulation, shouting, more sound, more fury? How can they be so calm yet do so well in today's "fast-paced, split-second, rate-of-change-was-never-greater" world?

Teamwork. That's how. Almost without exception, the successful people stress the importance of teamwork. It starts at the top.

Now, you may be thinking to yourself: "That's old news. Everyone understands the need for teamwork." Not so, according to a recent study conducted by Robert Lefton, president of the training company Psychological Associates. He found that many executives distrust collaboration because it seems "soft" and "unbusinesslike." They prefer instead the "hard-nosed," authoritarian approach. The result? "Less than 40 percent of the effort expended by top-level corporate teams can accurately be described as 'teamwork.' One-third of the time, the group leader calls the shots to head off opposition."

Every renewing organization has a clearly-in-charge chief executive. But this individual is so seldom the grandstanding, heroic figure—the hard-nosed authoritarian—that the popular press makes such leaders out to be. Leaders are supposed to be "charismatic," but that is not how you would necessarily describe the CEOs of renewing companies. Their personalities run the spectrum from voluble to taciturn, from extroverted to introverted.

Ralph Waldo Emerson said that an institution is simply the lengthened shadow of a single individual. This may be true for many organizations, especially new or smaller companies. American emphasis on individualism and our fixation with heroes encourages us to believe that the single individual at the top is more singular than he really is. In several of the big companies we talked to (e.g., Citicorp, Morgan, IBM, GE) I had the impression that a dozen or so of their top people had the raw capacity to be CEO at most any big company you would want to name. Their wealth of talent at the top, and the manifest teamwork, makes for what many described as seamless transition from one generation of management to the next.

It is truly a team at the top that makes renewal happen. Yes, there has to be a first among equals. Harry Quadracci has a rule he calls "president wins" for settling issues when his consensus-driven style doesn't yield a decision (or yields one he knows is wrong for the company). But, no, the top person is not as effective when operating as a loner.

At Steelcase, as you might expect for an office systems company, teamwork at the top is symbolized by office layout and reinforced by computer technology. The two top people, Bob Pew and Frank Merlotti, have offices that connect via an atriumlike conference room so that they can quickly confer. All Steelcase executives, managers, and supervisors are linked by IBM AT computer terminals that encourage electronic mail; they can call up everyone's schedule at the stroke of a few keys. That almost gimmicky-sounding device makes it so easy for the executive group to find one another, they end up communicating more often.

At Super Valu, CEO Mike Wright holds forth from a glassed-in office where he is visible to all. He wants to encourage others to treat him informally. The nameplate outside his office says MIKE WRIGHT. He tells everyone to call him Mike. "It's all first names around here; no 'mister,' " he says. By making his own office physically transparent, and by insisting on informality, he reinforces Super Valu's own brand of teamwork.

At Ford, it was hard to tell which individual was behind the turnaround symbolized by the Taurus/Sable. When people tell the story, former chief executive Philip Caldwell is mentioned often. So is current CEO Don Petersen. So is president Harold "Red" Poling. They all played a major role. The skills and personality of one complemented the skills and personalities of the others. When Petersen and Poling accepted their current jobs, they informally divided the work. Poling took financial controls and manufacturing; Petersen worked on the product line and the people side of the business. The two men worked naturally as a team, creating an atmosphere that was just the opposite of what Ford Motor was used to during the Henry Ford/Lee Iacocca era. As you move through the Ford organization, you get the same sense these days of pervasive teamwork. *Team Taurus* was the appellation they used to bond everyone who had anything to do with the product.

Ken Iverson is the main man at Nucor. Scratch the surface, though, and you find very strong support from Dave Aycock, who worked his way up from welder to president, and Sam Siegel, the chief financial officer, who has been with Iverson since the beginning. (Both he and Iverson laugh about the day they poured the first batch of metal out of the ladle. The accompanying fire and noise were so frightening that the newly trained employees ran out of the mill. But alarming as it was at the time, and humorous as it is in retrospect, it's just such a shared experience that builds teams.) Siegel's financial acumen is a nice balance to Iverson's metallurgy and steelmaking knowledge and Aycock's sales and operations savvy.

In companies that aren't as well managed as Nucor, there's an inverse relationship between the low amount of teamwork and a high amount of executive turf-grabbing, each fiefdom jealously duplicating and defending its staff and functions. These companies then wonder why they are so top-heavy with managers. When things get insufferable, they set about slashing staff without regard to who will fit into a new teamwork structure or who will simply re-create, on a decreased scale, the same fractious situation. A company with good teamwork and cooperation at the top enjoys a terrific multiplier effect; their close-knit gang of three or four accomplishes far more than a throng of managers (and supporting retinues and overhead) threefold in size. The teamwork companies enjoy a communication level that seems uncanny to outsiders; important ideas move like quicksilver. Decisions are made in hallways and on telephones. Formal meetings are less frequent and not all that formal.

Even within the vastness of IBM, with its 400,000 employees, teamwork at the top provides a kind of intimacy. "We've all grown up together," says John Akers at IBM. "When we have a meeting of the top eighty-five or ninety people throughout the company—we call them 'Distribution A'—I know them all. Not because I've just met them; I've known them all for twenty years! Everybody started out as a clerk or a salesman or a junior engineer or something, and we all kind of moved forward together."

Smart chief executives like John Akers know that they won the top job through a combination of ability, luck, and perseverance. They accept the fact that if they were suddenly vaporized, a slew of highly talented, eminently qualified men and women in the organization would be available to fill the job. To a significant and beneficial degree, the people at the top of a renewing company are interchangeable, although that word is often cast as a pejorative, implying a sea of dull gray look-alikes. To believe that is to miss the point. The members of the senior team represent individual shadings of style and emphasis, but they share the fundamental beliefs, values, and skills that drive the company.

Does the certainty that one can be so easily replaced create fear and anxiety for top executives? It doesn't seem to; if anything, this knowledge adds to the calm at the top. An executive knows that he doesn't have to do everything himself, that some superhuman effort on his part is not only unnecessary but would probably be foolish. He knows he is surrounded by smart and capable people who can make the organization run effectively, preferably with him but, if necessary, without him. It's when you have a brilliant leader surrounded by people he thinks are incompetent that fear, uncertainty, and doubt take hold.

"At one company I visited, they were all terrified of the chairman," says Peter Buchanan, chief executive at First Boston. "On the company plane he sat off in his cabin and everyone else sat worrying about what he was thinking. It was worse than what I saw in the military." At First Boston, he says, "We look for the guys who will be team players. There's very little hierarchy here."

Teamwork doesn't mean cloning and conformity. A good team has plenty of room for stars. Alvin V. Shoemaker, First Boston's chairman, talks about the diverse personalities and styles now at the company and adds, "Ten years ago, when we weren't doing so well, everyone looked the part and wore the same suit." Sportswriter Lowell Cohn puts the idea in a baseball context: "Most great players had a touch of egomania—Willie Mays, Joe Morgan, you name them. Their pride was part of their greatness, but they also learned how to fit into the team."

"I don't care whether they get along [with each other or with me]," said a CEO with a national bank, "as long as they do a good job." The position sounds reasonable. But the point is that they *couldn't* do a good job as long as they couldn't work effectively as a team. An "energy leak" is what physicists call a system that wastes a lot of heat in its effort to produce useful work. The top executive "team" at this company had a huge, politically generated energy leak. Executives spent too much time worrying about, imagining, and defending against one another's "hidden agenda." At lower levels, if one individual worked for one group executive while another worked in a different group, the two people could rarely collaborate. They either felt disloyal to their respective bosses or had been convinced by them that the "other side" was up to no good.

Contrast that with an experience at one of the renewing companies, where groups from various divisions were meeting to discuss their common interest in computer-aided design, engineering, and manufacturing technology. There was a lot of information-sharing going on. No posturing. Nothing held back. Just relaxed, open information exchange, an easy-going cooperative attitude. But it wasn't always this way. "Several years ago, you would have seen just the reverse," says the president. "Lots of politics, nobody working together. I finally got so fed up that I picked the two worst offenders among top management. I fired them and I told everyone why I fired them. We didn't have much trouble with politics after that."

We/They

Moving outside the executive suite, a formidable barrier to change and renewal is the we/they split that fragments an organization. The we/theys are all around us. The most obvious is the split between labor and management. Then there's the classic line-and-staff split. Marketing and manufacturing. The New York office versus Chicago. One division versus another (or versus the rest of the company). The German (or French, or European) operation versus the domestic operation. The common ingredient in we/they splits is that communication breaks down. Trust disappears—or never gets established. Organization gridlock is the result.

Sometimes the we/they split is blatantly adversarial. Other

times it is more subtle, and when it masquerades as consensus, it can be even more destructive. Symptoms include excessive politeness, excruciatingly correct behavior, and formal "agreements" that each side promptly goes about trying to undermine in private.

We/they barriers have to be removed, or at least dramatically lowered, in order for renewal to happen. That was the starting point for the phenomenal turnaround in the fortunes of GE's Appliance Park. Roger Schipke, the man who led it, recalls: "In the early 1970s we got ourselves in trouble with matrix management. It was the 'glamour' organization then." But it had the appliance division broken into so many small segments, with artificial walls between, that it was more confusing than helpful. Schipke remembers: "By the late 1970s we had thirteen corporate VPs in major appliances, and they all had different agendas. We were paralyzed. No one could make a decision."*

Schipke sat down with a clean sheet of paper and designed an organization that would foster teamwork and strike a balance between short- and long-range thinking. "I blew up the [separate] functions and created four major operating units. Two divisions—production, and sales and service—are 'now' organizations. The other two—technology and marketing—are futures groups. One problem was that 99.9 percent of the people here were so focused on making income for the quarter, they had no concern for two years down the road. I wanted each pair [of divisions] to get involved with the other—to talk to each other. Linkages between them are crucial." Schipke comments that swimming against the functional tide is one of the hardest things he's had to do. "People seem to want a narrow, functional self-concept. I'm trying to create a one-team business perspective."

---

* Schipke attributes much of the problem of the past to the fragmentation. Elsewhere, I've argued for "chunking" things up, being willing to pay the price of fragmentation to reap the innovativeness that seems to flow from smaller units. One of the best books I've ever read on organization, *It All Depends*, by Sherman Harrey, makes the point that trade-offs constantly have to be made. HP flourished with small, highly independent divisions. Then, as market conditions changed—i.e., requiring that the black boxes sold by one division be compatible with the black boxes sold by others— the very independence of the divisions led to problems. At the same time that GE moves away from the matrix, HP is moving toward a kind of matrix. But the specifics of each situation and each market are very different. The overriding point is that in both cases, the existing organization had created formidable we/they barriers within. In GE's case, everybody was guarding the walls defined by their matrix organization. In HP's case, everyone was protecting the sanctity of division boundaries. In both cases, fragmentation existed where communication was needed.

Schipke went to work on making sure the people who populated the new organization *would* work as a team, or at least "a well-coordinated dinosaur," as he refers to the place. "I said to Jack [Welch]: 'Now, you pick the fellow on the top block [Welch chose Schipke]; then he can pick his team. Each of them picks theirs, all the way down.' In early 1982 we were disjointed; it was a staging year. I worked on team building and relationships. In 1983 I added a strategic orientation."*

To further break down barriers within Appliance Park, Schipke and his new team made many symbolic moves. One was to take down all the signs from the factories. DISHWASHER, RANGE, LAUNDRY, and REFRIGERATION became buildings 1, 2, 3, and 4.†

Schipke reports almost immediate results from his efforts to lay waste to the old we/they boundaries. One group noted that customers often put liquid detergent directly on clothing stains and washed them in smaller loads with a greater concentration of soap. "Our washing machines had little lingerie baskets that not many people were using. So the group figured out a way to turn them into 'spot scrubbers.' It turned a disadvantage into an advantage. We had a six-month turnaround on that idea. With the old organization it would have taken three years—if we'd have done it at all."

One reason that Schipke was so effective is the strength of his relationships across organizational boundaries. He and Ken Cassady, the president of the local union, are on good terms. The bond started with their mutual concern for product quality, and was probably forged when Schipke "sent the message out that we would fire anyone who used anything that was tagged defective." Others commented on Schipke's singular ability to relate up, down, and sideways. Said Jim Allen, communications director at Appliance Park: "Roger has a 'good guy' reputation in the middle

---

* Note the reverse of the conventional wisdom here, which would say: first strategy, then organization. It is an interesting variant on the "implementation starts day one" theme presented in the chapter on direction and empowerment.

† Again there is an "all depends" quality to a move like this. One of the problems that Sir Michael Edwardes reports on his struggle to turn British Leyland around was that "Great names like Rover, Austin, Morris, Jaguar, and Land Rover were being subordinated to a Leyland uniformity that was stifling local enthusiasm and pride.... Nowhere did the product names appear in the organizational 'family trees.'" The difference in the Leyland and GE situations is that GE appliances had no great names of the kind Edwardes talks about.

and lower part of the organization. They think of him as 'one of us.' But Jack Welch handpicked him for the job. He can stir up the troops, but he also has a big power base from the top."

Another executive talked about how Schipke put an end to the old political game playing: "Before Roger took over, we had no leadership here. The guys at the top used to send people to corporate to get beat up. The leader would stand back and watch. 'Corporate assistance' was an oxymoron. Roger made corporate [headquarters] look like they went away." But Schipke explains that he could not have done that all by himself: "Paul Van Arden, our sector executive, ran air cover and interference before our success. Jack Welch helped too. I wanted to avoid political pressure as much as possible. My new staff wasn't as political, either. For the first time in at least six years, there was only one message coming out of Louisville. No second-guessing going to corporate to raise doubts."

Among the other things that Schipke talks about that help break down old walls:

I move people from manufacturing to marketing and the other way around. Sales trainees spend two weeks in the factories for orientation. I would love to have them spend six months on the factory floor and some time on the retail floor as well.

People are social; they want to be on a team. Plus, they really want to learn more about what's going on around them. So I started the Breakfast Club. The top sixty managers in the organization meet once a month at seven-thirty. Otherwise they'd never talk to each other.

Formerly central marketing would sign off on all prices. But I turned pricing over to the field. The response was, "That guy is crazy. The whole organization will fall apart tomorrow." So I started the Price Club, which brings marketing and finance together. They communicate. We haven't fallen apart.

A sampling of GE's work force who had been around awhile

confirmed the new sense of teamwork and the importance of breaking down old barriers:

On teamwork: "If I can get along with the next guy and he can get along with me, then that's a successful business. Of course, we aren't going to see eye-to-eye all the time, but it's far from how it used to be when the attitude was 'You're stupid and I'm not going to listen to you.'"

On the past management/labor gulf: "Prior to 1980 we had a communication gap in this building that was two miles wide and fourteen miles long. You saw the plant manager once a year and that was the last working day before the Christmas shutdown. He'd go around the plant and shake everybody's hand and wish you 'Merry Christmas.' That was the last you saw of him until the next Christmas."

On crossing functional and hierarchical lines: "When they first started out, management picked a few of us out to sit in on the engineering meetings and the meetings in the lab. I learned a lot, and I found myself paying attention to things on the floor that I'd never thought of before."

On blasting barriers with suppliers: "We have supplier days now twice a year. We bring them in as guests of Building 3 and they think it's the greatest thing in the world. It has made every supplier to this building work harder to maintain that parts-per-million. Zero defects is what we're shooting for. They know if they don't maintain that level, their parts won't be certified and we'll go back to checking them every time they ship to our building."

And more barriers coming down: "Before, management talked down to—not across—people. The media were our enemies. We were closed, even though we knew this place leaked like a sieve. We opened our doors to them [the media and the community], saying, 'We've got nothing to hide. You're going to get no more song and dance from us.'"

But, as with the other renewing companies, emphasis on teamwork at

Appliance Park doesn't mean that power disappears. The last word on Schipke's political instinct comes from one of his executives: "Roger picked his own team, and he knows just when to ignore it."

GE's Appliance Park bore an eerie similarity to Ford's Chicago plant, until recently a shrine to the past. It was built in 1926 and used, among other things, to manufacture the Edsel. One employee said, "Five years ago it was like war games out here—everyone mad all the time, shouting at each other." A manager remarked, "It was crazy in the past. Management never walked the plant floor unless something wrong was happening. Usually they came down to take disciplinary action against somebody." Someone else chimed in: "The other day we discovered we were getting faulty brake cylinders from a supplier. They weren't all bad, and the problem was hard to detect. I can't say for sure, but I think that in the old days we'd have shipped the cars and let the dealer or the customer find out. What we did this time was shut down the line, track all the cars with the suspect part, and get it fixed. Five years ago no one would have dreamed of shutting down the line for anything short of war or an act of God."

Ford's Chicago plant is one of the two factories producing the Taurus. (The other is in Atlanta.) Dick Ross, the plant's top personnel officer, points to a banner draped across a ceiling with the word QUALITY in bold letters at the top. At one end was the Ford logo, at the other the UAW symbol, and between the two were the words QUALITY IS NOT EXPENSIVE. IT IS PRICELESS.

With a sweeping gesture around the cavernous plant interior, Ross says, "See that? Two months ago it was like Beirut in here. Everything was leveled." They quite literally tore down all the walls. In the biggest single change ever made by Ford, they shut the plant down on November 8, 1985, gutted it, replaced everything with new technology, and had it back in operation, producing the new Taurus, on January 28, 1986. It took just under three months.

Ross said they couldn't have done it without a massive attitude shift that broke down most of the we/they barriers between work force, union, and management. Five years ago, Ford management and the local couldn't agree on much of anything. However, they could both concede that something had to change.

A handful of managers and the leaders of the local went to Japan to see how things worked there. "The most striking thing," says Ross, "was not the technology. And not the presence or absence of union. They have unions too. It was their attitude—their will to work together." From the devastation of the Ford facility three months before and the massive workload they carried during the conversion, there had emerged almost magically a top-quality, highly successful product. But the real magic happened earlier. It happened when they had the good sense to level the we/they barriers, much as they later leveled the interior of the plant.

Maytag is unionized. But the company owes much of its manufacturing proficiency to the absence of we/they barriers. "The UAW local understands our Work Simplification Program," says Sterling Swanger, the manufacturing vice-president, referring to a program at Maytag that trains and rewards everybody for productive ideas. "Their officers have been trained in it." Swanger proudly explains that no grievances were filed during their last big push to automate—a recent $60 million investment in productivity and quality. He feels the investment never would have paid off if "there were no room for communication between management and the employee. The philosophy behind the change must start with management and be understood throughout the company by the total work force."

As at Maytag, many of the companies we talked with stressed the importance of talking directly with the people. They pointed out how common it is for some managements to communicate with the work force only through the union. The union may like things that way; it preserves their own power position. Managers may even think it makes their job easier. But this habit leaves a canyon-size we/they gulf. I'm not arguing against unions, but for the rejection of any practice that fosters a we/they split.

Although the gulf that often exists between management and labor is the most obvious we/they barrier in companies, many others exist, and a host of potential schisms are waiting to open with only the slightest encouragement. There seems to be something about human nature that creates a need for an us-versus-them mentality. Martin Luther King, Jr. called it the "drum major instinct." By that he meant that each of us has a need to stand out, to be special in some way. But he warned of the good and the bad side of that instinct. We all like praise; it makes us feel important and lets us know we are being given attention. Good managers energize their people by recognizing that drum major instinct in us all, by paying attention to us, and making each of us feel special.

The destructive side of the drum major instinct is that it leads us to look for, form, join, create, and invent groups that will make us feel superior because we belong to that group. We are okay; you're so-so. It's all too easy to slip into the suit of metaphorical clothes that strongly identifies us with those most like us—the union local, the factory supervisors, the division, the skunkworks, the R&D labs, the top executives.

To a certain point, that ability to identify strongly with something small is good. Highly divisionalized, autonomous companies like HP, Johnson & Johnson, and 3M have been unusually innovative over the years. They renew by being small and big at the same time. But too much identification with the small unit has problems of its own. It creates too strong a sense of "us." "They" become not just the outsiders but the enemy. The benefit of being a part of a large organization is lost. The ability to renew falls prey to the negative side of Dr. King's drum major instinct.

Simple job rotation improves teamwork and stops the we/they boundaries before they form. Morgan Guaranty makes a regular practice of that, and Vice-President Maureen Hendricks explains its effects. "There's an appreciation at Morgan for the circumstances under which your colleagues are working, because you've either had their job or will someday have it. Since we've been 'on the other side,' people here tend to be very sympathetic, very willing to cooperate. Or let's say you make a marginal loan because you think you'll get credit for the additional business. Four years later you'll be in the special loan department working it out, ruing the day [the loan was made]."

Even with the accent this bank gives to teamwork, Morgan's president, Robert V. Lindsay, says recent thinking showed a clear customer need "for a close relationship between our [securities] traders and the people who produce [deals] for their clients." Morgan created a single division "which combined trading and capital market activities under one roof, thereby bringing together groups that tended to argue for their spread [their share of the profit margin] against the clients' needs." The reorganization accomplished two things, according to Lindsay: It eliminated the issue of who gets credit for the spread, and it formed the basis for better "chemistry" and closer relationships between the two groups.

Lindsay says that there was also continuing, perhaps increasing, friction between the banking relationship people (the old national and international divisions) and the capital markets people (the merger and acquisition folks). He explains: "There was a bit of a 'we and they,' particularly for young, entry-level people who viewed capital markets as the hot area. All we did in this last reorganization was eliminate the differentiation between the two, glob them together, and call it corporate finance. It wasn't very scientific, but we think it will serve to tighten those interrelationships and also bring the client a closer working basis between the two."

Jack Ruffle, vice-chairman, says that the top management team could see strong political camps forming and we/they attitudes hardening between operations (the administrative activities) and the line units. "We had to decentralize. We eliminated the operations division, and we placed a number of its components into the business units. We also made [the operations] people feel a part of the business; [that was] partly to get more of us oriented toward the client as our master."

New on the American scene is the shattering of an unobtrusive, yet influential, we/they barrier: the one between a company and its suppliers. Ford plant manager Joe Bobnar mused that the employee teams can get things done that management can't do. For example, they were not getting the kind of parts or service they needed from an ITT unit. When the problem was bounced up to Bobnar's level, he tried to go through the ITT management to get it fixed. Not much happened. Eventually one of Ford's employee teams met with their counterparts in the ITT organization, and the whole problem was solved with alacrity. Now it is common for the people on the production line at Ford to know their counterparts in supplier organizations. Most things that go wrong can get fixed at that level. Another we/they boundary zapped.

Steve Walleck, a McKinsey director who specializes in manufacturing, notes that not only are we/they barriers between companies and suppliers coming down, but that suppliers are playing an increasing role in helping their customers renew. "This is especially evident in manufacturing," he says, "where the very existence of many suppliers is dependent on the health of the companies they supply. Some of the important advances in robotics for a Ford, General Motors, or Chrysler are supplier-driven."

The conventional wisdom is to have multiple sources of supply, and let them compete for the business. Today the move is toward one, or a very few, trusted sources, trained in your methods and quality standards.

Trust

Dana's president, Woody Morcott, and chairman, Gerry Mitchell, talk about trust all the time. They explain that when you come to work for Dana, you automatically have their trust. It is not something you have to earn. The assumption is mutual trust. They trust you to "do what's right for Dana." You trust them to respect and build your dignity as an individual. (Dana people are quick to point out that there are always disappointments. Some who have had their trust don't live up to it, and they don't last long in the system.) Though Dana gives away trust for free, the people who work there are no patsies. They are better characterized as idealists without illusions.

Morgan Guaranty builds trust into the culture from day one of the training program. Art Rogers, executive vice-president, described the need for it in practical terms. The corporate business that Morgan specializes in moves very fast these days, crossing international boundaries and many areas of banking expertise. "Suppose someone from another part of the bank calls with a neat idea for the XYZ company. If any of us have to sit around for hours wondering [what's on the other guy's hidden agenda], we've almost certainly lost the sale."

Rogers explains that even a twenty-six-year-old officer at Morgan would have a clear sense of the kind of bank it is, the kind of business the bank wants to do. There is not the same feeling, as in many banks, "that someone is trying to zoom one by you as if you were a hockey goalie. All of us are on the same side of the table. You don't have to question others' motives all the time. Trust. We've all inherited it, and the culture passes it down."

Walter Gubert, a senior vice-president, feels the trust of a client is an extension of what Morgan practices within the bank. "It's easy to talk about computers, electronic mail, and other techniques. Sure you need the systems to communicate," he says, waving a bit impatiently at the formidable bank of computer screens and the printouts that surround his office. "But the key, I think, is the willingness of people to communicate—no, make that the *desire* to communicate. When you're working on a transaction, you don't look at the Morgan organization chart. There's no focus on rank—that's just not an issue. When I talk to our Zurich people, I don't care if I talk to the junior person or the senior person, and neither do they. When you are trying to do a transaction, it's better to talk to whoever has the best information at the time. It's important to have an organization where everyone is sharing information with others for results that are good for the firm and good for the client."

The word *trust* came up over and over again at Morgan, as did the word *integrity* at Citicorp. On one level, that doesn't seem unusual, given that both are banks. Trust and integrity are what you would expect. But they were talking about the trust and integrity of the culture, and my experience is that this part is unusual. In the past, banks were the most political of institutions—attributable largely to the fact that banks were protected for so long by regulation, and many managers got bored with the business of "just banking." A little politics added some intrigue.

How does Morgan achieve this internal culture of trust? The explanation given by the top officers was that the training program for every new Morgan officer is as much to help classmates establish a tight rapport as it is to build their technical banking skills. With their business dependent on rapid communication across time zones, countries, and continents, this rapport means everything. If you know and trust the person on the other end of the telephone, you can put a deal together fast that meets the customer's needs. Mimi Willoughby, a new employee with six months of training at the bank's Manhattan headquarters, describes her experience: "We worked twelve-hour days and would go out to dinner together after that. It was hard but it never felt like work. Many of the people I met there will be friends for life."

Trust is essential to a business society that works. A senior bank executive advises: "Don't do business with people you don't trust." He then explains that all the lawyers, contracts, and rules in the world will not protect you from somebody who is out to cheat you.

Harry Quadracci makes a similar point. "We have three simple guidelines at Quad/Graphics: Make money, have fun, and don't do business with people we don't like." On the last point he elaborates that business is hard enough anyway. Why complicate it by doing deals with customers or suppliers where the relationship is destined to be one of constant hassle and distrust?

Don Kelley at GE's Appliance Park talked about a system he had installed. It resembles those at Maytag and Ford in that it empowers production-line workers to shut the line down for bad quality. What about the potential for industrial sabotage? "Many of us were worried about that," he said. "But it never happened. Even in the early days, when there was great animosity, no one used the system for sabotage." Kelley trusted the work force, and they lived up to it.

Here is a perspective from inside the electronics industry. Frank J. Burge, publisher of the trade newspaper *Electronic Engineering Times*, was formerly a sales manager for Fairchild Semiconductor Systems Division. He writes of that experience:

*I*BM *was a big customer. A good customer. A customer that dealt with us fair and square and expected the same treatment in return. When they had problems we worked them out together. And they paid their bills. On time. But not all our customers were as good as IBM. Some were absolute scoundrels. Instead of being professional in their dealings with us, they were often rude, unethical, and would sell their grandmother for a nickel. They expected their customers to pay them within 30 days, but would stretch out payments to their suppliers to 120 or 180 days. Getting them to honor commitments was like pulling teeth.*

Several months ago I was returning from the West Coast,

and happened to sit next to the vice-president of marketing for an East Coast components supplier. He had just been at Hewlett-Packard negotiating a big buy. He was generous in his praise of what a great company Hewlett-Packard was to sell to. So I asked him: "What is the worst company you sell to?" Without hesitation he mentioned the company's name. I laughed. Laughed because virtually every salesman that calls on the company, regardless of the product being sold, would rank the company as one of the worst in the business. Arrogant. Rude. A bunch of shysters. Getting this company to honor its commitments or pay its bill on time is next to impossible. Yet this same company has recently launched an internal campaign to get their employees to treat the customer like a king. Meanwhile they treat their suppliers like bums.

Why Vie?

It's "common knowledge" around many organizations that the way to get people to work the hardest is to pit them against one another. Give similar assignments to two or more people, and you don't have to be concerned any further about whether they do their best. It's a safe bet those involved will scramble to be the first with the most. Sure, some fur will fly—they may even undermine each other in the process—but it's worth the results. If there's going to be a winner, someone's got to lose. Right?

Wrong. Recent findings from the behavioral sciences suggest that cooperation is much more effective than competition. These studies support what the renewing companies were telling us about the role of trust and teamwork. Alfie Kohn, author of *No Contest,* describes a piece of classic research done in 1954 by sociologist Peter Blau of Columbia University, who studied two groups of interviewers in an employment agency. The first group was extremely competitive, personally ambitious, and concerned about their own productivity. The second group was naturally cooperative and worked as a team. The second group's results in filling jobs were much higher than the first.

Two and a half decades later, Robert Helmreich of the University of Texas used questionnaires to relate achievement among a sample of scientists with various personality traits. He found that the most productive scientists (as measured by how often their work was cited by others) ranked high on traits like work orientation and preference for challenging tasks. But they ranked low on competitiveness.

This intrigued Helmreich and his colleagues, who went on to study other groups. By 1985 they had covered seven categories, including airline pilots, airline reservation agents, college undergraduates (using grade point average as measure of success), and businessmen (using salary as measure of achievement). In each case the result was the same. He found a negative correlation between achievement and competitiveness.

In the literature about competition and cooperation, virtually every experiment about cooperation yielded much better results than competition. Why? Author Alfie Kohn provides some clues. "Success often depends on sharing resources efficiently, and this is nearly impossible when people have to work against each other. Cooperation takes advantage of all the skills represented in a group as well as the mysterious process by which that group becomes more than the sum of its parts. By contrast, competition makes people suspicious and hostile toward one another and actively discourages this process." Furthermore, "competition generally does not promote excellence because trying to do well and trying to beat others are simply two different things."

Even so, people often remain in a competitive situation long after it has become a self-defeating course of action. In an experiment called the Dollar Auction game, participants often end up bidding as much as $5 or $6 for a $1 bill. What motivates them to press ahead to win something that obviously will cost them more than it's worth? Initially they are influenced by economic motives—the hope of winning the dollar bill easily and inexpensively. Later in the bidding, interpersonal motives—a desire to save face or to prove one is the best player—drive their behavior.

If the research is correct, or even directionally right, we need immediately to reassess our assumptions about "making it," in school, in business, in life. It is no wonder that the companies we interviewed, who are best at renewal, put such heavy emphasis on teamwork and trust.

Sometimes it's hard to see high achievers as "noncompetitive." Perhaps the difference is the degree to which they wear it on their sleeve. People who are obviously combative, confrontational, and prone to win/lose situations don't get very far in organizations. They may win a lot of battles one-on-one, but their peers make sure they lose the war. Moreover, there are situations where the outcome is too important to leave it to one department or project team. Companies deliberately set up two or more teams to develop the same product. Then they have a performance "shoot-out" to see which one works the best. This approach is common in computer development. The difference is the competition is open, aboveboard, and free of the "win at someone else's expense" mentality. The reason for the competition—urgency of the project—is thoroughly explained.

At Morgan the fervor for collegiality has added a new word to the vocabulary of business. "We try to avoid 'profit-centeritis,' " said Vice-Chairman Jack Ruffle. Morgan people are acutely aware of the artificiality of trying to measure profit contribution at any level below that of the bank itself (the various units are dependent on one another). Morgan understands how easily profit centers can subvert team play, and has coined and often uses the word *profit-centeritis* to discourage the tendency. "It's not that we don't have profit centers," says Ruffle, "but [the profit center] is an indicator of results, not the be-all and end-all that you see in other institutions. There's a very strong desire to get this bank operating together as a team and pulling together for the long term—doing our best to have every decision we make be the best decision for the long haul." Adds Bruce Breckenridge, chairman of the Administrative Policy Committee, "The way to get on the manure list around here is *not* to do something because the profit doesn't go to your unit."

Breckenridge emphasizes teamwork, even—maybe especially —at a stressful time like the recent reorganization, which was big enough to be considered revolution-equivalent. But the trauma, dust, and fuss surrounding revolutionary change never appeared. Breckenridge attributes this to the bank's team-driven, consensus style. Most organizations are afraid to talk much to their staffs

about major reorganization for fear that the uncertainties generated will be more disruptive than a swift stroke of the structural
scalpel. For companies and cultures less secure than Morgan, the
fear may be justified. But of the recent reorganization, Breckenridge
says, "There was lots of consensus-building. [By the time we
reorganized] everyone understood that we wanted to get banking
and corporate finance together. We talked about it so much that
the actual change was 'ho-hum.' " Here is another fine example of
decision and implementation marching in parallel.

On the teamwork point, Morgan's Ruffle adds, "The other
thing that exists around here that has to be credited to [CEO]
Lew Preston and his predecessors is that when a problem develops, you run a high risk of being fired if you try to solve it totally
on your own. Don't be a hero. Expand the horizon quickly. Tell
others about it. You'll probably find someone who's had experience dealing with a problem like that. Lack of profit-centeritis
helps in this regard."

At Morgan the spirit of teamwork extends into the marketplace. Ruffle says that they tried to make their last reorganization
almost entirely transparent to their customers. They hoped that
the customers, knowing what was going on, would understand
and perhaps even be helpful in the process.

Morgan seems also to understand the value of "the facts" in
building teamwork. Observes Ruffle: "We don't have meetings
where people go in and argue over numbers. Today we have, as
of the close of business every Wednesday night, a worldwide
interest-rate and liquidity position put together by Major Currency. We can calculate the absolute risk to this institution to
changes in interest rates. So we know what it is, and it's right
because it's tied right into the books. We are not guessing the
earnings impact of interest-rate changes."

Historically, Citicorp has been such an entrepreneurial culture that teamwork comes less naturally. But they seem to be just
as thoughtful as Morgan on the issue of good politics and bad.
Larry Small says he finds politics an intriguing and complex question. He believes that at Citicorp they have two main ways of
combating the bad aspects: integrity and what he calls "the actuals." On integrity, he says, if you are determined, over a long
period of time, that everything you do will be done with complete

integrity, then you make that ideal believable. People just start to behave that way. Politics, in its ugly form, fades into the background.

By "the actuals," Small means that Citicorp measures and rewards people on the basis of their actual accomplishments. Then you get away from the outrageous kinds of political behavior. If you are backstabbing and otherwise not being nice, it shows up in the actuals. If you have the actuals, then it's easy to show that people are getting ahead on performance, not power games.

Small is quite proud that they are starting to count the actuals on what he calls an "adult," not "juvenile" grouping of activities. In Small's view, the complete manager is just that: complete. He or she is successful because earnings have grown, because revenues have improved, because the number of products has expanded, because stability has been built, because returns have improved, because people have been developed, and so on. In other words, lots of things contribute to an individual's success as a manager. Small believes they are way ahead of their industry in that they've stopped measuring people in a unilateral way.

Citicorp's "adult" accounting system helps them combat the same thing Morgan calls profit-centeritis. Larry Small asserts that a large business these days is horribly complex, whether you want it to be or not. Your ways of managing must correspond. Small has a personal view that the only way you can understand an organization like Citibank is to think of it as a prism—or better yet, a multifaceted gemstone. Their accounting system is now such that data can be cut by customers, by products, by geographies—all the facets that make up the business. There is no one way of understanding the whole all at once, and their information system recognizes that. In doing so it cuts down on silly jurisdictional we/they disputes.

Positive Politics, Productive Power

In his *Essence of Decision,* Graham Allison argues that organizations are creatures of habit as well as creatures of rational choice.

In that same book, he introduces yet a third model of organization behavior: a political model. Allison's neat trick in the book is to make all three models of the way organizations work believable by "explaining" the Cuban missile crisis in terms of each. As you read each "explanation," you find yourself in hearty agreement with it. His point, of course, is that the dynamics of all three models are simultaneously at play in any organization. To understand organizations, you can't just look at them one way. They are rational decision-makers. They are "irrational" creatures of habit. They are "irrational" (and unpredictable) products of internal politics and power.

Explaining his political model, Allison says:

M*en share power. Men differ about what must be done. The differences matter. This milieu necessitates that government decisions and actions result from a political process. In this process, sometimes one group committed to a course of action triumphs over other groups fighting for other alternatives. Equally often, however, different groups pulling in different directions produce a result, or better a resultant—a mixture of conflicting preferences and unequal power of various individuals—distinct from what any person or group intended. In both cases, what moves the chess pieces is not simply the reasons that support a course of action, or the routines of organizations that enact an alternative, but the power and skill of proponents and opponents of the action in question.*

Political behavior in organizations is perfectly natural and legitimate. Sometimes it is the *only* way to get things done. Among the more obvious examples:

Every organization, no matter how well managed, has multiple goals, values, and interests. It is never possible to align every person's objectives with every other's or with broader corporate goals. Political discussion, conflict, persuasion, bargaining, and consensus building are the only way to resolve disagreement and get on with things.

The convention you often hear in the well-managed companies is that responsibility always exceeds authority. If you see something that needs doing, do it, whether or not it fits your job description.* In other words, if you have to operate outside channels, you have to work the informal organization in order to be an effective manager. That is not classic organization theory. It is political behavior. The people who are good at it have a power that doesn't show up on the organization charts, but it is power nonetheless. It is the way much gets accomplished in this world. (Think of the green second-lieutenant versus the master sergeant in the army. On paper the officer is in command; in reality the sergeant gets things done.)

The nonprofit sector of the economy serves a wider, more diverse, more complex set of constituents than do most for-profit companies. This multiplicity of interest groups makes nonprofit organizations inevitably more political. Business-people who join their boards have trouble appreciating this dimension; therefore, they are less helpful than they could be if they would simply recognize the inherent political nature of these institutions. Further, as prevailing political winds with their reduced government subsidies have forced the nonprofit organizations to "go private," many have tried to adopt management tools from the private sector. A fine arts museum or a community hospital will introduce a long-range planning process. But the fit is rarely an easy one, because the process assumes more "rationality" than you find in the nonprofit world. Going back to Allison's models, nonprofits have had to be more political in the past to survive. They can, in fact, be managed less politically, but they cannot be understood or managed without more allowance and tolerance for the inevitable political dimension.

---

* A General Motors executive says that H. Ross Perot saw something that needed doing inside GM and told a GM manager to do it. The man replied that it was not part of his job description. "You need a job description," fumed Perot, "I'll give you a job description: Use your head." The bemused GM executive said, "Can you imagine what chaos we'd have around here if everybody did that?"

Politics and power are neither good nor bad. They're neutral. Their misuse, perversion, and occasional excesses lead us to be rightfully suspicious. What all of us are afraid of is the kind of behavior that Niccolo Machiavelli so eloquently expresses in *The Prince*.

It must be evident to everyone that it is more praiseworthy for a prince always to maintain good faith, and practice integrity rather than craft and deceit. And yet the experience of our own times has shown that those princes have achieved great things who made small account of good faith, and who understood by cunning to circumvent the intelligence of others; and that in the end they got the better of those whose actions were dictated by loyalty and good faith. You must know therefore, that there are two ways of carrying on a contest; the one by law, and the other by force. The first is practiced by men and the other by animals; and as the first is often insufficient, it becomes necessary to resort to the second.

Was he right? Must you engage in force, cunning, and deceit to succeed? Many key events in history say yes, but we're fools if we give in to that inevitability. Our collective distaste for politics and power leads us to an innocence about politics and power that forces us either to bow to those who use force, or to use it ourselves. We can do better than that. We can start by recognizing that organizations run, in part, on political dimensions. Then we can be explicit about the benefits of politics as well as the drawbacks.

The fact remains that the role of the manager is to get things done. Little change, let alone renewal, happens in this world without a power base. Remember Roger Schipke's experience in Appliance Park. People felt that one of the reasons he was effective was that he had support from all sides—the people in the plant, the union leadership, the chief executive, and, of course, the management team that was brought in from other GE operations. He had a power base. He was very effective politically, but nobody would label him as "political."

The key to being good politically without being political lies in the way historian James MacGregor Burns defines leadership. He calls for recognition of collective purpose between leaders and followers: The followers need something, leadership fills their needs, and the followers yield power to the leaders. In his classic book *Leadership*, Burns contrasts two styles. He calls the first "transactional leadership," which stresses the interaction between leader and follower in "exchanging gratifications in a political marketplace."

"Thus Dutchmen (colonists in America) give beads to Indians in exchange for real estate, and French legislators trade votes in the Assembly on unrelated pieces of legislation. . . . The object in these cases is not a joint effort for persons with common aims acting for the collective interests of followers but a bargain to aid the individual interests of persons or groups going their separate ways."

In contrast, the result of "transforming leadership" is to raise the sights and aspirations of the followers to a greater degree. Both kinds of leader, says Burns, can contribute to human purpose. Both operate off value sets, but the transactional leader's values are those of "means—honesty, responsibility, fairness, the honoring of commitments." The transforming leaders elevate the aspirations of the followers through their teaching, mentoring, and coaching rule. They are more concerned with end values— "liberty, justice, equality." Roger Schipke at GE, Caldwell and Petersen at Ford, and Iacocca at Chrysler, along with many of the other executives, are playing that transforming role.

It is the transforming leader who renews institutions, not the transactional leader. And that person need not be a top executive. In one of his most compelling paragraphs, Burns says:

Leadership—especially transforming leadership—is far more pervasive, widespread—indeed, common—than we generally recognize; it is also much more bounded, limited, and uncommon. Common, because acts of leadership occur not simply in presidential mansions and parliamentary assemblies but far more widely and powerfully in the day-to-day pursuit of collective goals. . . . It is an affair of parents, teachers and peers as well as of preachers and politicians [and executives]. Uncommon, because many acts heralded or bemoaned as instances of leadership—acts of oratory, manipulation, sheer self-advancement, brute coercion—are not such. Much of what commonly passes as leadership—conspicuous position-taking without followers or follow-through, posturing on various public stages, manipulation without general purpose, authoritarianism—is no more leadership than the behavior of small boys marching in front of a parade, who continue to strut along Main Street after the procession has turned down a side street toward the fairgrounds. Also, many apparent leaders will be only partial leaders. They may tap follow-ers' motives or power bases; or they may take value-laden positions, . . . or they may operate at the final policy-making or implementation stages; or they may do some or all of these. The test of their leadership function is their contribu-tion to change, measured by purpose drawn from collective motives and values.

Bill McCormick, CEO of Fireman's Fund Insurance Company, believes that all leaders are political and there's nothing necessarily wrong with that. Many leaders are smart and talented—you don't get to the top without that—but they are focused mainly on acquiring position. They want to get into the next-bigger chair. Those are the ones who get to the top without having earned it. Others also want to move ahead, but their main concern is "What can I do to fill the chair when I'm in it?" Their purpose is much bigger than occupying the position; it's to make a difference in the organization. McCormick is clearly in favor of this kind of leader, and believes that a big problem in corporate leadership is that too many of the former are in positions of power. In his own company he hopes that he is able to stop people who are inter-ested only in their own advancement, or lead them to change their ways.

The most effective leaders can take on a challenge without getting swallowed up by it. They're willing to walk if they are no longer in a position to lead. Listen for a moment to Jack MacAllister, who accomplished a lot in the Bell System before he left to head US West: "I wanted a management challenge, and I guess the Bell System was the biggest one I could find. I decided that never, under any circumstances, was I going to be intimidated by the organization or anyone in it. And, yes, I thought many times about leaving." GE's Schipke reinforces Jack's point: "I've always been willing to walk. I say what I think, and I don't get mad at people if they criticize me." That state of mind gives Roger a tremendous source of power, although he says, "I'm not a political animal."

Every individual's true source of power over the organization that employs him is his willingness to walk. It's too big a stick to use often, but unwillingness to use it always puts people in a subservient role to organizations. Companies should encourage people to see this; the last thing organizations need are leaders, managers, and people who are overly dependent and submissive. They will not speak up on the tough issues. No individual security and toughness—no renewal.

Clarity about your own purpose in the organization—and how far you're willing to go to accomplish it—is crucial. But that doesn't mean you can do everything by yourself or by decree. The most effective leaders recognize these limitations and understand the importance of building support networks throughout the organization. That's what led IBM's John Akers to comment, "You have to be politically capable. You have to be able to sell your ideas, to get people on the team. Those who can't get things done, who can't get people to work on their problems, don't rise as high as people who can."

Fireman's Fund's Bill McCormick has made a career of resuscitating troubled businesses. He got his start in the renewal game with the American Express banking subsidiary; more specifically, his charge was to "automate the bank." He said the biggest problem was that the bank operated in more than twenty-five countries, and he wanted to design a system that would work for all of them. He remembers: "I kept worrying, 'Is the design right?' But Pano, a member of my team, said, 'Bill, you don't understand. The political risk is greater than the technical risk;

everybody will want to go their own way.' And I said to myself, 'The son of a gun is right.' " So they shipped the equipment to the banks in countries most critical to the project's success, and gave each country the lead on a part of the total project: financial accounting to Italy, client accounts to Germany, foreign exchange to the United Kingdom, fixed asset accounting to France, and so on. McCormick says, "That step, which was Pano's idea, made it work. And every time we brought another country into the system, we gave them a piece to design. Go anywhere in the world and they say, 'That's our system. We built this piece.' "

Another source of power for negotiators and politicians is simply staying power. Like politics itself, this power source is neither good nor bad. It can be used for the wrong ends as easily as for the right ends, so a part of being political and positive within this dimension is to keep questioning the merit of causes for which you persevere. But given integrity and legitimate purpose, simply hanging in there is another way to get things done without having the power of office.

For years, one of the top performing companies in the broadcasting industry has been King Broadcasting in Seattle. King's CEO is Mrs. Stimson Bullitt, now in her nineties. As a fairly young woman she had inherited a small radio station from her father. She decided to do something with it and, since Seattle is in King county, went after the call letters "KING," which at the time were the property of an inactive station. Later she went for, and got, an affiliation with NBC. Still later she picked up the NBC affiliate in Portland and the ABC affiliate in Spokane. Quite a success, especially when you consider that she started long before there were many women managers.

Why has she been so effective? "Good negotiator," one of her colleagues explains. "She just wears you down. She knows what she wants and she just leans on you until you say 'okay.' " She understands the power of persistence.

Lamar Alexander, the recent governor of Tennessee who was so effective in bringing industry to the state, creating jobs, and generally getting things done, talks about the difficulty of implementation in the private sector, expressing no small amount of wonder that he got so much done in his eight years as governor. He said, "Well, the governor has to know what he wants." He explains that not much of significance can get done unless the chief executive supports it. What about all the people and forces that oppose action in government? "You just have to wear them down."

Politics and renewal are not incompatible. Political power can be used for destructive or beneficial ends. It's obvious that back-stabbing politics have no place in any organization. Yet our culture is so suspicious of both politics and power that we barely have a language for talking about their good side. Some executives told us that the "good guys" will figure it out anyway. Some *will* figure it out; others will believe management's refrain of "no politics around here." The trouble is that the latter group will be "had" too often by those who have figured it out. They will be less effective leaders because they don't understand the political dimensions of organizations. What to do?

Another political skill on the positive side is to attack issues, not people. A study of thousands of successful negotiations done by a group of Harvard researchers showed that one of the many skills of good negotiators was their ability to shift the discussion away from personalities. They concentrate instead on the issues. Poor negotiators and negative politicians do just the reverse. They attack people.

Steps for Getting There

One way to halt negative politicking and move toward the positive is to make your organization one where teamwork counts. Teams generally get things done in organizations—not Lone Rangers, not "yes people," and especially not people who are out to serve their own ends. Does your company reward teamwork? Do the people in it *like* working with one another?

Teamwork is a tricky business; it requires people to pull together toward a set of shared goals or values. It does not mean that they always agree on the best way to get there. When they don't agree, they should discuss—even argue—those differences. Vibrant teams should do just that: vibrate. But don't let the quest for teamwork pull down the heroes. Teams need great quarter-backs and gifted players. Many organizations undermine their heroes in the name of "teamwork." That's not teamwork, but just another form of politics on the seamy side. To strengthen the sense of teamwork:

1. Pick people on the basis of both qualification for the job and fit with the culture. Most companies told us that one key to their success was having the best people. But how can they all have the best people? What they *can* have is the best people *for their own business*. IBM has the best people, and Nucor has the best people—for their respective businesses. There's a danger with too many like-minded team players: You could get blindsided by big change. But the renewing companies have plenty of wild ducks, who may be several standard deviations off the cultural norm but who fit in the cultural envelope nonetheless.

2. Destroy at least one we/they barrier a year. Start with a tiny one for practice. Then, with some we/they combat experience under your belt, knock down some of the big ones. Do not assume the barriers will stay down. They are deeply rooted in every human being's need to feel special as an individual and as part of a broader whole. And recognize the healthy potential in multiple loyalties. Just as you can be proud of your town, state or country, people in organizations can feel a part of multiple groups in the organization without erecting impassible we/they barriers.

3. Communicate. Share information. Encourage direct talk across the we/they boundaries. Ford used Interaction Associates of San Francisco, a firm of professional facili-tators, to help break down all the old barriers as they set about to rebuild and renew the company.* But bringing in specialists in group dynamics isn't the only way to

---

* Facilitators are people who act as catalysts to make meetings work. They "facilitate" in the sense that they help make sure that everyone has a chance to talk, nobody dominates the meeting, different points of view get aired, and conflict is channeled into productive discussion. Good facilitators can be invaluable in helping to erase the lines between "us" and "them" in meetings.

open up communication. You can start with your own attitude toward other people's ideas and opinions.

4. Look not only inside but outside the company for needless we/they barriers. The one that cries out for continuing attention, no matter how many times it has been said, is between a company and its customers. The one receiving increasing attention these days is between a business and its suppliers.

5. Use training programs not just to "train" in the narrow sense, but to build relationships, as Morgan does. This needn't apply only to the new hires. Learning is a lifelong process. IBM understands that, and all of their people arc continuously being trained and retrained. But while they are learning, they are also forging new, cross-company bonds.

6. Recognize that persuasion is not a one-way street but a means for problem-solving. Look for that area where your interests overlap. Look at the problem from the other person's point of view. Try to enlarge that area of overlap so that you both "win" in the end. Citicorp's Tom Theobald makes the point: "If you are referring to politics as the art of persuasion, when a number of people have to cooperate on something and we have to persuade them one at a time, then it's a noble cause. Around here there's a pretty decent level of recognition that change requires the consent of a wide variety of people. A little bit of it is even institutionalized—like getting sign-offs from certain people for certain projects."

7. Build networks. Much of what happens in the daily life of companies happens through informal channels. You will be effective in organizations to the extent that people throughout the organization know you, like you, and trust your motives. That's why Schipke was so successful in Appliance Park, and that's why Morgan puts so much stress on relationship building as part of the training program. The lack of it is also a main reason why strategies, decisions, and consultants fail. Rational argument does not carry the day in organizations. Rationality

points the way, but whether anything gets done is directly related to whether people support it. Consultants are not stupid, and their recommendations are often annoyingly right. But the reason they often fail to get things done is their myopic trust in rationality and in their own brilliance. Their attitude is: "Of course people will do this, because it's right." That's where they're wrong.

8. Think of the political process as one of conflict resolution. To a great extent, good politics is the ability to negotiate well. Imagine negotiation in terms of a different kind of solution space from the one we talked about before. Good deals benefit both parties, and good negotiators don't try to beat the other guy. They solve problems. They look for areas of overlapping interest and expand on those. The diagram below pictures optimal solution space for negotiation. What you are trying to do is find and enlarge that area of mutual interest.

NEGOTIATION AS SOLUTION SPACE

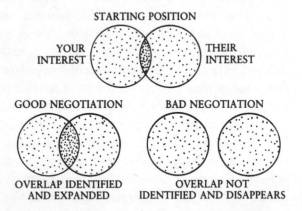

9. Get the facts. Information is a source of positive power. If you know what is going on when others do not, you are immediately in a position of power. If you try to hold

on to that position by not sharing information, you lose trust and, in turn, the power you had.

10. Win support from the boss. While you can get much accomplished through sheer negotiating ability, you'll get much more accomplished if the boss supports it. The situation is circular, however. Trust and integrity are the basis for keeping politics and power positive. Misuse of the boss's support gets you in the soup (or it ought to).

11. Take special pains to discourage behavior that has no other purpose than to meet someone's own political ends. Weed out those who are politicking in the negative sense. The more blatant ones are easy to spot. The difficult ones are those who are especially good at relating upward, but not sideways or down, in the organization. They are so good at getting along with the boss, and so effective at helping him, that they mask the fact that their actions are fundamentally divisive.

12. Come down hard on political infighting. It is a huge energy leak. Take a cue from that executive who picked the worst offenders, fired them, and told everyone why. The action seems unduly harsh, but in considering the vigor lost by businesses that tolerate politics, the punishment fits the crime. (You can get sued for whimsical firings these days, so you have to be a little careful with this remedy.)

13. Be absolutely intolerant of lack of integrity or lack of trustworthy behavior. Dana, IBM, Citicorp, and Morgan return to this point over and over. An atmosphere that lacks trust breeds the worst sort of politics. Don't do business on the outside with people you don't trust. Avoid those people inside the organization you don't trust.

14. If your company runs on mistrust, leave. This is easier said than done, but the alternatives are bleak: Become political yourself or watch well-intended programs constantly being steamrollered.

15. If you are the boss, promote transforming leaders at all levels of the organization. Look for several characteris-

tics: a vision that says "This is what the organization needs, and here is the mark I will make on it"; a track record of accomplishment—the person really has made a difference; the ability to bring out the best in others; and, of course, integrity.

SEVEN

Stability in Motion

Nothing endures but change.

—HERACLITUS (c. 500 B.C.)

If there's a magic to renewal, it is the magic of the *status quo*. The renewing companies understand the need for consistency, for order, for norms, and—yes—habit. They also understand that the only constant is change. This is a wonderful state of paradox, where people see the need for enduring norms, and one of those norms is change. In companies that are able continuously to renew, the management system is best described as consistency with constant experimentation. Quantum change over time, as a product of tiny steps every day. At companies where renewal comes to pass as the result of crisis, stability gives way to lurching, jarring change. The jolt is needed—it can even be exhilarating for the few who thrive on high adventure—but it's no fun for most of the people affected by it. Crisis-driven renewal means loss of jobs. Stability disappears for a while and so does the magic.

In writing about self-renewal, John Gardner states, "The only stability possible is stability in motion." This captures the essence of what the renewing organizations try to achieve. There is a kind of rhythm to the process: first, a constant search for standard ways of doing things. That makes life easier. Then the deliberate breaking of old rules, familiar patterns, past practice; that is the only way to respond to change.

The truly difficult challenge is to find and keep the balance—or perhaps a better phrase would be the *dynamic imbalance*. To change is to risk something. That makes us insecure. Not to change is the bigger risk, but it seldom feels that way. Renewing organizations lay a stable foundation. They build it from sets of core beliefs, constant reminders that change is the norm, and policies that furnish security of employment without promising security of position. They find and manage a delicate balance: enough security so that people will take risks, enough uncertainty so that people will strive.

Change Is the Norm

One cornerstone for the stabilizing base is the leaders' disposition—their knack for welcoming change as the norm. Leaders at renewing companies often mention their acceptance of the inevitability of change. This mirrors the intensity of internal communication on the same point. By talking about it, by treating change as normal (instead of as something you do only when you have to), these leaders take away much of the fear and anxiety that surround change.

As much like common sense as this seems, there is tremendous stabilizing power in contantly reminding folks that change is normal. Most companies don't do this. But without a fluent and continuing reminder that change is the order of things, people assume the opposite. They structure plans on business-as-usual base cases. They tell the troops they want no surprises. They seem both dumbfounded and paralyzed when blindsided by change. The renewers behave the reverse way. They keep reminding themselves to expect change. Their willingness to understand and exploit change is a powerful competitive weapon.

Bob Pew, Steelcase's chairman, is by nature a taciturn man, but Pew is voluble regarding the need for constant change: "I have regular opportunities to speak with our managers. My theme is almost always the necessity to manage change and the dangers of complacency and self-satisfaction." Pew reminds his managers that Steelcase's current industry leadership doesn't mean a thing. Two decades ago, a roster of top U.S. companies would have included Revere Copper & Brass, W.T. Grant, and Addressograph-Multigraph. All three went bankrupt. He talks about other companies who led the office furniture industry in years past. "One is out of business and the other is second class; I saw them both get pompous, then complacent."

Mike Wright, CEO of the Super Valu empire, strikes a similar chord. "Markets can change overnight. One morning you wake up and you are dead in the water. We remind ourselves of that often; we have a sense of urgency." Super Valu makes that "sense of urgency," and the need to change, a part of the institutional fabric by spurning written contracts with its customers. They don't want the small grocer in Aberdeen, South Dakota, locked in. They'd rather the relationship be sustained day to day; having no written contracts forces Super Valu to constantly read the needs of both grocers and consumers and to react.

Wright credits his predecessor, Jack Crocker, for instilling this philosophy. Crocker's single-minded emphasis on "Change is a good thing" made it the mantra of his leadership. "Time after time, he'd keep pounding it in," says a Super Valu executive who recalls Crocker carrying around a can of peas for his standard lecture of how inflation creates illusionary profits. Crocker would gesture to the peas, saying that unless Super Valu people changed the way they managed costs during inflation, they would lose money every time they sold a can of peas. Super Valu today keeps changing and growing, thanks to what Gene Hoffman, chairman of the wholesale food division, calls "our philosophical zero-based budgeting."

Citicorp's Larry Small sings a similar tune. He generalizes that in Citibank's customer base he sees two kinds of company. There are the "BAUs," the ones whose operating assumption is "business as usual." They do change from time to time, but when they do, it's a big deal—disconcerting to everyone. Others— Larry Small puts Citicorp in this category—are habituated to change. They change more rapidly and more easily because their folks expect it; it's part of the culture. Citicorp's Dick Huber explains further: "When things are growing we can make a bundle; when things are shrinking we can make a bundle. We thrive on change. A turbulent environment plays to our strengths."

Deliberate Bureaucracy-Busting

Dick Huber says, "Citicorp manages by shuffling the deck once in a while, and we do it when we aren't in trouble. Reorganize on the crest of the wave, not when you are down in the trough."

This is a phenomenon demonstrated by renewing businesses in a variety of ways. They are deliberate bureaucracy-busters. The trait is a hallmark of IBM. Remember John Akers on their propensity to reorganize. "We organize for good business reasons. One of the good business reasons is that we haven't reorganized for a while."

Akers, an outgoing, gregarious individual, gets really animated on this point. "We're a collection of habits. Good and bad." He elaborates: "It's very healthy to take all those institutional habits that you and I have been talking about, and if they've been in place for five years"—he snaps his fingers with an explosive crack—"change them."

He explains: By changing, you learn. Your habits, good and bad, are exposed and you have a chance to look at them. Drawing an analogy to a card game, Akers says that reorganization gives you a chance to improve your management hand. Change, in and of itself, can force a fresh look if you're willing to look. But while he and others see arbitrary change as a sign of health and argue the case for change for its own sake, most everyone would agree that they could not do that without other sources of stability.

Fellow IBMer Tom Liptak amplifies Akers's comments. "Here is a company in excess of fifty billion dollars in sales, and over four hundred thousand employees, and we have completely reorganized every major unit at least once in the last two and one-half years. Now, that's a fairly significant amount of change. I literally hear this—I'm not making it up—if I go to some division that hasn't been reorganized in a couple of years, they start getting nervous. [They wonder]: 'We must be doing something wrong.' " Liptak reflects on that statement. "I think we probably reorganize too much. But if we were arguing the polarized case—should we err on the side of reorganizing too little or too much—I can tell you where I am." He hammers the desk with a fist for emphasis. "Do it too much!"

Potlatch's Dick Madden explains the case for bureaucracy containment: "You want to make general rules because that simplifies management. But the truth is that there is no complete and proper answer even for one point in time, let alone over a period of time. So you have to review policies from year to year, or at least from time to time, to see if they are still applicable. Many large companies have policies dating back five, ten, or fifteen years just because they haven't taken the time to go back and look at them." Peter Drucker expresses the same sentiment when he suggests that every three years or so, a company should be put on trial for its life—every product, process, technology, service, and market.

The most unique approach to stirring up the bureaucratic pot comes from Japan. Chiyoshi Misawa, founder and president of Misawa Homes, the largest home builder in Japan, "dies" at least once every decade to arrest the momentum of out-of-date assumptions and policies. He sends a memo to his company—the most recent one was last year; the one before that was after the last energy crisis—that formally announces "the death of your president." This is his way of forcing the whole company to rethink everything. When employees resist change because they are used to the old way of doing things, Misawa-san declares: "That was the way things were done under Mr. Misawa. He is now dead. Now, how shall we proceed?"

McKinsey director Kenichi Ohmae says that behavior like this may be a singular example, but that the attitude it conveys is not uncommon in Japan. Both Nomura Securities, the big brokerage house, and Toshiba, the electronics firm, force a periodic change in their chief executive. At Nomura it happens every ten years; at Toshiba, every six. Each new chief executive is expected to be able to answer the question "What mark will you have left on this organization?" It is a way of breaking with the past and encouraging a focus for the future. At Toshiba, the current chief executive's top priorities are attaining globalization .and encouraging internal entrepreneurship. His predecessor's top priority was to bring Toshiba to the state of the art in technology. For the CEO before, the priority was to improve the company's profitability, which then trailed the competition's.

The approaches to bureaucracy-smashing in the renewing companies are many and ingenious. One of the standouts at IBM is the "IBU," their code for the independent business unit. It works like this: From time to time they identify a business or product area where they think they should be better positioned. They also know they can't force any new project into the plans of any of the existing divisions. It just wouldn't get the proper attention. Or it is too different. The momentum of the IBM culture would kill it before it had half a chance to develop. So the company has a portfolio of independent business units. They're managed much like a venture capital portfolio. They run almost completely outside the IBM management structure and systems. IBM has over a dozen such activities in operation now.

Like any successful venture capitalist, IBM expects to hit it big on some, do all right on others, and lose on a few. That is, in fact, the way it works. When we interviewed the IBMers, management was about to write a few ventures off to experience. Many others were doing fine but had yet to come into their own. Several were big successes. Among these they count their computer-aided design, engineering, and manufacturing IBU, where they believe IBM came from behind to take industry leadership.

Their most visible success with the IBU is what they call the "Entry Systems Division," and what most of us know as their Charlie Chaplin/personal-computer family of products. The late Don Estridge (he died tragically in a 1985 airplane crash) and his "gang of twelve" cut themselves loose from the IBM culture in 1978. They went to Boca Raton, Florida, to set up headquarters and do battle in the personal-computer business, which was then dominated by Commodore, Apple, and Radio Shack. Five years later, the Entry Systems Division was generating over $5 billion in revenue. They became the dominant force in the market. Through the IBU approach, IBM had added a company to its empire that was approximately the size of a Hewlett-Packard, and they hadn't been forced to make an acquisition. They had built it from scratch. Most IBMers will tell you that their success with the PC never would have occurred had Estridge and his colleagues been operating from a command post inside IBM's formal structure.

Another bureaucracy-buster inside IBM is the Fellows Program—the institutionalized recognition of the importance of what Thomas Watson, Sr., called "wild ducks," those especially creative people who don't fly well in formation. Ore-Ida took a cue from the IBM catalog of bureaucracy-busters and started its own Fellows Program as part of a drive to become more innovative. Ore-Ida's Fellows are not like IBM's. They are not detached from their regular duties and they do not have much by way of resources at their disposal. They do have a similar function. They act as a channel around the normal bureaucracy so that good ideas will not get crushed by the force of business-as-usual. Here's how it works: Each year Ore-Ida appoints five Fellows. They come from the ranks of middle management and represent different business and functional areas. Their main qualification is zest for the program. Each has a small budget, around $50,000, which he or she uses to ferret out and sponsor ideas that might otherwise have gotten tangled in the system.

The first year the program was in place, Ore-Ida Fellows reported that they were a little discouraged. They had identified no new products or product-line extensions. They had "only" managed to uncover one million dollars' worth of cost saving. By three years into the program, they had proved to be the major source of new products and line extensions.

One of IBM's manufacturing and development czars, Executive Vice-President Jack Kuehler, describes another way his company fights bureaucracy. If there's a hole in a product area which the team responsible for the product is unable to fill, Kuehler will go to a different location and ask another team to take a crack at it. If they're willing to take it on, he goes back to the first team and lets them know someone else is taking a look at their product area. He does the same if a manufacturing cost doesn't really look competitive. He might go to another manufacturing plant and ask if they'd like to bid on a product. This strategy gets results. It "stimulates an absolute fuss between the two groups."*

What Kuehler has done here—and what others like HP or Dana or Super Valu do by keeping divisions small—is push an element of the free market system into the hierarchy. It cuts through bureaucracy.

Stable Beliefs

Warren Phillips of Dow Jones calls his organization's shared values "the bedrocks." Tom Watson, Jr., called them "basic beliefs." Whatever the name, they add up to the values that supply another source of stability for the motion that surrounds the renewing companies.

Maytag's well-deserved reputation for building outrageously reliable major appliances is rooted in the clearly articulated, simple, shared values that drive the company. Walk into their huge plant in Newton, Iowa, and what's the first thing you see? A sign that says QUALITY PRODUCTS BUILT BY QUALITY PEOPLE. CEO Dan Krumm keeps things just as simple, but uses a few more words: "What are we good at? The appliance business. There may be more interesting things to do, but this is what we do well. Our goals have always been a little bit different from those in other companies. We build only one kind of quality." Belief in quality— Maytag's kind of quality—supports the company as it responds continuously to the kind of industry change that almost defeated General Electric's Major Appliance Business Group.

But in companies that had changed over time, do shared values get redefined as well? Well, Maytag, Steelcase, IBM, all had Rock of Gibraltar values that hadn't budged a millimeter for decades. There may be a direct relationship between the quality of their value statements and their ability to renew continuously. At

---

* This has obvious political danger and Kuehler knows it. He says you have to monitor it very closely so that it doesn't get out of hand. IBM's close culture and abhorrence of negative politics make this sort of thing possible. On the other hand, if the stakes are high enough, a company might take the political risk. Unless Steven Jobs had left Apple's Lisa project and started a parallel one, flying pirate flags in defiance, there might not have been a Macintosh.

other companies that renewed as a result of crisis—Ryder, Ford, GE's Appliance Park—one of the early actions was to go to work on reviewing core values.

Following its near failure, and the wave of change that hit the trucking industry after deregulation, Ryder's business has been moving almost as continuously as its fleet of yellow trucks. Tony Burns believes in the need for change and growth; that's the energy source for keeping Ryder people vigorous, challenged, and renewed. But as Ryder has moved from the truck leasing to the transportation business, they have continued to follow their guiding values.

You don't have to look too far to discover those values. They are on plaques and posters all over Ryder's Miami offices. And to assure that every employee keeps them always up-front, a pocket-sized plastic card has been distributed to everyone. On one side of the card are statements prefaced by: FOR OUR BUSINESS WE WILL STRIVE. Included here are affirmations about everything from providing the best possible products and services to being a positive contributor to society. On the other side is: FOR OUR EMPLOYEES WE WILL STRIVE, followed by pledges ranging from providing "a working climate of mutual trust, respect, and support" to paying for performance.

Like many leaders of renewing companies, Tony Burns is often on videotapes which circulate around the company, talking about what Ryder stands for, making the Ryder leadership less remote. One video format is "CEO Forum," which shows Burns in a press-conference-style meeting answering questions submitted anonymously by employees. According to Ryder's corporate communications staff: "Burns reiterates the same five values every time he stands up and talks." The specifics of his taped message change, but one way or another in each message, he finds a way to talk about the things Ryder believes in: service, quality, transportation (not just trucking), growth, and financial strength.

"Ryder Magazine," another regular video production for employees at Ryder, communicates the motion and stability that characterize the company. The segment on Ryder's acquisition of Aviall, for instance, is the perfect way of saying "We're in transportation—not trucking," "We're changing," and "We haven't gone that far afield." Aviall, "Ryder Magazine" tells everyone, is one of the best at jet engine overhauls, just as Ryder is among the best at truck engine overhauls.

The Pathfinders

One of the most difficult challenges in management is developing a sense of value and vision. Stanford's Hal Leavitt calls this part of the manager's job "pathfinding," and he distinguishes the thought process it requires from the way a manager thinks when he is making decisions or carrying them out. "The pathfinding part of managing is the homeland of the visionary, the dreamer, the innovator, the creator, the entrepreneur. . . . The central questions are very difficult and often unaddressed: How do I decide what I want to be when I grow up? What should this organization try to become if it could become anything imaginable? What do we really want to do with this company?"

How do leaders do the pathfinding that leads to vision, value, and stability? By finding a way to give the organization a sense of pride. The questions that seem most helpful in translating the need for vision and values into specific statements are: 1) Looking back on the history of our organization, what have we done that gives us the most pride? 2) Looking back on our history, what ought we to be ashamed of? 3) What could we do now that would make us all proud? 4) Ten years from now, looking back, what will we have done that will have made us most proud?

A part of Ford's renewal was rooted in questions exactly like these. According to chief designer Jack Telnack, it started under former CEO Phil Caldwell, who kept encouraging the designers to do something different. It crystallized early in Petersen's presidency when he wandered out to the design center and asked, "Do you really like this stuff you're building? Is this what you like to drive? Would you want to see it parked in your driveway?" Telnack says, with some lingering astonishment, "I first thought, 'God, is this guy for real?' Then I said, 'No, sir.' And when he asked me, 'What would you like to drive?' I told him, 'If you come back in a couple of weeks we will have something to show you.'"

Petersen recalls the same incident: "I was feeling worse and worse about what we were introducing [in 1978 and 1979]." Early on, he made a visit to the design center "just to find out what was going on." He says that he hadn't talked to them in years. He was head of international and "couldn't talk about North American matters. It just wasn't done. Now that I could talk to them, I asked them whether they actually were designing cars the way they thought they should be." (Notice the high-level we/they barrier here.)

Petersen says they all looked at each other and shook their heads. "That's when I asked them to show me a car they would be proud to be seen driving." Petersen asserts, and Telnack confirms, that "designers always have that advanced area behind some closed door where they can take out their frustrations. It turned out they had a beauty back there."

Pathfinding starts with the leadership, but it is not just the job of a small group at the top. Hal Leavitt notes: "Large complex organizations simply cannot afford to isolate pathfinding as the special province of a small set of people. These days no CEO, even the brilliant founder ... can generate all of the adventurous explorations, large and small, that organizations need to maintain their vitality." And that is how the Ford vision began to build.

Petersen talks about the days when he was first made chairman and chief executive, and Harold "Red" Poling was made president: "In the early years, struggling with the question of what we wanted our cars to represent was something I probably spent as much time on as anything else." He says the issue was addressed through a multitude of small get-togethers and off-site meetings. "Sooner or later all these groups would come to a point in their deliberations where they wished there were a better explanation of just what Ford stood for." Petersen and Poling pressed the Ford employees to select from their own ranks some individuals to represent them, to meet with the top officers and work on the central question of core values.

Says Petersen: "People got very excited about this idea." The representatives were chosen quickly. "Over about a six-month period, Red and I met with the same group of ten people. We had no idea how long it would take us." They worked at it until they had produced something that felt right to the top, to the individuals involved, and to the people they represented.

The result is a statement of mission, values, and guiding principles. In essence it says, just as you read in the ads: "Quality Is Job One." It says that Ford will be a customer-driven company (no pun intended). And it emphasizes the importance of employee involvement.

Some companies, such as Citicorp, recently have reexamined their shared values—not because of crisis, but because of inconsistency between their values as practiced and their understanding of the needs of the market. Despite the many positive attributes of the Citicorp value system—they're innovative, aggressive, competitive—they have a reputation for being, in their words, "combative and truculent." Larry Small has a colorful way of putting it: "We have a clear tendency toward arrogance. We occasionally show an almost uncontrollable urge for confrontation. We are a Maserati or a Ferrari, tearing down the highway at great speed, taking corners with screaming tires, and stopping and starting in clouds of dust. Many of our competitors may be compared with cargo trucks, station wagons, limousines, or stately sedans.

"We want to switch to being a touring car—a high-performance machine with great power and handling ability, but with a touch more grace, elegance, and dignity. An IBM. A General Electric. Or a Sony. They are each viewed as a force for good in the world. People tend to see them as additive to the process of improving the welfare of humankind." Small tells Citicorp people that they ought to strive for the same image and the reality that underlies it.

Whether core beliefs were old and unchanged or more recently developed and modified, all the companies we interviewed thought them to be a source of stability in a changing world. All felt that core beliefs should be carefully developed, continuously interpreted, and changed slowly if at all.*

---

* The only thing I would add is that any company in crisis has to challenge everything, including the set of beliefs, written or not, that got them into the pickle in the first place.

The pattern persists: stability and motion. Stability from a value set that can make everyone proud, stability from the constant reminder that change is the order of things, and motion from the zest for breaking up bureaucratic patterns.

Tiny Steps

One way to keep change as the norm is to change all the time—in tiny steps. This goes against the grain of a lot of management thinking, which calls for the quantum leap. The reasoning is this: As a company grows and gets a few big successes under its belt, only big successes will count in the future. This attitude probably gets in the way of renewal.

To understand the fallacy of the Big Win mentality, look first at fields other than business. Organizational theorist Karl Weick says, "There is widespread agreement that social science research has done relatively little to solve social problems." One reason, he suggests, is that we tend to define social problems in such grand terms that we paralyze our ability to act. The problem seems so big—e.g., "the drug problem," "the national debt," "the bomb" —that we either freeze up at the enormity of the issue or we become apathetic. Weick observes: "Ironically, people often can't solve problems unless they think they aren't problems."

The comparable cycle in business goes something like this: The problem is defined in big terms. It is conveyed to down-line management along with the demand for a quantum-leap solution. Then what the psychologists call "arousal" sets in. In other words, anxiety increases. When this happens we fall back on old, less complex ways of dealing with problems. We panic and forget what we know. In situations when all our recently acquired skills and new habits are needed the most, we fall back on the old stuff. Seeing something as a "mere problem" instead of a BIG PROBLEM is easier for us.*

One advocate for the small win is IBM's Ralph Gomory,

---

* Tom Peters introduced the concept of "small wins" in his doctoral thesis for Stanford University, entitled *Patterns of Winning and Losing: Effect on Approach and Avoidance By Friends and Enemies.*

who puts special emphasis on the importance of continuous small steps. The contrast is curious because, when entering the lobby of IBM's famous research facility in Yorktown, New York, the first thing that catches your attention is a big display of the important scientific breakthroughs IBM has made: the disc drive, a new branch of mathematics called fractals, magnetic core memories, and recently, the one megabite chip. Gomory himself was responsible for a breakthrough in a branch of mathematics called integer programming. Yet he advocates the small win.

IBM is constantly criticized for being behind in technology. It's a bum rap. Their sales and service stars have shined so bright that people often miss the company's luster in basic science. Further, IBM is not especially concerned with being first to market with a new technology, preferring, it seems, to let others test the market for them. Sometimes this backfires. But in spending $5 billion on basic research annually, they are a major contributor to science in this country. Apple computer founder Steve Jobs has said, "IBM is a national treasure." Nowhere is this comment more applicable than in their contribution to technology.*

Gomory's basic position remains. It is the small stuff, not the breakthroughs, that provide the backbone for technical advance. The misperception, he says, is due to the way people are brought up. "The world of industrial development is invisible to most people. In school most of us learn about the heroes of science. We go to college, and many of the people there don't understand the technology development world either. So we are trained on great events and breakthroughs, but when people go to work they find that most progress is of an incremental nature. Breakthroughs are relatively rare."

He relates his own experiences in computing, asserting that in some sense nothing fundamentally important has happened since the transistor was invented in 1947. "In this industry it is possible to improve products by about twenty percent a year. That has been possible for the last twenty years and it probably will be possible for the next twenty years." This sustained rate of

---

* One striking example: Alex Müller, an IBM Fellow and physicist in IBM's Zurich research laboratories, and his colleague J. Georg Bednorz made the breakthrough in superconductivity at relatively high temperatures. Many believe this development could be at least as important as the transistor.

progress is extraordinary, he says, but it doesn't rely on break-throughs. It rests on something rather fundamental—the idea that IBM's business is information processing.

Information can be processed as marks, or bits. Little "ones" and zeros. "Marks have the property, that small 'ones' are just as good as big 'ones,' as long as you can still read them and maneu-ver them. When you make them smaller you can store them in less silicon on fewer circles on a disc. Most of the progress in the last twenty years can be traced to learning how to make these marks smaller. Today we have no trouble putting a million bits where we put one before. The result is a million times better, yet no fundamental breakthroughs were required." Gomory reinforces his premise that advances in information-processing are driven more by rapid evolution of technology than by breakthroughs.

It takes a lot of skill and investment to do the kind of thing he is talking about. But it *is* doable. "You invent on a micro scale. You have to learn how to make smaller and smaller structures, thinner and thinner layers. For that you need bigger tools, greater understanding of the materials, and more expensive facilities," Gomory says.

He brings the point home with the example of word process-ing. Something like word processing—or its numerical cousin, the spreadsheet—looks like a breakthrough to most of us because suddenly it's widely available. Word processing would have been doable on the very early computers, but you never would have used them for that: The economics would have been absurd. But as "invention at a micro level" has made computing power widely available and cheap, we suddenly get a "breakthrough" like word processing.

Potlatch's Dick Madden contributes another illustration from the pulp and paper business. "We had been on a constant but rather slow track with regard to technological change. But in the last eight years," Madden says, "our industry has exploded with technical change." He explains that measuring techniques have suddenly come into their own in the business. As recently as a decade ago, there was a lot of art in the pulp-and-paper-making process. (Madden didn't say this, but I can remember having seen machine tenders tasting the pulp.) "Now you can measure the chemistry of the process itself and feed that back in real time." What this makes possible—with computers and computer models to support the technique—is materials and chemical balance. Says Madden: "You can measure the chemicals and heat that you add to the pulping process so you're not wasting anything. On the paper side of the business, thickness can be measured with precision so that you don't waste paper trying to make sure that what is coming off the paper machine meets minimum standards." These days, technology has made possible better coatings and in turn better gloss finishes, better color, and layered sheets: "What may look like a single layer to the user may be several [with better properties]."

The change looks, and is, explosive. But behind it lie the efforts of companies like Measurex and Accuray, which have been working at the technology of measuring pulp and paper processes for more than twenty years. Another case of the collection of small victories that leads to the quantum leap.

Karl Weick chimes in from an entirely different field. He argues that Alcoholics Anonymous has been successful because it doesn't insist on huge change. Though the goal of the program is lifetime abstinence, AA doesn't ask for that. "The impossibility of lifetime abstinence is scaled down to the more workable task of not taking a drink for the next twenty-four hours, drastically reducing the size of a win necessary to maintain sobriety. Actually gaining that small win is then aided by several other small measures, such as phone calls, one-hour meetings, slogans, pamphlets, and mediations, which themselves are easy to acquire and implement."

Change the People

HP's executive vice-president, John Doyle, smiles wryly and comments that one reason organizations are creatures of habit is that the people in them are creatures of habit. "If you want to change habits, change the people." He is right of course. And in changing people you do get motion. What about the stability side?

Renewing companies generate motion, break habits, and scrape the barnacles of bureaucracy by changing people. They start at the senior management levels, where entrenched habits can be most harmful. The main difference among the renewing companies is the degree and rapidity of people change. It relates to the lumpiness of the renewal process. Where renewal seems a continuous state, people move from job to job, but most of the changes are internal and there is a secure base for most who move. Where renewal begins with crisis, wholesale change in management seems an inevitable part of the process.

Those companies that continuously renew enact a policy of security of employment but not position. Many have explicit no-layoff policies. They have both tough performance expectations and safety nets.

Nucor is a good illustration of this apparent paradox. Nucor has a no-layoff policy. It doesn't have a mandatory retirement age. But the company is absolutely dependent on making more steel with fewer people to maintain cost competitiveness. Here is what they do: First, they let everyone know that if they can possibly avoid it, they will not lay anybody off. Second, they scour the world looking for ways to make better steel at a lower cost. They find and install a new machine that makes half the work crew on a line redundant. People on the crew tell us: "Sure, we are scared when something like this comes along." But instead of being laid off, some are retrained to run the new equipment while others find new positions elsewhere in the company. Nucor has all of them on incentive; a big part of their generous paychecks comes from the company's continuous push to automate, and Nucor's willingness to share the results. Nucor reminds its people, and the people remind each other, that they are in world competition; if they cannot keep productivity marching forward, there won't be jobs for anyone. Nucor grows as it prospers; between growth and normal attrition, there are always openings for people whose jobs have been made redundant.

Dana, Maytag, and IBM have policies that are similar to Nucor's. They actively solicit ideas for better productivity, pay people for the ideas, avoid layoffs, and retrain where displacement occurs.

IBM and Hewlett-Packard are well known for their no-layoff and lifetime-employment policies. Steelcase and Dana have had layoffs on rare occasions, but their flexibility and the lengths to which they go before taking those steps are impressive. When Steelcase had a sales slump in 1982, they cut back from a normal forty-five-hour week to forty, then thirty-eight hours. The company kept sending letters to employees informing them where the company stood and what the outlook was.

"Finally, we were down to thirty-six hours. It was costing our employees a lot of money and that didn't seem fair. We had to lay off eleven hundred people," recalls President Frank Merlotti. "It made the headlines: 'Steelcase lays off.' It was like the end of the world. There were television cameras out there. The laid-off employees said, 'We know the company is doing everything it can. It won't be long before we'll be back.' Sure enough, although we had prepared them for a long layoff, things turned out pretty nice. In three months we had them all back and we hired about a thousand more."

Employment security is not intended as a sinecure that will create a sterile, civil-service environment. The safety net is there, but people are still held to tough performance standards. The quid pro quo of the pact is that employees will be willing to change jobs, locations, or career paths to help the total balance. The company says, in effect, "We don't reserve the right to lay you off," and the employees, in turn, grant a high degree of latitude in what they'll do to cooperate.

IBM has a carefully planned series of steps, calibrated to increasing degrees of severity, in order to adjust their employment ratios. On the lower end, outside services are pared back, travel expenses are reduced, and summer hiring is lowered. On the higher end, employees change locations, are retrained to new jobs, or switch from staff to line or vice versa.

In one instance, IBM employees were requested to take all their deferred vacation time, with pay; the company estimated that the total bank of deferred vacation days came to about 17,000 *years*, which the company had to add to its business expense. In addition, increased use of vacation helped spread the workload at IBM facilities where the workload was light. "We've been there before," says *Think,* the IBM company magazine, referring to previous computer-industry slumps in 1957–58,

1961–62, 1971–72, and 1974–75. There were no layoffs during those slumps, but IBM did plenty of "resource-balancing."

The idea is that there isn't just one giant switch labeled LAYOFFS that a company must pull when in a slump. There are plenty of intermediary steps, which can be a challenge to administer but which help the company in the long run. Frank Merlotti recalls the "tremendous shuffling" that Steelcase went through to preserve jobs: "It was a real nightmare for personnel, but we did it because we thought it was the fair way."

Another example from Steelcase illustrates the curious blend of the hard and soft in their culture. There is a demerit system that assigns points for things like excessive tardiness. A certain level of points triggers a warning, then meetings with supervisors, and finally, dismissal. Most companies would treat a high-demerit employee as if he were radioactive, never mind one they had dismissed. Steelcase takes a different approach. Duane Sayer, a forklift driver in Steelcase's Grand Rapids plant, explains:

If you're a good employee, the company will bend over backward for you. If you're a bad employee—well, I've been with the company for eleven years. When I started I was single, I liked to have a good time, and I got a lot of points, but they gave me a chance. A lot of guys here might be going through a divorce, or have problems. They might put him on the night shift if he can't get up in the morning. Then there are second-chance employees. They might send you out the door, and a few weeks later call you up and say, "Have you straightened out yet?" It's a chance to come back, start fresh.

This kind of leniency might sound like an invitation for abuse. But somehow it works at Steelcase, which has high productivity in its plants and good relations with its employees. We asked President Frank Merlotti about second-chance employees; his answer showed the realism of the Steelcase method. "Sure, we hire back people we've fired all the time. Which may be dumb . . . Many of them get fired a second time. But every now and then one of them will turn around and become a damn good employee."

Just as the no-layoff-unless-we-have-no-choice policy provides a basis for tough standards and security at lower levels, so do expectations of "promote from within" and "company as career" at management levels. Managers at IBM, HP, or Super Valu move up, down, and sideways with surprising fluidity. It's not unusual for managers to move up; they do that everywhere. The sideways part is far more rare, while in most companies, to be moved down means, in effect, you're out. The culture expects you to leave and makes it all but impossible for anyone who has been demoted to stay. By contrast, it is not unusual at IBM or HP that an individual gets promoted, does not cut it in the new job, and is transferred to a job that he can handle. At Super Valu a similar policy prevails. A young manager, who was put in charge of a struggling regional operation that eventually got shut down, was welcomed back to headquarters and given a choice new assignment. He says of the experience: "I was part of the decision, not the victim. The signals sent were 'You're not here alone in the wilderness.' "

Most of the renewing companies put great emphasis on shuffling the assignments of their executives, both to give the executives broader exposure and to break the force of old habits. As Dick Madden rebuilt Potlatch, he worked with the people who were already there. He brought in very few outsiders, but rather broadened the insider base through rotational assignments. Carlo De Benedetti took the same approach at Olivetti.

At Club Med, the French resort company, CEO Gilbert Trigano says, "Every three or four years the management concept of Club Med changes. This winter we will change some of the structure. If you are a general manager in Europe, you go to America; if you are a general manager in America, you go to Asia. All the system changes. *La mode dangereuse* for the company is *habitude*. If you use *la même méthologie* for ten years, you are finished. If a person works in the same place for a long time—eight years or so—it may be impossible then to move. The weight of the habit may be too heavy to break. Between three and five years is the time to move."

Trigano elaborates: "When you move, the first year you study and learn. Your productivity is sixty percent. The second year your productivity is eighty percent. The next year it is eighty to ninety percent. Afterwards, it starts to decrease. After ten years, I think your productivity [on the same job] is twenty-five percent."

Trigano's comments sound a lot like a pet theory of Citicorp's Dick Huber regarding job performance. You take a new job, all charged up to achieve a set of goals. If you're good at your job, you've attained maybe 80 percent of those goals after three or four years. The remaining 20 percent don't seem that urgent anymore; you're already looking ahead to the next challenge. If someone new takes over, your leftover 20 percent becomes the top slice of his or her 100 percent—and the cycle continues. The goals remain the same, but the sense of urgency is critically different.

The renewing companies take this theory to heart. IBM, many say, stands for "I've been moved." They, Citicorp, Morgan, and others keep their managers in motion. Of particular interest is the way they are willing to pay the cost of shifting managers across functions and from line to staff in order to build leaders who have experience across a variety of fields.

At IBM, Tom Liptak cites an example of the kind of movement in the management ranks that IBM is famous for: "I had just come out of the field where I had been a branch manager. We had just launched the 360 Series, so we were gearing up all the factories around the world to produce it. After ten months Opel said to me: 'How would you like to be director of scheduling for manufacturing?' Not only did I not know how to schedule, I didn't even know where the factories were! Talk about taking a fresh look. But I know I brought to that job a very current feeling of what customers' needs were. Since I had just come out of the field, I tended to bias the system toward being very responsive." The Series 360 proved to be a huge success and entrenched IBM's leadership in mainframe computers.

Change the Leadership

At another end of the renewal spectrum is the company *driven to renewal by crisis*. There the need for radical and dramatic shifts in the people, especially among the top managers, is a common element of renewal. The worse the situation, the less time there is for change and the more radical the shift. Stability gives way to quick, decisive action. A more positive way of looking at it is that in crisis, the only way to regain the stabilizing base is to replace the people who led the company into near-collapse.

That was the predicament facing Heinz after its takeover of Ore-Ida in 1965. Now one of the best companies within Heinz, this producer of frozen potatoes ("If it's Ore-Ida, it's all righta") was not always that good. Although the company had a hefty retail market share when Heinz bought it—thus its attraction for the Pittsburgh ketchup and pickle people—the problems within Ore-Ida were considerable. The plants were run down and poorly maintained, and that caused severe quality and cost problems. What's more, a grave conflict of interest was built into the system. Many of the top executives were also independent potato farmers who contracted crops to Ore-Ida. Since the ability to buy potatoes effectively has everything to do with Ore-Ida's success, that practice, so open to possible abuse, had to stop. Heinz had to take drastic action.

On what Ore-Ida historians now call Black Monday, the Heinz board, led by CEO Burt Gookin, visited the subsidiary and summarily fired the top seven executives. A new team was quickly put in place. Bob Pedersen, a vice-president of operations at a Heinz subsidiary, Star-Kist, was brought in to take charge. Pedersen, then in his mid-forties, recruited a management board "not one of whom was a day older than thirty-two," who met every Monday morning to clean up the company. Included in this group were Paul Corddry, who was then brand manager of Heinz ketchup, brought in to head marketing, and J. Wray Connolly, a Heinz lawyer, recruited to revamp potato purchasing. Gerry Herrick, one of the few who survived Black Monday, rose to head manufacturing.

Beyond the simple lesson—make big and swift people changes when we have no other option—there's another renewal message that's only slightly hidden in the Black Monday story. As unpleasant as an event like that is, and as reluctant as managers ought to be to use Black Monday medicine, the learning experience is huge for those brought in to fix things. As the Heinz example suggests, the people who turn things around often become an organization's heartiest future executives. Corddry was to become Ore-Ida's CEO and, very recently, president of Heinz USA. Connolly preceded Corddry as president of Heinz USA. Herrick was appointed president of Ore-Ida's Foodways subsidiary and has recently succeeded Corddry as president of Ore-Ida. If an executive has lived through near-failure, especially early in his career, he is more likely to sense the signals of incipient heavy weather next time around, and tighten ship.

When Dana Corporation's past CEO, Rene (pronounced "wren") McPherson, talks of his earliest experience at renewal, it sounds like an Ore-Ida Black Monday story. His boss, Jack Martin, asked him to help salvage Dana's failing Canadian operation. Soon after his arrival, McPherson found himself in an untenable situation: trying to change things while under the direction of the old regime. After about four months he called Martin and said, "I'm leaving. As long as this guy is here, I can't get anything done." Martin put Rene in charge and moved the other guy out.

This illustrates a common mistake in renewal. The executive group wants, understandably, to be humane. Reasoning that the new management team will "learn" from the old, they create a transition period where the old guard remains in charge while the new guard is getting up to speed. It seldom works. The old guard's main agenda has to be that of keeping collective egos intact, proving that what it had been doing made sense. The new guard needs to deny the past in order to get on with the future. The attempt to be humane has just the reverse effect.

Free now to act, McPherson—wisely—didn't. Instead he talked and listened for six months. Only then did he decide to make some changes. And he made some biggies. McPherson says, "What you want to do [when things are bad] is get everyone's attention. Mix things up at the top. Change everybody." He continues: "At business school there was a phrase for the way you were supposed to do things like this, called 'ad prac.' " The phrase stands for "administrative practices" and it means to proceed gently. In his early days at the Canadian plant, McPherson was ad prac-ing like mad and nothing was changing. Eventually, he called in all the top people and said, "You know the old organization chart. Here's the new one." Except for one person (and McPherson), of all the people in that meeting, everyone got a new assignment.

McPherson's story is intentionally harsh, because a common mistake in turnarounds is to be too gentle with the ones you see every day and who are most nearly your peers. That "gentleness" completely ignores the damage ultimately being done to people down the line and to customers.

Moving managers to ensure renewal is not just an American and Japanese phenomenon. Sandoz, the Swiss drug company, had been doing fine by most standards. But insiders felt it was swollen, lethargic, and overstaffed in almost every department except research. When Dr. Marc Moret took power, he brought in a new executive team whose first priority was to diet away the excess layers, departments, and people. They did this, explaining all the while to the Swiss people and government why they felt it necessary to make changes in a company that was, by all surface measures, doing just fine. Under Moret's leadership, the company has moved from the "just fine" category to the rare stratum of a top company like Swissair.

Steps for Getting There

Because change is the norm, renewal must be continuous. That means giving up any notion you might have that change is something you do only when you're forced to—when your back's against the wall. It also means that you're not likely to accomplish change in one quantum leap, then go back to business as usual. That just isn't the way the world works.

1. Create broad-based acceptance of change as the order of things; paradoxically, that helps stabilize the organization. It goes further. Change is a positive indicator, a sign of health and vigor. Remember the way IBM's divisions start worrying if they haven't reorganized in a while? Make change the expectation. You should worry, and so should your people, if things have been left alone too long. No change ought to feel too good to be true. What are you doing wrong?

2. Stop asking people for no-surprise results. That's a quick

way to neutralize your staff's open attitude toward change. First, it predisposes them to deny anything threatening that might be occurring. It also encourages them to avoid the risks inherent in change, since risk-taking begets more surprises than following a known path. This in turn digs you deeper into your habit and isolation holes.

3. Don't be afraid to change "for no good reason," provided that the people involved have a basis for stability other than their position. Shuffle the deck and see what you learn. There's nothing like a new vantage point to help you break out of your former mind-set. The change doesn't have to be drastic: start a new task force; schedule some field trips; drop some committees and join others. Keep your antennae up. When you start to get too comfortable, when there aren't many questions you can't answer, it's time for a change.

4. Make bureaucracy-busting a habit throughout your organization. Take a layer out of the hierarchy. Put staff in line jobs and vice versa. Recentralize something and decentralize something else. Look for ways to organize so that innovation doesn't get buried; the force of tradition can kill a good idea in no time. The "we've always done it this way" attitude makes people intolerant of anything different and unwilling to pay attention to something new. IBM's independent business units and Ore-Ida's Fellows Program are great examples of efforts designed specifically to make an end run around the insidious forces of structure and tradition. If the outcome is critical, set up competing projects. Spend more on the research end of R&D; it's cheap. Encourage people to speak up when something they're doing seems irrelevant or a waste of time.

5. Memorize the phrase *markets and hierarchies*. To oversimplify things a little, there are two ways that decisions get made in the business world: by the marketplace and through the hierarchy. The former is generally more efficient and the latter prevails in big companies. Markets are automatic bureaucracy-busters. Look for ways of pushing the marketplace into the hierarchy. Allow

divisions to use outside supply if sources inside the company are not competitive. Look for ways to break big units into smaller ones. Don't do your own market research if you can buy it outside. Don't staff up for functions that can be obtained from other divisions. Dana doesn't even have the same personnel policies from division to division; if someone moves from one division to the next, the salary and benefits package is renegotiated. Dana headquarters doesn't have its own data processing, but buys that service from its divisions.

6. Shared values contribute greatly to the stability that people feel, even in turbulent times, and should be managed. Occasionally do a "values check." Talk informally with your folks to see how they perceive the values. Look at what has happened in times of crisis or abrupt change to see what the shared values are. If the values need stating, or restating, ask: "In what ought we to take pride?" Remember Don Petersen's question to the designers: "Do you really like this stuff?" Every few years organize a task force to reinterpret the main values in your culture. At least once a year give a speech that reiterates what you stand for. Don't worry about sounding repetitive; almost every CEO we talked with seemed a little embarrassed at how often he repeated the same message, and all the down-line people felt that they could not hear that message often enough.

7. Look for discrepancies between the values that influence the work that people do every day and the ones that are supposed to be guiding your company. If differences exist, try to identify their source. When people are getting mixed signals— ones that sound like "we do care about quality, but in a pinch it's more important to get the product out the door"—it's a sure bet your value base is eroding. Clearing up the discrepancy strengthens and reinforces the base.

You may go for years, even decades, without needing to redefine your company's core beliefs. Then again, a significant shift in the environment may require a similar shift in values. Deregulation, for instance, has forced the introduction of more entrepreneurial, market-driven values in the banking, transportation, and communication industries. Foreign competition has thrust many companies toward new high-quality, low-cost values. Understand the important role played by stable values, but also recognize when they need to be updated.

8. When you're hiring staff, pick people who reflect the values of your company's culture. IBM recruits heavily from universities in the Midwest, and that's not surprising; midwestern graduates are more likely to live by an ethic that is similar to IBM's basic values. Ask yourself: "Are we hiring people who fit in with the way we do things around here?"

   The importance of value consistency goes even further than your staffing decisions. When you are doing business with outsiders, if you have a choice, pick ones who have a value set you admire. This is particularly true for suppliers and outside consultants. Suppliers are providing your raw materials; every time they compromise on quality or default on a delivery, your own quality and productivity costs are affected. Consultants supply advice—something much more intangible. If their basis for viewing the world is out of sync with yours— let's say, their typical solution for cutting costs is to cut staff, and you have a no-layoff policy—it's not likely you are going to get much useful advice from them.

9. Keep reminding yourself that big issues can be solved best by breaking them down into smaller ones. Although you may be tempted to engage in dramatic exhortations about impending catastrophe, such excursions usually paralyze rather than motivate people. Large-scale problems seem impenetrable, whereas incremental steps are both doable and consistently rewarding.

   Even so, the cumulative effect of many small wins can't always alleviate a more massive need to change. Sometimes experimentation around the edges just doesn't provide the major course correction that you need. When it's time for a fundamental reassessment of the business you're in, don't settle for stopgap measures. They give an illusion of progress that masks the pressing need for broad-based change.

Let go of the notion that the technological breakthrough is the only way to measure whether your investment in innovation has reaped results. That's just another version of the "big win" mentality, which doesn't recognize the collective power of many tiny steps. When breakthroughs do occur, they're often based on the impact of lots of unrecognized steps forward.

10. Besides shared values, security of employment contributes greatly to the stabilizing base that makes change less threatening to most people. The first thing we want to know whenever we are faced with impending change is: "How will this affect me?" At work we want to know: "Will I get laid off, transferred to another office, reassigned to another position here?" Full-employment policies make it clear to everyone that the first of these options will not be exercised. That alone makes people much more willing to respond flexibly to necessary changes in their position or location.

11. Like the renewing companies, you may want to build in opportunities to move people around the organization before they start to get stale in their current positions. These shifts help people break old habits and build a broader experience base. Ideally, managers and employees alike should be on some sort of a learning curve, even if it's not too steep. One of the most effective ways of making sure that's happening is to give them new job responsibilities every few years, at least.

12. Like massive layoffs, wholesale replacement of the team at the top is justifiable only under conditions of extreme crisis. Sometimes, however, such action is unavoidable. When there's no other choice but to bring in new leaders, it's best to be quick and decisive about it. Protracted transition periods may assuage bruised egos, but they don't do much to get the company back on track.

Remember that healthy organizations, like healthy people, simultaneously experience stability and motion, continuity and change. Too much stability leads to stagnation; too much change results in chaos. Both are debilitating, and neither one by itself leads to renewal.

In the concept of stability in motion, we have a continuity that allows for change, a stable system with renewal as a built-in part. The ideal is an organization that preserves its base but learns as the environment changes. In *Self-Renewal*, John Gardner puts the concept eloquently:

Our thinking about growth and decay is dominated by the image of a single life-span, animal or vegetable. Seedling, full flower, and death ... But for an ever-renewing society, the appropriate image is a total garden, a balanced aquarium or other ecological system. Some things are being born, other things are flourishing, still other things are dying—but the system lives on.

EIGHT

Attitudes and Attention

*What you are stands over you the while, and
thunders so that I cannot hear what you
say to the contrary.*

—RALPH WALDO EMERSON

—

Develop a healthy disrespect for the impossible.

—SUPER VALU'S GENE HOFFMAN

*Productivity is a function of attitude, and cost
is a function of productivity. So it all comes
down to attitude.*

—ZEBCO'S JOHN CHARVAT

They can because they think they can.

—VIRGIL

Attitudes count. First Boston's president and CEO, Peter Buchanan, strives to set the example. He tries to pay as much
attention to his family as his work. "It must be a macho thing to
work until eleven o'clock every night. I've heard that one of our
competitors tells you the firm comes first in your life, and then

your family. I think that's *appalling*. It comes around later to hurt the firm. Granted, there is no way we can take the pressure off if a client wants to start a merger the day before Thanksgiving. But I take my vacations every year. I go skiing for two weeks and leave instructions that I'm not to be called." His attitude pervades the firm; the recruiting brochure talks about the need to balance one's personal and professional life. Buchanan emphasizes: "If people here don't think their family comes first, I don't want to hear it." No wonder one third of Yale's graduating class this year signed up to interview with First Boston.

Attitude makes the difference. Discussing his approach to renewing Olivetti, Carlo De Benedetti told us, "I gave a little *courage* to the company. We were discounting our products. We were always ten percent to fifteen percent lower than the competition, not because we were more clever [or had lower costs] but because we were more shy. Normally, when you lose money, you cut prices. But then you have a losing attitude. I increased the prices, without looking at the products, by 15 percent. The market reacted the way I was convinced it would: Immediately the volume increased. The Olivetti people began to believe in themselves when they stopped discounting." De Benedetti's move to raise prices signaled a winning attitude; everyone began living up. to winning expectations.

Expectations are everything. Three years after American Express Banking operations were automated, there were half as many people processing twice the volume of work. Bill McCormick, who oversaw the operation and now runs Fireman's Fund Insurance, says that it was the vision of what could be that turned things around. At first he was not optimistic. "The back office looked like the Lower Slobovian civil service. My first thought was, 'Man, if we automate this we either have to retrain everybody, or there has to be a wholesale change of people.' " But McCormick talked to them about his vision. "We're going to automate the bank because we can't compete otherwise. Life should be more fun—and easier. There will be fewer jobs of the kind you know, but there will also be more jobs of a different kind, so we aren't going to fire anyone. We need your help to figure out how to do it." McCormick says that even then he had his doubts: "I could have sworn we would eventually have to hire all new people from the likes of EDS or Arthur Anderson." And he did bring in a couple of people. "But," he says, "out of this pile of people you would swear couldn't do anything, a few started hanging around after work asking questions. In six months some clerks were becoming systems designers." McCormick declares that those people had more talent than anyone would have imagined. "They weren't dumb. They were fully competent. They responded once we hung a sign on the wall that said 'We are going to automate; we are going to capture data only once; we're going to design reports the way people want them; we're going to try to be the best in the world.' "

Attention is all there is. For several years innovation had been a strategic priority at Ore-Ida, but little happened. Then top management added the missing ingredient: attention. Through their sponsorship of the Fellows Program, and the way they put their own time behind the innovation priority, leadership support for innovation became palpable. They got the results they had wanted all along. For example, $15,000 in seed money from the Fellows Program led to a computerized scale that is now saving the company more than $2 million annually. Over in R&D a staff member received a $2,000 Fellows grant to develop a process to turn potato skins into a product, an idea his boss had previously rejected. Now there's a patent application and a product that management says could sell 10 million pounds annually.

All these stories echo a familiar refrain. Attitudes, expectations, and attention establish what gets done. The most sophisticated marketing plan, the most complex strategic analysis, the most up-to-the-minute personnel policies are moot in comparison with the power of a single manager's attitudes, and his visible attention.

Toughminded Optimism

Lou Holtz, Notre Dame's recently appointed football coach, is celebrated for both his wit and his ability to turn college teams around. He is eloquent on the subject of attitudes. Holtz describes how he once breathed life into the University of Minnesota's moribund football team:

The program at Minnesota was down, not because of the previous coach but because of the attitudes that permeated the entire organization. Somewhere along the line some people got the misconception you cannot win in Minnesota. All I heard was how cold it gets. When I found out that the state bird was a mosquito, I got a little nervous myself.

The whole attitude was: "We can't win anyway. What's the sense in even trying?" And then you have failure and you get away from fundamentals and you become aggressive with one another. Then you become insecure and begin to worry whether you can win. Then you lose your leadership. Then you become undisciplined. Then resentment sets in, and you lose your enthusiasm. That spells failure.

I'll never forget the first speech I made to the Chamber of Commerce. I said, "We can win at Minnesota, and we can win with in-state athletes. The heart and soul of our team must come from the state of Minnesota. . . . You do understand that the arms and legs have to come from somewhere else."

Minnesota's program came a good eighteen months later with five seniors and twenty-eight red-shirted freshmen, and we had that football team in a bowl game. We had changed the attitude. We were saying, "Hey, we can win!"

De Benedetti's ability to coach the Olivetti team out of the doldrums mirrors Holtz's approach. De Benedetti says, "The first thing I did was to select twenty people who were willing to try to help turn the company around, who were prepared to dedicate themselves, and who wanted to switch from losing to winning. I didn't bring anybody in from outside. All the work has been done with people who were already at Olivetti."

Identifying the core group of twenty was the first step. Enabling them to work effectively within an unmotivated organization was the next, tougher step. De Benedetti removed the first line of management and promoted down-line managers. He explains: "The company had been a loser for ten years. That attitude is hard to change. It was too big an effort to try to change people who were already skeptical about what was feasible. They were also, in a certain sense, trying to defend what they did. I needed people who were not afraid and not used to losing."

In *Self-Renewal*, John Gardner notes that continuous renewal requires a confident, realistic stance toward the future. Blind optimism isn't the answer. "High hopes that are dashed by the first failure are precisely what we don't need," he cautions. Hopelessness does not make for renewal. "Individuals cannot achieve renewal if they do not believe in the possibility of it. Nor can a society," he observes. "We need to believe in ourselves," Gardner encourages us, "but not to believe that life is easy."

The renewing companies have confidence, even in the face of relentless competition. But it isn't a Pollyanna optimism rooted in myopia, naïveté or a refusal to face the facts. Rather, it springs from the Lou Holtz kind of understanding that the world is tough, but pessimism and cynicism make it impossible. The tough and the optimistic keep reminding us: Don't rest on your laurels if things look good; don't give up hope if things look bleak. A senior executive at Digital Equipment Corporation captured it nicely when he said: "We were never as good as the analysts thought when times were good and never as bad as they thought when times were bad."

Times *were* bad for Digital in the early 1980s, and times seem remarkably good for the company today. Pier-Carlo Falotti, who heads the company's European operations, attributes much of their renewal to a change in attitude: specifically to moving away from what Gardner would probably characterize as soft-minded optimism. In the euphoria of Digital's halcyon days, when the annual growth rate routinely exceeded 30 percent, he says: "We forgot. We forgot that we used to make fast decisions. We forgot to watch what was going on outside. We forgot about the interdependence it takes to service a customer or build product." According to Falotti, Digital took refuge in an old company attitude: "Do the right thing." That was fine when the company was smaller, but it became increasingly unworkable as the company grew. Digital had gotten too complex, too big, and too rich.

An attitude of justified pride had lapsed into arrogance and, apparently, unjustified optimism about the status quo. The Digital example is a fascinating case of the difficulty of double-loop learning and the importance of bureaucracy-busting. Since they were growing so fast, they assumed they were changing. But their own growth masked the changes in the fundamentals of the market. For a while, they missed that.

One aspect of the renewal program that put Digital so nicely back on course was aimed squarely at attitudes. Challenge the past; be realistic about the future. Like Ford, Digital reexamined everything, including their shared values. "Companies with strong shared values seem universally to be outstanding performers as long as their values are relevant to the environmental conditions," Falotti says. The old "Do the right thing" was too often interpreted as "Do your own thing." Digital had to reinterpret that and put boundaries around the way they did business. They found themselves very strong in technical markets but virtually ignoring others, so they examined their attitudes about the business they were in. Too many were thinking "computers" and too few thought "information systems." Another big problem was salesmen's attitudes—convincing them, according to Digital executives, that "their first priority was customer satisfaction, not selling computers."

Other dysfunctional attitudes stemming from the good old days were ferreted out, challenged, and changed. According to Falotti, "We had to become aggressive again—not to defend our territories, but to go after the competition." As people grew with the company, they carried all the old responsibilities with them instead of delegating. Entrepreneurial spirit was killed as a result. "We had lost the old sense of excitement that was pervasive in the company and felt we had to bring that back." The focus on quality service had faded among the whole staff. "Our attitude on superior service had to be there in everyone, from the people who answered the phone to the people who sent the bills; we had to make it very clear that customer satisfaction was the number one priority."

Of course, the turnaround at Digital was much more complicated than challenging and changing attitudes. But without examining the soft-minded attitudes that were a byproduct of the good times, questioning those, and showing the will to change, my belief is that Digital would not have bounced back the way it did.

An attitude that some call FUD—fear, uncertainty, and doubt— is the nemesis of the toughminded optimism that sustains renewal. The FUD factor is a particularly insidious barrier to change because it is a byproduct of the change process itself. Morgan's Jack Ruffle observes that people in changing situations experience "fear about themselves and fear about what's happening to the institution." Talking about the recent organization change that he led, Ruffle says, "It was a situation where one had to look fear in the eye and try to arrest it. If we could win the confidence of the people by involving those people, we had a much greater chance of doing it right." About his company he observes: "We have a fantastic benefit here at Morgan in that there is a fair amount of security; we're not out to dump a lot of people." At Morgan, the organizational attitude fights FUD and embraces change.

IBM is having a rough time now (though many would trade IBM's problems for their own). However, the underlying strength of the company is the combination of realism and optimism that CEO John Akers epitomizes when he talks about the future: "Do we have faith in the future of the industry? Yes. In technological advance? Yes. Keep asking these questions, and if the answer keeps coming back 'Yes,' then it's a question of execution. The computer industry looks a little dull right now. . . . Those things [like the current slowdown] aren't fundamental to a business like IBM."

IBM's no-layoff, full-employment policy, like the company itself, is toughminded optimism in action. It is based on respect for the individual, a tenet deeply embedded in the company's culture and central to all management decision-making. This means that when work-force adjustments are necessary, due to factors such as automation or a slowdown in the market, no employee with satisfactory performance involuntarily loses employment. It's a gutsy posture. Many would urge IBM to abandon that policy in tough times to sustain earnings performance. The issue is one of costs. It costs money to retrain and rebalance the work force when times are tough, just as it costs money for companies to clean up their waste—to stop polluting. But one way or another, society pays the cost—just as it does for pollution—if IBM starts laying off when trouble hits. IBM takes a longer, broader view of things instead of buckling under pressure to prove its "worth" by keeping quarterly earnings up.

In his book *The American Vision*, Michael Novak, a theologian and resident scholar at the American Enterprise Institute, writes that the great strength of democratic capitalism is pragmatism: "Our culture encourages a pervasive recognition of the limits of theory and of the intractability of the real world. . . . Our businessmen prize doing rather than theorizing." Novak argues that our bent for pragmatism is also our great weakness. Man will continue to seek meaning, needs something to believe in, and no matter how efficient the system, will lose tolerance for it if it "merely" creates wealth and is callous to the other needs of human beings. Writes Novak:

C*oncentration upon the empirical and the pragmatic makes the practitioners of democratic capitalism effective and powerful; it does not make them noble, virtuous, or happy. In an ironic way, the very successes of democratic capitalism lay it open to the charge of spiritual poverty. The habit of evading questions of "meaning" in order to concentrate upon what may be done in the world of fact renders the human person disappointed, in the end, with his or her own performance. The hunger for "meaning" is spoken of with longing by many successful persons today.*

A wonderful response to Novak's concerns is IBM's Lexington, Kentucky, plant, which manufactures typewriters, keyboards, and printers. Over the years, IBM's Selectric typewriter had become more and more complicated internally. Labor costs for building the machine and fine-tuning it by hand became uncompetitive. Starting in the early 1980s, when competitors began producing a less expensive typewriter that rivaled IBM's, the company knew its product had met its match. The best long-range solution was to completely redesign both the typewriter and the way it was manufactured.

The Lexington facility underwent a metamorphosis. So did its staff. Site general manager Ted Lassetter recalls: "The key philosophy from the beginning was to design for automation. We automated the factory and changed our way of thinking about manufacturing." The new typewriter was designed to be produced robotically; the new design reduced the number of parts from 2,500 to 1,000. Now it's simpler and more reliable; it goes together more easily and requires a minimum of adjustments. But, in an example of double-loop thinking, IBM's intent was to automate a factory with machines that could be programmed to make anything from typewriters to toasters. They are now set up to make "keyboards"—not just typewriters. The factory has since expanded and picked up the manufacture of printers and keyboards for IBM's personal computers as well as typewriters.

These changes were necessary to increase quality and lower costs, but they also displaced hundreds of assembly-line workers in Lexington. In characteristic IBM style, the prospect of redeploying large numbers of people was met head-on. Lassetter explains: "In 1981 and 1982 we began to communicate to people about the automation that was coming up. We started out early [five years in advance, to be exact], being open with the staff through all-employee meetings, department meetings, and videotapes. We told them about the competition and what we were doing, why, and when. We had rooms with competitive products and videotapes on the competition. We were candid about the risks that were out there, and the staff responded to the challenge."

From the beginning, management's messages and actions were straightforward and honest—the embodiment of optimism with no illusions. Managers told everyone that it was necessary to modify the skill base in Lexington. Some people would probably be relocated to other offices; many would have different career paths. In the end, hundreds of people were retrained instead of being laid off. Assembly workers were retrained. Some became programmers, others secretaries, others equipment supervisors, and others "owner-operators" of a work station in the newly automated factory. Some people took an eighteen-month course in technical maintenance. Many of the skilled staff who were no longer needed were transferred elsewhere in IBM. Despite massive personnel shifts affecting virtually everyone in Lexington, morale improved during the change.

People's feelings for the company run deep. We spent an afternoon in Lexington talking with some of the people who had been retrained. Based on advice she got from her manager and others in Lexington, Mary Briggs decided to be retrained as a programmer. "They talked to me about where the company was going and gave me a lot of guidance on what skills were going to be marketable—what they were going to be looking for in the future. I didn't just let things happen or wait for somebody else to make them happen. I attribute that to the willingness of the managers to work with me."

Barry Crump started out on the line in Lexington. He was so determined to go to work for IBM, he presented himself at the personnel office four times a week for two months straight until he was hired. Then, on the assembly line, he says he got to thinking: "Well, typewriters are okay, but they don't give any feedback. I'm a people-oriented person." So he chose to be retrained as a secretary, "to have more contact with people." Barry's gratitude to IBM was clear when we talked to him: "IBM gave me so much that I didn't have before. They taught me how to deal with people, be professional—not artificial—how to do the best I can in life. It's hard to uproot, but if IBM said, 'You've got to go; your check's in Austin,' Barry Crump would be gone."

IBM is tough. It had to automate and displace hundreds of people. IBM is optimistic. The company believes that investment in Lexington, and continuing investment in its people, will have healthy long-run returns. IBM sets a standard for all of us to watch in trying to balance the conflicting pressures of return for the shareholders, world competitiveness, and belief in its people. In doing so, IBM may well show that there is no conflict in the long run between pragmatism and high ideals.

Paying Attention

In an important way, the business of change is a Hawthorne effect—the term that comes from experiments conducted by Harvard's Elton Mayo, Fritz Rothlisberger, and William Dickson in Western Electric's Hawthorne plants during the 1930s. The goal was to measure the impact of work conditions on productivity.' The experimenters would change something in the environment and observe the effect. For example, they'd improve the lighting. Productivity would go up. Then they'd turn the lights down, anticipating a drop in productivity. But productivity would go . . . up.

Confusing things like this kept happening throughout the course of the decade-long experiments. What they were investigating is complicated, and the interpretation of their results is still controversial. But the prevalent interpretation—and the one that appeals to me—is that work conditions were not the prime thing in productivity. It was attention. In the Hawthorne plants we have a work force that, like most, received virtually no attention before the study. Suddenly a group of Harvard researchers appeared and started paying close attention to what the workers were doing, with management looking over the researchers' shoulders. The workers were getting attention. No wonder productivity kept going up. As Stanford's Jeffrey Pfeffer, a leading contributor to the theory of organizations, observes: "The placebo effect occurs in organizational contexts as well as in medicine." To some extent, and at least initially, the content of the attention is less relevant than the fact that someone is paying attention.

The history of Ore-Ida's attempts to get good at product and process improvement makes a lively story of the importance of attention. In 1981 their strategy called for more R&D productivity. New-product development had almost come to a halt during the past several years. There had not been a major cost reduction idea carried out in the factories for more than a year, even though over 80 percent of the projects on the research slate were for process improvement and cost reduction. Ore-Ida needed line extensions, new products, and continued cost reduction to defend their high market share, and high margins, against private-label competition. They figured product variety and process automation were the best ways to accomplish their goals. The source for that should be their own R&D labs.

The trouble was that their strategy in 1980 had called for roughly the same thing as it had in 1979. Despite the high priority that CEO Paul Corddry was giving the issue, there was little progress to show for it. Paul asked McKinsey to bring an outsider's perspective to the problem and make some recommendations.

We talked to just about everybody who could shed any light, analyzed case histories of past R&D projects (looking for habit patterns that would explain recurring failure), reviewed the structure and the strategy. About halfway through the project, a progress review was held with Corddry and his top managers. There was a presentation, a two-page, single-spaced memo that started with the phrase "Assuming Ore-Ida is serious about an active product line extension strategy . . ." The phrase provoked the intended immediate reaction from the top brass. "Of course we're serious," they objected. "Otherwise it wouldn't be in the strategy."

Maybe top management was completely serious, but the Ore-Ida research people didn't see it that way. Sure, they knew it was in the strategy, but they rarely if ever saw Paul Corddry or other members of the top management team. They took the top brass's inattention to mean lack of interest. The point of how much attention they got from Corddry and colleagues became the issue. The brass felt they were lavishing more attention on R&D than the research folks were giving them credit for. Shortly after the progress review, the calendars of top management were analyzed to see how much time executives had actually spent at the central research facility in Ontario, Oregon, about an hour's drive from headquarters in Boise. The cold fact was: near zero. Confronted with that, management sheepishly admitted that at heart they were marketing guys, not too comfortable around the research folks, who, for their taste, talked funny and dressed a little weird.

Top management did not intend to give the impression that they were not interested in research. In their own minds they were vitally interested. But they did not feel comfortable with the folks in Ontario; there was very little personal interaction between Corddry and the people a few levels down, in dramatic contrast to the constant interaction on the marketing side of the business. Without intending to, management came across as "not really serious about research."

The people at Ore-Ida were, and are, good managers. It had simply never occurred to them that they came across as disingenuous on their research priority. Once Corddry was convinced that his own lack of visible attention was the problem, he moved fast to correct the situation. He initiated the Fellows Program. He led a series of meetings in the Ontario facility, sharing his thinking, answering questions, and going over the consulting team's complete report. The reaction of the research people was mixed: delight and cynicism. "We love what's happening now," they said in effect, "but Paul will never sustain his interest. This is not his field. Besides, he's too busy. Right?"

Wrong. Corddry and his top team committed themselves with a vengeance. Their main tool for doing so was to set up a product review committee—the PRC. Together with the R&D people, the PRC agenda was carefully developed. The group would meet for two days each quarter. The typical meeting would last two days. The first day and a half would be devoted to a detailed review of the ten or so top-priority projects: Where did they expect each project to be? How much did they plan to spend? Where did they actually stand? How much had been spent? Should any of the projects already on the schedule be dropped?

The last half-day would be devoted to idea encouragement: a review of all the ideas in the pipeline for future product development and consideration of the top-priority ideas for future development. Should any of the hot ideas replace the portfolio of projects on the main slate?

But the most important agenda item of all was that Corddry was committed to spending—and from that point forward, did spend—the full two days per quarter on the PRC. Within six months after the start of the PRC meetings, new products at Ore-Ida were starting to see daylight. Within a year some line extensions were winning broad acceptance in the marketplace. These days Ore-Ida has a product-development skill that begins to match its consumer-marketing skill.

A paraphrase of Ralph Waldo Emerson circulates around HP: "What you do is so loud, I can't hear what you say." If ever there was a perfect example of that, it was Ore-Ida's predicament before the innovation. The R&D people couldn't hear what management was saying because actions didn't match words.

The reason that attention—"what you do"—is so loud is that

it's a visible commitment of your scarcest resource: your time. There is not much that a company can't get more of with a little effort. For the reasonably healthy corporation, money is available. Capital equipment is available. Manpower is available. The one thing in truly short supply is management time and attention, especially top management time and attention.

What Gets Measured Gets Done

A behaviorist from the University of California's Institute of Industrial Relations, Mason Haire, once said, "What gets measured gets done." If you're looking for quick ways to change how an organization behaves, he suggested, change the measurement system, or change even one measure. Conversely, if you can't figure out why things aren't changing, look to the measurement system. Measures are an important part of both the explicit and implicit systems for paying attention.

Humana's hospital-performance standards and their accompanying measurement system dramatize Haire's point. Humana's founders, David Jones and Wendell Cherry, met with Peter Drucker and took away from the encounter Drucker's insistence that they couldn't really manage their hospitals unless they had a way of measuring things.

As a result, they set about to determine what processes could be measured and how. Work groups from each hospital department, led by either Jones or Cherry, spotted the activities with the highest impact on departmental performance. Which ones contributed most to patient care? Which ones were the most prone to mistakes? Which were the most costly?

To illustrate, X-rays regularly get botched and have to be redone. The problem is common at most hospitals. That's expensive for the hospital. For the patient, it's distressing. Everyone knows the danger of too much radiation. Besides, what does an all-too-obvious snafu in taking X-rays—an apparently simple procedure—say about the care you are receiving from the system in general? A Humana "radiology work group" established X-ray performance standards, now routinely measured in every hospital. If an X-ray technician falls below standard, the supervisor intervenes to determine the reason. Perhaps more training is in order. Maybe something is wrong with the equipment. Whatever the cause, the problem is solved before it gets worse.

Another early finding of the work groups was that typical emergency room procedures drive everyone nuts. Even serious cases are often not attended to promptly by a professional. Patients get mired in the glacial paperwork of the admitting procedure, usually before they have a chance to see a nurse or a doctor. The result of Humana's study of their own emergency room procedures: Anyone coming to the emergency room is seen by a medically trained professional within sixty seconds of arrival. If the pro determines that the patient needs immediate attention, that's what is provided.

Humana now has a happy combination of higher-quality care, better patient perception of that care, lower costs (the system is more efficient because of the measures), and higher morale among the hospital professionals. The last point is an interesting sidelight. With the identification of common mistakes, and the installation of system measures, the professionals are spending more time doing what they were trained to do—delivering quality care. They spend less time correcting mistakes or trying to support defective administrative processes. What's more, recognizing that the hospital is delivering better care, they are proud to be associated with it.

Measures work. The thing to watch out for is that they do what they're designed to do. A California banker said his bank was having difficulty retaining the accounts of people who move (a pervasive problem—Californians are peripatetic). Management would like to hang on to its existing customer base by simplifying the transfer of accounts from one branch to another. But the branch staff take no interest in making it happen. The reason is that the branches are measured exclusively as individual profit centers. It makes no difference to a particular branch whether an account they lost stays within the bank. In fact, it costs them money.

Total Quality

One of the better examples of Hawthorne effects and measures in action is demonstrated at Hewlett-Packard. HP's approach is simple. The HP program sails under the "TQC" flag. These initials stand for total quality control. Since its inception in the late 1970s, TQC has moved from idea to program to cause to way of life at HP. This is a story of shifting attention and measurement.

If one could pinpoint a starting point for total quality, it would probably be in 1973, when HP's Japanese joint venture YHP (Yokogawa-Hewlett-Packard) was the recipient of an automatic, wave-soldering machine that one of the U.S. divisions considered obsolete. Started in 1963, YHP served mainly as a window on Japan for Hewlett-Packard. According to HP's Craig Walter, who oversees the TQC program, "YHP was never very profitable—always near the bottom when compared with all our other operations." In 1977, YHP changed. Within two years, they had reduced manufacturing costs by 40 percent. By 1982 the failure rate of products had been reduced by two thirds; YHP's productivity (as measured by revenue per employee) was up 100 percent. Market share had tripled in Japan and had grown by 60 percent outside Japan. R&D cycle time was cut by a factor of three. Profitability had trebled. Since 1982, YHP has been one of HP's top-performing operations; their proprietary products were among the most profitable in the Hewlett-Packard company. The main thing they did was start *paying attention* to quality.

In 1976, YHP's president, Ken Saito, saw the "total approach that other Japanese companies were taking to quality." In early 1977 he made total quality a strategic priority for YHP. To get it started he decided to focus his attention on an area where the opportunity would be large and the potential impact relatively easy. He did this to set the example, the tone, the symbol for the whole approach. As Saito was later to explain: "We call it our 'shining star,' our 'sparkler.' "

YHP picked a manufacturing process—printed circuit assembly using the hand-me-down wave-soldering equipment. The equipment had been in use since YHP received it in 1973. But in the period before 1977—before total attention to quality—the defect rate on this machine was running at four failures per thousand. By the end of 1979, failures were down to forty per million, and recently defects were at the near-zero rate of three per million. HP's Craig Walter explains:

Of real interest is the history of this particular machine. It's not a new one. It was considered obsolete in 1973 by one of our domestic divisions. Yet its present performance is still ten to one hundred times better than any other in the company. They had lived with the inferior performance for five years. It wasn't until they made a commitment to improving the process that the spectacular improvement took place.

Using wave-soldering as the flagship, YHP went on to improve quality in other manufacturing processes, in research and in all other business activities including service (e.g., the downtime of products undergoing repair) and customer satisfaction.

As an HP-wide priority, the program got its real impetus when Chief Executive John Young decided that, based on what he had seen at YHP and in manufacturing operations elsewhere, higher reliability *and* lower cost would be a major priority for the whole organization. His way of getting it going was mainly symbolic.

In 1979, Young told his general managers that over the next decade they ought to be able to improve product reliability by at least an order of magnitude—in other words, tenfold—and reduce costs in doing so. Many of them, who already saw their company as the industry quality leader, thought Young was nuts. Order-of-magnitude changes are big stuff. An order of magnitude in speed is the difference between walking and cycling, between running fast and riding in an auto on the freeway, between the auto and the jet aircraft.

Talking about the early years of TQC, Young says, "It was as if I were the only guy who showed up for the parade, and I don't mind telling you, I felt a little foolish. It was like being out in a vacant street, waving my arms, yelling, waving a flag. There were a few curious onlookers at first. Then people started following, and pretty soon we had a mob of people headed in the right direction."

Among the early marchers in Young's parade was one of HP's Colorado divisions and the Avondale division. Both adopted the quality program as a symbol for the division manager's belief that they could simultaneously achieve lower manufacturing costs, higher productivity, lower inventory, and better product quality and reliability. They started with products still in development as a way of challenging everything: the way they design products, the way they manufacture, and the way they sell and service. The attention shift was crucial: from "manage by exception" (fix it after it goes wrong) to "do it right from the outset."

The programs were numbingly successful. In the Colorado division, defect rates went from a few parts per hundred to a few parts per million. Manufacturing cycle time was improved by a factor of ten; inventory was reduced by half. Product made by the Avondale division was redesigned, and the number of assembly parts was cut by a factor of three and a half (compared to previous generations of similar equipment). Assembly errors were reduced by a factor of fifteen, cycle time by a factor of seven, and inventory cut by 40 percent. These results would be striking in any setting; at HP, they are astonishing.

TQC, as it now operates within HP, "starts with a management and operating philosophy that is absolutely and totally committed to quality," says Craig Walter. Jim Fischer, who is now charged with renewing HP's competitiveness in printed circuit boards, explains the difference between the quality philosophy today versus that of several years ago. "Imagine that you have a manufacturing line that is supposed to produce cats," says Jim. "Every now and then, for no apparent reason, the line spits out a dog instead of a cat. In the old days we used to say, 'Yup, it'll do that.' These days we say, 'The damn thing is not supposed to be producing a dog; let's find out why.'"

HP's TQC program treats every part of the business as a process that can be improved. Although the program started with manufacturing, the folks at HP found that the same ideas could be applied to anything—literally anything—they do. The program is just as applicable to the way they market, or to the way they account, as to the way they manufacture.

They break the business down—at least conceptually—into sets of processes. People are encouraged to diagram in great detail the way the process works, starting with the customer and working backward. "Every process in the business has one or several customers," explains Senior Vice-President Bill Terry, "even if the processes and customers are external. To illustrate, the main output of a staff group might be a report or set of reports, but those reports go somewhere. And the people on the receiving end are thought of as customers, even though they may be internal customers."

The next step is very straightforward. HP goes to the customers and finds out what they like and don't like about the product they are receiving. "Simply by diagramming the process and talking to customers about it, you often discover that fifty percent of it is not working the way it should be," says John Young.

Then they put measures against various parts of the process. Say, for example, that last year, of every million boards produced, customers were returning 6,000. The goal might be to reduce that to 1,000 for this year, to 300 by next year, and to 50 by the following year. Measuring product quality is the obvious part of the process. Less obvious but just as important is putting measures on all aspects of the business system—everything from late customer deliveries to internal communication (measured, at least at first, by the number of informal meetings). When HP says "total quality," it means *total*.

Others have tried programs similar to HP's TQC, sometimes with disastrous results. As put forward by some, the method can be Draconian. Its vicious potential is in the way people are treated. A process like this, whether called "total quality" or something else, suggests cost reduction. At HP this is no big deal, because of the way they treat people and their security of employment policy. Other organizations using the same approach can be seen to be—often are—asking people for ideas on how to cut their own jobs.

Another potential trouble area is timing. Projects like this are often on a very short time-fuse. Management expects too much too soon. At HP "all" that's being asked is tenfold improvement.

But it's up to the people way down the line, and their own sense of urgency and doability, to specify the time frame. This is like the solution-space idea presented earlier in the chapter on empowerment.

A final place to look for trouble is in the inherent nobility—or ignobility—of the cause. If the focus is only on cost reduction, the atmosphere that surrounds it is usually dour. If the focus is on quality, service, or revenue enhancement, the process has an inherently positive spirit. Individuals can identify with it and get excited about it.

The Pygmalion Effect

The Hawthorne studies brought to the forefront the idea that a manager's attention, no matter what it is about, can increase productivity. Sounds easy. Focus on an ailing department for a while, and the staff will shape up. But more recent research shows that it's not that simple. Long-term improvement comes only if the attention employees receive communicates their manager's genuine belief that they can do what is expected of them. Believable, positive expectations yield positive results. Unbelievable or negative expectations beget the opposite. This phenomenon is called the Pygmalion effect.

The original Pygmalion was the king of Cyprus, who also happened to have a penchant for sculpting. He fell in love with a statue of a woman he'd created of ivory, because it represented his own desires and expectations. His repeated overtures to the gods finally persuaded Venus to give life to the statue. (So it goes with mythology.)

George Bernard Shaw sculpted his own version of the same tale in his familiar stage play *Pygmalion,* involving Henry Higgins's transformation of a Cockney flower girl into a woman who successfully convinces others she's an aristocrat. More than a half century after Eliza Doolittle learned the King's English, *Pygmalion in the Classroom*, by Robert Rosenthal and Lenore Jacobson, burst upon the education scene. It argues the startling research conclusion that student achievement mirrors teacher expectations more than it does actual student ability.

Despite its many incarnations, the story of Pygmalion rests on an unwavering premise: People behave in a way that reflects our own expectations of them. Expectations can exercise a significant positive or negative role on both academic and job performance. When others believe our images of how things should be, they become self-fulfilling prophecies—a term coined by Robert Merton in 1948 to refer to the tendency of people to perform in accordance with what is expected of them, as well as their own expectations of success or failure.*

Carlo De Benedetti's belief in people, and his ability to translate that value into words and deeds, helped set Olivetti on its new course. His philosophy was both optimistic and straightforward. Its result? The self-fulfilling prophecy in action: "I don't believe in being condemned to be a loser or in being blessed as a winner. You have to gain your day every morning. As long as you are convinced that you are not stupid, as long as you are committed, as long as you are convinced that you can do it, it is feasible."

Robert Rosenthal studied the notion of the power of expectation—the self-fulfilling prophecy—with research that began rather unpretentiously with laboratory rats. Half of the college students participating in an experiment were told that they had been given "maze-bright" laboratory rats, a more intelligent strain that had been developed through inbreeding. Actually, these rats were no different from the ones given to the other half of the students, who were told they had stupid rats. Sounds crazy. A shot in the dark. But the results were astounding. The "maze-bright" rats outperformed the others!

---

* Note the importance of a significant outside influence in the change process. This is not at all uncommon. In talking to the very successful Melville Company, a specialty retailer who got its start with the famous (to those old enough to remember the radio commercials) Buster Brown line of shoes, we find that Peter Drucker also had a very powerful influence there. In the case of Melville, Drucker kept pushing them on the question "What business are you in?" Though it's a seemingly trivial question, it is always hard to answer. In Melville's case, would they answer "Shoes"? "Making money?" "Retailing?" These responses—and many others—are possible. Melville's answer was "specialty retailing." They went on to define as precisely as they could what they meant by *specialty retailing*. Melville keeps asking themselves this question. They assert that the answer and its details, which change with the times, are a powerful reason for their success.

Rosenthal and colleague Lenore Jacobson reasoned: "If rats act smarter because their experimenters think they are smarter, perhaps the same phenomenon was at work in the classroom. So in the mid-1960s [we] launched what was to become a most controversial study." They gave all the elementary school students in a lower-class neighborhood a pseudo-test that was supposed to identify "intellectual bloomers." Then they randomly labeled 20 percent of the students as "intellectual bloomers." The teachers were led to believe that the "bloomers" had greater potential, even though there was no correlation between their actual ability and their being given the label. Eight months later, at the end of the school year, these students showed significantly higher IQ gains than their peers.

Why did this happen? Rosenthal reports that "teachers encourage greater responsiveness from students of whom they expect more. They call on such students more often, ask them harder questions, give them more time to answer, and prompt them toward the correct answer."

Since the publication of Rosenthal and Jacobson's *Pygmalion in the Classroom*, some three hundred studies have been conducted to determine whether or not similar results can be found in varying situations. (As you can well imagine, the original study became a source of controversy because of the inadvertent harm done to some of the students. Subsequent research eliminated the chances that this would happen to participants.) These studies involved a wide range of people and environments—everything from teaching children at summer camp how to swim, to increasing the work effectiveness of undermotivated Navy sailors.

If a manager believes that an employee is competent and that his or her work is worthwhile, the subordinate is likely both to be more effective and to see the job as more rewarding. That's because an employee's performance is greatly affected by his or her self-image. Self-concept sets the boundaries of individual accomplishment; we can do something only as well as we believe we can. Expanding employees' self-confidence increases what they can accomplish.

The Pygmalion effect was at work all over GE's Appliance Park. When Roger Schipke brought in Don Kelley from another GE facility to manage their refrigeration plant, Kelley found disillusioned line operators and defensive foremen. Whenever they attempted to communicate with one another, an explosion of previously pent-up anger occurred instead. Despite these entrenched problems, Kelley's strategy was to accentuate the positive. He harnessed the power of the Pygmalion effect by *expecting* people to be responsible for quality, then recognizing their efforts to do so.

Working with people who had not previously been respected by their bosses and who felt more hostility than loyalty toward GE, Kelley set up a system that shut down the line if quality fell below a certain standard. That seemed like an outrageous thing to do. After all, wouldn't the union guys sabotage the line? The sabotage never occurred. Why? Because Kelley trusted the employees and believed in their desire to produce a quality product. Expect sabotage and you get it. Expect quality and that's what you get.

Kelley says, "I recognized the need for a rallying point so that the hourly people and salaried people could have something in common. The hourly people were interested in building a quality product if given the chance. In truth, the greatest inhibition to doing that was coming from some of the managers and supervisors who were under the gun to get the product out the door."

Kelley had to do something radical to communicate to everyone his commitment to quality improvement. How did he go about it? "We went out and bought traffic lights, installing three lights out in the aisle of each assembly line. We do a quality check called 'end-of-line audit' where we take about two percent of the product (about three units a line) every hour, and then, based on a demerit system, we turn on the green light if everything is acceptable. If we find a 'class one defect' (where the defect would result in a service call seventy to one hundred percent of the time) the end-of-line auditor switches on the red light, which stops the line.

"At first everyone thought I was crazy. They figured that the system would last two weeks at the most. For about the first six months, once the red light went on, nobody could start the assembly line again except me. I did that because the culture change we needed was so drastic. I would adhere to that rule even if I was five buildings away in a meeting. After a few months, they were convinced that we were serious. After about six months, we backed that responsibility down to the quality-control manager. Now it's the responsibility of the process-control engineering manager. But now the line rarely stops.

"Our people are paid an incentive based on production. We made a decision that we were not going to penalize them from a pay standpoint when the line shut down. I recall having quite a go-around with a corporate auditor who wrote me up for costing the company something like a hundred and eighty thousand dollars. He felt that when the line was down we shouldn't continue to pay at the incentive rate. Our point was that we did not want to turn the quality around at the expense of the operators. We didn't want any negativity associated with improved quality. I was also told that people would make mistakes on purpose to stop the line, but that never happened, *even in the early days when there was a lot of animosity.*"

So, contrary to expectation, no one sabotaged the line. The reasons are many, but two stand out. First, Kelley's traffic lights were constant reminders that quality was a priority, all the time, every day. When quality dropped below acceptable levels, he acted decisively and in a way that did not penalize employees. But more important, from the beginning—even when no one else trusted the guys on the line—he did. He *anticipated responsible behavior* on their part, and they lived up to his respect.

Attention Through Symbolism

People are symbol manipulators. Words provide the set of symbols we manipulate most often. We do it so much and so well that most managers rely too heavily on language and not enough on the great wealth of other symbols available to them. We have talked about measurement and attention, two alternative ways managers can support change and renewal. Our research uncovered many other creative ways people have devised to tell the organization that "this time we're serious."

The most effective symbols are symbolic *and* functional. What symbol, for instance, could be more powerful and pervasive than the IBM White Shirt? It presents a quandary to IBM competitors. Do we wear a white shirt and appear imitative, or do we wear striped and colored shirts and appear to be somehow less professional? This distinctive IBM look stems from Tom Watson, Sr.'s conviction that being a salesman was a respectable, desirable calling, far from the reputation for double-dealing and phoniness that salesmen carried in the first half of the century. Business author Robert Sobel writes: "Older Americans may still recall jokes about traveling salesmen that portrayed them as boozing, wenching, unscrupulous individuals out to cheat customers; and the 'drummer' was always identifiable by his flashy clothes. Watson would have none of this. His salesmen would be impeccably and conservatively dressed and altogether respectable and sober."

Allen J. Krowe, a senior executive at IBM, told us the legend (which may be somewhat apocryphal) of how the White Shirt got started. "You've heard it a hundred times," he protested, but we assured him we hadn't. "Tom Watson, Jr. is visiting a bank president and they get on an elevator. Another guy gets on who is dressed like he's heading out to the racetrack—big loud tie, garish suit. Tom says to the bank president: 'I'm surprised one of your employees is allowed to dress like that.' And the bank president says, 'Tom, he works for you.' That's all that Tom Junior needed. He decided we were going to have a dress code.* He didn't *want* his people looking like they were heading out to the racetrack.

"I dress like this [classic IBM white shirt and dark suit] because it gives me an edge," Krowe continues. "I remember very early in my career with IBM, negotiating for our Federal Systems Division out on the West Coast. My opponent came in with his pink shades and his Nehru jacket. I felt I had an advantage over him. I had a couple of things going for me anyway—being better briefed, having done my homework. But now I had another advantage! People now ask if there is a dress code. No, there isn't a dress code. We dress this way because we think it is a good idea."

Then there are the different uses of the "head office" symbol. It was said of the late Sy Newhouse, founder of the Newhouse

---

*IBM never had a written dress code, as Krowe later points out, but Thomas Watson, Jr. did continuously urge all his people to dress conservatively, and once he did so in a memo. It had the power of a written code.

publishing empire, that he hated overhead so much that he had no office; he carried the corporation around in his briefcase. Harry Quadracci of Quad/Graphics has a president's office built in each of his four main facilities. This is no ego trip. He wants each facility to feel important enough to have an office for the top guy. As he travels from plant to plant, Quadracci carries a big canvas mail sack for correspondence and company papers. "This is a standing joke," he says, pointing to the mail sack. "We call this 'the corporation,' and I carry it around with me everywhere." Quadracci feels the symbolism of the bag helps maintain Quad's informality and his accessibility.

Decentralized companies with loose structures often have stories that involve someone literally smashing down a barrier or obstacle. They serve as metaphors for the bureaucracy-busting that is essential to the corporation's vitality. *In Search of Excellence* told of Bill Hewlett, co-founder of Hewlett-Packard, visiting a plant on Saturday and finding a lab stock area locked. This bothered Bill, who wanted HP scientists to have access to the labs at their own choosing, not the company's. So he immediately went down to maintenance, grabbed a bolt cutter, and cut the padlock off the lab stock door. He left a note that was found on Monday morning: "Don't ever lock this door again. Thanks, Bill."

An analogous tale comes from Super Valu in Eden Prairie, Minnesota. Larry Anderson, a regional vice-president, described something that happened at a bureaucratic supermarket chain where he used to work. Anderson was responsible for opening a new store in Miami, and time was getting tight. The day before the opening he greeted a fleet of delivery trucks, only to find that the loading-dock doors were padlocked. As the truckers and loaders stood around waiting, Anderson sought in vain for the company employee who could unlock the doors. Finally he found a sledgehammer, smashed off the padlock, and proceeded to stock the shelves. Sure enough, a few weeks later a reprimand arrived from corporate headquarters chastising Anderson for breaking company policy and invoicing him $52 for a new padlock. Not long after this incident Anderson joined Super Valu. He commented that the contrast in styles between the companies is still obvious to him.

There are a variety of symbols for keeping costs down. "We're squeezing each buck until the eagle grins," says Ken Iverson of Nucor. He's not much on frills. He runs $750 million Nucor with a skeleton staff, out of an austere corporate office in a nondescript building next to a Charlotte, North Carolina, shopping center. There's not even a sign out front with Nucor's name. Consistent with the nonexistent sign, the rest of Nucor's public image exudes Iverson's frugality and economy. The annual report, which Iverson writes himself, is only eighteen pages long and has no color photographs. A business magazine profile of Iverson marveled that when he briefed financial analysts in Manhattan, he took a subway to the meeting. (New Yorkers might argue that this is a sign not of frugality but of recklessness.) To partake of the fare in Nucor's "executive dining room," one must sprint across a highway and choose between a Chinese restaurant and a delicatessen that adjoins a shoe store. The power of this symbolism isn't lost on Nucor employees, especially those who have worked elsewhere in American steel. Nucor's mill manager in Darlington, South Carolina, who worked for two other steel companies before joining Nucor, recalls hearing how the senior executives at another steel company ate lunch on fine china in a chandeliered private dining room while mills were being closed and steelworkers thrown out of jobs.

Bankers Trust is one service firm that understands the power of symbols. When the firm decided to leave retail and become a merchant bank, they wanted their new organization to seem less like a traditional bank and more like a Salomon Brothers or Goldman Sachs. So they stopped using titles like senior vice-president and executive vice-president and started calling people "partners." Junior officers used to be loan officers; now they are called associates. Base salaries were frozen, with compensation tied to performance incentives. By paying attention to the messages embedded in titles and rewards, they communicated to everyone that there were some significant changes in "the way we do things around here."

When EG&G accepts a government contract to run a complex military/defense installation, the first thing they do is to make sure the cafeteria works and that the mail gets to people's desks on time. "That's what the average Joe sees," says Bernie

O'Keefe. "If you can do those things, they assume you can do the other stuff well." Taking care of the details early on says implicitly, "Things are running smoothly; we're in control."

Organizational anthropologist Joanne Martin has spent years documenting and analyzing organizational stories for the messages embedded in them. She has found that the stories people tell about the company, its leaders, or their peers perpetuate the culture of the place much more significantly than do official policies, systems, and structures. Procedures manuals might have rules, but stories have morals. The latter tend to influence thinking and action more than the former.

For instance, a security guard may wonder what to do if the CEO starts to enter a restricted area without safety goggles. The rule book dictates that the CEO should not be allowed in. But then, he's at the top of the heap; he might pull rank and reprimand the guard for not recognizing that he's above following the rules. The fallback position for the guard is to remember the stories people have told him about the CEO. If the scuttlebutt is that the CEO believes he is exempt from the rules, he may let him pass. If, on the other hand, the stories indicate that the CEO believes everyone should be treated equally, the guard will probably ask him to don the goggles.

It matters little whether the stories are true or fictitious. The fact is, stories—and that includes rumor mills—perpetuate the culture. Toughminded optimism, then, can be either strengthened or discredited by the stories people are telling. A CEO can give all the rah-rah speeches and hand out all the T-shirts he wants. But if the legends or the current desk-to-desk whispers are about actions he took that discredit his symbolic behavior, he may as well save his breath. What's the moral in all of this? There are three of them: Listen carefully to the stories that are circulating around your organization; remember that the false stories are just as influential as the true ones; and never underestimate the power of the grapevine.

A recurring theme in the stories people tell is: "We're a special bunch here." And nowhere is that more pervasive than at Steelcase. The company takes a great deal of pride in its fleet of fifty-nine blue-and-chrome eighteen-wheelers. The drivers are full-time Steelcase employees. A new driver isn't allowed to take his wheels on the road right away, regardless of prior experience. For the first six months he is on washing detail (the trucks must be washed down and scrubbed after every trip). Then he graduates to parking and backing up the trucks in the Steelcase lot. Finally he's allowed out on the road. One Steelcase driver, an aspiring songwriter, penned a country-and-western ode to his truck called "The Blue and Chrome."

Here's a story told often around Steelcase: Apparently, at a big employee picnic they ran out of hot dog buns and dispatched a driver in a Steelcase truck to pick up the 10,000 originally ordered. Everyone stood around, eyeing the grill, waiting for the driver to return with the goods. It seemed to take an eternity. Finally he showed up, apologizing for the delay. It seems he felt obliged to wash down the truck after driving it back from the bakery. Like many other corporate legends, it is hard to determine whether this tale is apocryphal, but the glee Steelcasers take in retelling it provides the story with its own dimension of credibility and usefulness.

Symbolism can have unintended results. When Ford Motor wanted to emphasize quality back in 1979, it put a bunch of Japanese cars in the plant to show employees what you could do if you really put your mind to quality. The result was that employees went out and bought Japanese cars. A few years later, though, when the Taurus project got under way, another symbolic idea worked out much better. To usher in a new era, one of the plants threw a Christmas party in which all the employees were served a sit-down dinner. Rather than getting their own food buffet-style, as in the past, everyone was waited on. The sharpness of this departure from previous parties greatly impressed the employees and sent a reverberating signal that things were truly different.

At Dow Jones, many of the symbols and stories concern the late Bernard (Barney) Kilgore, who shaped the company first as *The Wall Street Journal*'s managing editor and then as company chairman. He wanted business news delivered in a crisp, terse style without jargon. Veteran reporters tell rookie recruits the story about the time Kilgore became distressed at the overuse of the word *upcoming* in *Journal* stories. Finally, Kilgore dispatched a note to an offending reporter: "If I see 'upcoming' in the paper again, I'll be downcoming and someone will be outgoing."

This discussion of symbolic behavior wouldn't be complete without recognition of two of its major pitfalls. First and most important is assuring the sincerity of what you are communicating and how you are doing it. Because symbolism is such a potent source of influence, it can be used to manipulate people. We all know of the ways it has been put to unscrupulous use in the past. Rather, a reminder that symbolism should never compromise one's integrity is enough.

Second, symbolic behavior can be a substitute for doing what you're supposed to do. It can convincingly give the appearance that you are going along with written or unwritten rules and norms, while all along you are undercutting them. Dick Huber of Citicorp, who spent many years in Brazil, has a neat Portuguese phrase that describes this phenomenon: *paro Inglese ver*. Literally, it means "for the Englishmen to see." In practice, it manifests as the make-work boondoggles, procrastinations, and rearguard actions that look like cooperative activity, even though those involved have absolutely no intention of doing what's wanted.

Lamar Alexander, the former governor of Tennessee, dealt with *paro Inglese ver* by devising a bit of symbolism called "Who's on the flagpole?" He recalls his early Cabinet meetings: "I would say, 'Why don't we do X?' Everyone would agree, 'Let's all do X.' A month later, X wasn't done. I learned the hard way that everybody does nothing." So when the governor wanted something done, he'd select an individual and say, "Jim, you're on the flagpole." There would be laughter and everyone else had to pitch in to help, of course, but it was up to the flagpole person to make things happen. "Otherwise," says Alexander, "he would have been flapping at the top of the tallest flagpole on Capitol Hill."

Steps for Getting There

1. Start with the attitudes of the people who report to you. Do they feel as if they're part of a winning team? If not,

figure out why. They may feel insecure about their ability to do what's expected of them, or the team may have an embarrassing track record looming in the not-so-distant past. Their shaky self-concepts may mirror the way you have been treating them. (That's a tough one to look at.) Remember the FUD—fear, uncertainty, doubt—factor and actively counteract it.

2. Find something you can win at. One of the nice things about business is that it is complex; there are many ways to approach being "the best." Your company is engaged in multiple games of business all the time. If you can't win the game you're playing, change the game. Pick one product and set out to be the best in quality or service. Select a market niche that you can serve better than anyone else in your neck of the woods; then make it happen.

3. Take a chapter from the Lou Holtz, Carlo De Benedetti, or Bill McCormick handbook on being a winner. Hang your aspirations on the wall. Create high standards for achievement, and let people know you believe they can live up to them. Give your people a little courage to test their limits.

   Think Pygmalion. People succeed if someone they respect thinks they can. Expect people to be trustworthy and competent, and they will be. A recent group explored the subject of "the leader as coach." One of the exercises was to list people who had been powerful influences in their lives, then identify what made them effective as coaches or mentors. When the group compared notes, they found these coaches had consistently believed in them and had high expectations. A frequent comment was: "He (or she) knew I had it in me before I knew I had it in me." How good a mentor are you? How do you let your staff know that they're better than they may think they are?

4. Check your own attitudes about yourself and the people you work with. How do they stack up against Gardner's benchmark of toughminded optimism? Are you both confident and realistic? You probably cannot lead an

organization toward continual learning and renewal without the ability to see future possibilities. At the same time, getting there is never easy; temporary setbacks are not unusual, even when you're making long-term progress. Don't let them take the wind out of your sails.

Check to see if you are confident in your own ability to be the best at your job. If you are, how does this attitude come across to your troops? If you aren't confident, why not? It may be a function of the game you're playing; get into one you can win if you aren't there now. If you're being unjustifiably "down" on yourself, do everything you can to get out of the tailspin. Remember that attitude and mood are contagious both with yourself and others. One caution: You can carry even confidence too far. The higher up the corporate ladder you go, the more people expect quiet confidence.

5. Consider this: Failure is not an absolute; it's a mind-set. Something doesn't have to be considered a "failure" unless you label it that way. Warren Bennis and Burt Nanus, who interviewed more than one hundred successful leaders in preparation for their book on leadership, observe: "Perhaps the most impressive and memorable quality of the leaders we studied was the way they responded to failure. . . . They simply don't think about failure, don't even use the word, relying on such synonyms as 'mistake,' 'glitch,' 'bungle,' or countless others." These people do have their failures just like everyone else, but they don't allow themselves to see them as such. Instead of taking the negative, limiting view embedded in the word *failure*, they just think of them as mistakes they can learn from.

6. Your program for making a top priority happen ought to include ways you can show that it *is* your priority. One of the best approaches is to spend a lot of your time on it. Everybody knows that time is your scarce resource. If they see you investing time in a priority, they will too.

Do a "content analysis" on your calendar for the last year to determine how much time you spent on various activities. Match time spent against your priorities during that same twelve months. Were there priorities you neglected? Or, do it a different way. What is not getting done that you think is important? How much visible time and attention are you giving that priority? Time spent sitting in the office thinking about it doesn't count; you must be visibly paying attention to the matters that matter to you.

Do another kind of content analysis. Look through your old speeches, memos, letters, and other verbal material to find out how much you said about your top-priority issues. If putting out brush fires consistently took precedence over supporting "priorities," maybe they weren't really priorities for you. Or maybe you allowed yourself to get sidetracked too easily. People assume (and rightfully so) that whatever you are talking or writing about is the priority for the moment.

7. Remind yourself that another way of paying attention to something is to measure it. Involve your staff in setting realistic performance standards; then measure them regularly. Measurement systems that are done right help people do a better job. But measures that are either unrealistic or are used to manipulate people get in the way of job performance by destroying morale and trust.

8. There is *always* room for improvement, even if your company is solidly successful. Increasing quality organization-wide requires people to pay attention to quality and to measure it in all areas of the business. If you're considering a broad-based effort like Hewlett-Packard's total quality program, remember that it requires the unflagging and unified attention of your entire top management group. Further, recall that John Young "felt a little foolish" at first; no one took him seriously when he announced the program. But he kept paying attention to it—talking about it—and eventually it caught on.

9. Listen for the stories that are now finding their way around your organization. What underlying messages are they communicating? Don't get hung up on whether or not they are based on reality; perceptions *are* reality and as such influence employee attitudes more than official

reports and organization-wide memos. If the grapevine persists in perpetuating caustic rumors, nip them in the bud. Over the long haul they can erode your company's shared values. Remember that, on a broader scale, organizational stories help perpetuate your corporate culture.

10. Use symbols to strengthen what you communicate verbally about your priorities. There's nothing like a well-placed slogan or an unexpected bit of adventure to kick off a new priority. It's amazing how much T-shirts and coffee mugs can do to help focus attention that "something's changed around here." But hollow symbolic gestures usually get the superficial results they deserve. Symbols are not a substitute for commitment and hard work, and they should never be used to compromise integrity.

N I N E

Causes and Commitment

*To venture causes anxiety, but not to venture is to
lose one's self. . . . And to venture in the
highest sense is precisely to become
conscious of one's self.*

—SØREN KIERKEGAARD

*When great causes are on the move in the world
. . . we learn that we are spirits, not
animals.*

—WINSTON CHURCHILL

Man seeks meaning in organizations. Theorists Michael Cohen
and James March argue that an organization is "a collection of
choices looking for problems . . . solutions looking for issues . . .
and decision makers looking for work." Sound familiar? Karl
Weick suggests that people in organizations make meanings by
engaging in "retrospective sense-making"; they identify the "decision" they've made *after* they act—not before.

Meaning contributes fundamentally to survival, just as food
and water do. Viktor Frankl makes this point most powerfully in
his book *Man's Search for Meaning*. Frankl, a survivor of Auschwitz
and Dachau, was profoundly influenced by what he observed

during his agonizing years at the death camps. If ever there was an event in history that challenged meaning, it was the Holocaust. The message that many took from that event, from the two World Wars, from the bomb, is that life is *not* meaningful. But Frankl saw the reverse. The concentration camp survivors, in his view, were not necessarily the strongest physically. They were the ones who could cling to a shard of hope in a hopeless situation— those who could hang on to meaning under conditions that defied all meaning.

The need for meaning runs so deep in people that organizations must supply it if they are to renew. Many don't. The best they can come up with is "more profit, continued growth." Serve the shareholder, and the rest will take care of itself. That is a dangerous perspective. For most of us, "the shareholder" is an abstraction—that fickle and faceless money manager who buys shares on rumors of good news and sells on hints of adversity.* If this view gives meaning, it does so for only a few. Pursuit of profit is hardly a cause that inspires loyalty or makes life meaningful for most people, unless company survival is at issue, and even then it may not be enough. Meaning should be bound up in the work we do. If we cannot find meaning in work, we spend our eight hours every weekday in quiet desperation. If we can find meaning in work, we can keep ourselves recharged, and the organizations we work for stand a chance of staying renewed themselves.

Leaders who are successful seem to understand the importance of making work meaningful for themselves and the people who work for them. The pattern that emerges is one of a constantly shifting set of issues that surface as the organization sails into uncharted waters. Some managers avoid the issues or put them in the "too hard" basket; their organizations don't renew. Others not only welcome the issues but take some pains to dig

---

* Making the employee a shareholder through an employee stock ownership plan (the ESOP) helps a little but doesn't solve the problem. ESOPs are just a nonsalary or nonwage way of distributing wealth to the employees. But money is not necessarily a prime motivator. Research shows that when people aren't paid fairly they lose motivation; but given fair compensation, money is far down on the list of what motivates most people. ESOPs have other problems. They used to have a tax advantage; with the new tax law, that is gone. ESOPs signal ownership, which is good, but the fraction of employee ownership is so small that no participation in company affairs is implied. What's more, ESOPs put the burden of market risk on the employee.

them out and turn them into causes. Their organizations have a chance. A few leaders are able to find adventure and nobility in the causes. Their companies will probably stay fresh. Some are able to turn organizational causes into individual commitment. Their organizations will almost certainly regenerate.

Moveable Issues

Andy Pearson says that when he was president of PepsiCo, one of his most valuable management tools was a handwritten list that he kept and updated three or four times a year. On the list were the short- and long-term problems and opportunities for each division he managed. He says, "You'd be amazed how helpful that is to keep things in focus."

Pearson's management tool might be called a "moveable-issues list." For different companies it takes different forms. It is not always as explicit as Pearson's list. Or it might be more formal than his handwritten notes. The concept behind it is simple. At any point a company is faced with a set of problems and opportunities. A good brainstorming session will bring most of these out. A little more attention and they can be stated as issues to be addressed. A touch more work and they can be summarized into a few top-priority, must-deal-with items.

In some situations the issues are obvious. When Manufacturing VP Dick Burke joined the Schipke team at GE, he says, "I was sitting in a meeting when I first arrived here and someone was reporting that we had an SCR of sixty-five for one of our products. I asked what that was, and he said that sixty-five percent of the appliances needed a service call during the warranty period. I was appalled. He asked, 'What's wrong with that? It used to be a hundred and thirty-five percent.'" That's more than one service call per appliance while it was under warranty. Burke had come from GE's turbine division, where even a minor glitch in quality could knock out a city's electric power. Quality went straight to the top of his issue list.

Priorities are not always obvious; the important thing is to pick one that is directionally right and let it stand for the rest. In

1980, when John Egan took the helm of the Jaguar automobile company, the whole company was on strike. We/they fences were everywhere, especially in the form of job boundaries dictated by the trade unions. The company was losing money. Jaguar wasn't even a complete company; only engineering and manufacturing were on-site. Sales, marketing, and other activities had vanished into the functional structure that had resulted from the nationalization of Jaguar's predecessor, British Leyland. Everything was a problem, an issue, and a potential cause.

Egan says he decided that the place to start was with quality. "Companies in crisis cannot tackle too many things at the same time," he says. He reasons that in times of crisis there will always seem to be a crushing list of conflicting problems and priorities. But Egan knows that you have to make it simple; he picked quality as the top issue and cause.

His choice showed a good understanding of the market situation. Jaguar has always had a strong following in the luxury car market, but in the late 1970s and early 1980s the standing joke was that you had to own two—one to drive and the other to have at the shop, being fixed. Quality as cause gave focus to the company's energies. They looked at their internal inspection system, which demerited the cars with faults. They looked at the warranty numbers and the problems those numbers reflected. Then they got a quick fix on how their own numbers stacked up by phoning a sample of one hundred Jaguar customers, one hundred Mercedes Benz owners, one hundred BMW owners, and so on, to ask about their experience in using each car over a twelve-month period. "We mobilized the whole company to solve these problems [the ones they pinpointed from their own analysis and market feedback]," Egan says. There were about two hundred of them: paint work, steering gear that leaked, gear boxes that failed, and so on. That information provided a way to target their "quality" push.

Morgan Bank recognizes the importance of articulating the issues and of keeping the issues list in motion as times change. Says one executive: "We haven't done a detailed five-year plan in quite some time. We realized that we can't do them anyway, so we're better off taking strategic issues and dealing with them. Our strategic planning meetings for the last two or three years have been highly issue-oriented. First the staff puts together a long paper on the issue; then it's discussed extensively."

At IBM a very similar process is at work. Bernard Puckett describes it: "One of the parts of the planning system is something we call strategic planning conferences. Twice a year Akers takes his top twenty executives and goes off for two and a half days. What we do is try to focus on some area. In my former job I'd go in to [Akers] and say, 'John, I think we ought to look at . . .' I'd pick a specific issue, try to sell it, and if he bought it, he'd select people to work on it. Then we'd sit in a room for two and a half days with people from all over the world. That's really where we set the rudder [IBM's major directions], as far as I'm concerned."

To explain the value of focusing on a few issues, Puckett elaborates: "You never notice any red cars when you're driving around; now you'll see twice as many because I mentioned it." At the time of our talk, IBM had just announced a major thrust in systems integration. Puckett commented that only two years before, that concept had been viewed negatively around IBM. People felt getting into systems integration would require IBM to take on much more responsibility for the total package than the company had been used to assuming. Then, many believed, IBM would run the risk of not living up to customer expectations. "In a *relatively* short period of time—less than twelve months—the attitude switched from 'I'm not interested in doing that at all' to Akers's saying 'That's a major thrust for the IBM company.' The change resulted from spending time at these conferences discussing the issue. You put something on the table there, and then guys like Rizzo, or Akers, or Phyphers [all very senior IBM executives] who have their own close contacts with customers, ask 'How are you buying things now?' The customers tell them something like: 'I've got seven vendors; the equipment never all works together; I don't know how to install it myself; I need somebody to come take that problem off my hands.' "

According to Puckett, it was a similar set of meetings that led IBM to conclude that, despite their sales prowess, they were never as market-oriented as legend made them out to be. This issue, combined with the need for systems integration and their determination to keep costs down while keeping their no-layoff policy, has led to a massive shift of people within IBM. They are moving away from factory, staff, and office positions and into the field, where the customers are.

My own certitude about the value of a moveable-issues list comes from my days with the Long Range Planning Committee for the San Francisco Symphony. One of the committee's first actions was to frame a very complete list of issues. To do that, we interviewed everyone who was influential and knowledgeable about the Symphony, to find out what bothered them.

In the first year, there were two priority issues. First, what could be done about the deficit? Second, did everyone truly buy into the Symphony's stated aspiration to become a great symphony, one recognized as world class?

As the years went by, the committee, and the rest of the Symphony in turn, kept updating the issues list and setting new priorities. By the end of the second year the deficit had been erased, but if the Symphony was going to be world class, it needed more world-class musicians. It also needed to tour more and find a way to attract more top-flight guest conductors. Those became priority issues.

A few years later, the deficit that had been so nicely erased several years back wouldn't stay erased. By that time, the financials on a "what-if" computer model were completed, but no matter how the budget was cut, the Symphony would probably be bathing in red ink five years out. Building the size of the endowment and thinking of new ways to do that were problems that got moved to the top of the issues list.

One of the recent issues has been to knock down some we/they barriers between board members, staff, and musicians. During one meeting, a musician who had been quiet for most of the session said, "I'll tell you what the biggest we/they barrier is: us and the hall." The new Davies Symphony Hall was giving the musicians fits—it's built with adjustable curtains and reflectors so that it can be "tuned." Every time it gets tuned right for the audience, or for recording, the musicians have difficulty hearing one another. There are some dead spots on stage, and one section of the orchestra might hear an echo from another section rather than the direct sound. The strings can't be sure they are precisely with the horns—and so on. Acoustics in the hall moved right to the top of the issues list.

What makes the issues list work is that it was conceived as an "issue broker," not an "issue resolver." The concern was with implementation. To get anything done, the committee had to enlist the people who could resolve the issue. Who were those people? It depended on the issue. Sometimes it was another board committee member, sometimes a person on the Symphony staff, sometimes the president, the executive director, or the conductor, sometimes a task force involving musicians.

Another part of the process that made it practical was that although we were called the Long Range Planning Committee, there was never a long-range plan. There was plenty of documentation. But it was flexibility that made the planning process a force for renewal.

The *moveable* part of the moveable-issues concept reminds us that the world keeps changing, that it does so in hard-to-predict ways, and that renewal is a constant challenge, something you live with—not solve. H. Ross Perot has a sign in his office that captures this spirit: EVERY GOOD AND EXCELLENT THING STANDS MOMENT BY MOMENT ON THE RAZOR'S EDGE OF DANGER AND MUST BE FOUGHT FOR. In a lighter vein, John Gardner remarks that Sisyphus just misses being a good metaphor for renewal. For those of you who don't remember, he's the fellow from Greek mythology who is eternally condemned to push a rock up a hill, only to have it roll back down as he nears the top. "But," Gardner says, deadpan, "Sisyphus had a very flat learning curve."

Refreshing the Cause

"We run on causes around here," declared many of the executives we interviewed. Their way of keeping their companies fresh was to keep their causes fresh—and inspiring. A moveable-issues list can be the source of the cause that refreshes and renews organizations. The flip side of any top-priority issue is a top-priority cause. As the Symphony example suggests, it's not that hard for most organizations to list and to rank issues. The challenge for leadership is adding the magic—transforming the issue from just another dreary problem to a cause that inspires people.

Porsche's CEO, Peter Schutz, brings the point to life with this story: "Three people were at work on a construction site. All were doing the same job, but when each was asked what his job was, the answers varied. 'Breaking rocks,' the first replied. 'Earning my living,' said the second. 'Helping to build a cathedral,' said the third.' " In his classic book *Working,* Studs Terkel found that some of the happiest manual laborers were stonemasons. They could look back on what they'd built and take pride in it.

Few of us can build cathedrals or work as stonemasons. But to the extent we can see the cathedral in whatever cause we are following, the job seems more worthwhile. Good leaders help us find those cathedrals in what otherwise could be dismal issues and empty causes. The point seems obvious, but failure to pay it any heed was one of the main problems CEO John Egan inherited at Jaguar. Executives there report that in 1975 an effort was made to subjugate Jaguar under the umbrella of Leyland cars. The Jaguar signs at the entry to the factory were torn down. Only Leyland flags could be flown on the premises. Switchboard operators were threatened with disciplinary action if they answered, "Good morning, Jaguar Cars." Instead they were supposed to say: "Good morning, Leyland Cars—large car assembly plant number one."

The assortment of causes among the renewing organizations was as varied and individual as the organizations themselves. At Children's Television Workshop the original cause was to use the television medium to teach economically disadvantaged preschoolers. As time passed the cause was broadened to include all preschoolers and then children worldwide. Today's cause, and the basis for their new program, *3-2-1 Contact,* is to use television to help rectify America's decline in math scores.

One cause that most of the renewing companies seem to have moved away from is growth for its own sake. The volume-oriented, shove-it-out-the-door mentality, which went unchallenged for too long, put many organizations on the brink of disaster. Many of the leading banks, for example, were preoccupied with growth. When the American market for big lending dried up, the banks went after foreign credits, which turned out to be much riskier than the banks had ever imagined.

The volume cause was what got GE, Ford, and other manufacturers into so much trouble in the late 1970s and early 1980s. It was also one culprit behind Jaguar's troubles. Jaguar executives say that those were the days of the dual ethic; "big is beautiful" and "economies of scale" were everything.

The situation at GE typified what happened when volume stood as the premier, unchallenged cause. An assembly worker said, "Back then, if you said that you had a bad part, and if they felt they had to get the job done, they'd tell you to run it anyway. They didn't want to hear any more about it. We had to supply John Q. Customer, and if he got a bad [product], why we'd just go out later and fix it."

GE managers, along with many others in the Western world, were transfixed with volume, quite possibly trapped by group-think, and could not make the necessary common-sense decisions. Faulty product was pushed out the factory door despite the fact that GE knew it cost them $3.50 to fix a defect in the factory and $60 to fix it in the home. Several people told us that bad parts received from suppliers would often be rejected, but not dis-carded. In a production bind, people would fish out the bad parts and build them into the appliances to meet the targeted volume. Another trick for meeting production targets was to produce the appliance short an unavailable part or two, send it to the ware-house to get production credit, then try to find and fix it later in the warehouse.

As long as quality was sacrificed in the name of volume, worker unrest had to follow. Their work lost its meaning; people had no source of pride in what they were doing. Folks were treated as if they were stupid. GE's Dick Burke says, "The biggest problem in U.S. industry today is the arrogance of management. We had nineteen thousand people here—a tremendous resource—but our management team hadn't communicated anything to them [except, implicitly, the importance of volume]." According to Burke, the attitude of past management was "Hourly people aren't very bright; why should we take the trouble to instruct them or ask them for help?" Contrast his depiction with what we heard from one of the hourly employees who had lived through the old era: "Just like all these child psychologists say, 'If your child has an inquiring mind, teach him.' My mind's not stagnant. Teach me." The simple act of informing people down the line and asking for their help goes a long way toward making their jobs meaningful.

At Appliance Park the situation had gotten so bad that work had lost meaning even for the middle managers. An executive told us: "For eight to ten years management had been saying, 'We don't want any strikes,' and tried to buy their way out with sweetheart deals. We had double-digit absenteeism. Time clocks were broken. Restrooms were a mess. There were no employee cafeterias. Management was accustomed to not being backed." In one outrageous incident, an employee threw a cup of coffee in his supervisor's face, the supervisor tried to take disciplinary action, there was a strike, and the *supervisor* was fired. Burke says, "In 1982 only a tiny percent of the middle managers trusted upper management. The middle managers looked, acted, and smelled like losers—they had to be the most beat group I've ever seen."

For Roger Schipke, finding a renewing cause was easy. He says, "*I got mad!* I saw all the fumbling and waste here. The Japanese were beating us. American manufacturing was going down. People were saying our factory workers weren't as good as they used to be, and certainly not as good as the Japanese." With so much wrong, there was no lack of causes. But, as people who survived the worst of it recall, the problems seemed insurmountable. Focus was desperately needed. When Schipke got mad, he was heading up dishwasher manufacturing in Building C within Appliance Park. His initial cause was not to take on the problems of a Don Quixote-like joust with all the issues at Appliance Park. It was to make something called "Project C" work—automating the dishwasher line in Building C.

Better quality and better treatment of people are the causes most frequently heard about. Each of these comes inherently packaged with themes that motivate. Each has a kind of Golden Rule quality to it. Do a better job on quality or on treating your employees well, and you display an attitude that says "We care." The quality and employee-involvement themes, newly instituted at Jaguar, Ford, GE—and historically in place at Maytag, IBM, HP—are natural sources of pride.

The push for quality at Jaguar has done the seemingly impossible: It's turned a near-failing British company into one that is competitive on a world scale. J.D. Powers is a company that ranks automobile manufacturers in terms of customer satisfaction. Egan told us: "In 1980 we were so bad we weren't even on the [Powers] list; last year we were fifth."

In recent years Jaguar has been gaining a share in the U.S. luxury car market segment—the only company other than BMW to do so. Even more recently, Jaguar picked up a small share of the market in that bastion of quality luxury cars, West Germany.

As a cause, better service has precisely the same attributes to recommend it that better quality has. But, despite the fact that a large number of the companies we interviewed are in the service business, and that 85 percent of the new jobs being created these days are in the service sector, we didn't hear "better service" put forward as a cause nearly as often as "better quality" was. There are some notable exceptions, but the fact remains: We heard more about quality products than about quality service. The reason could easily be that because of poor quality, American manufacturing has recently suffered mightily at the hands of foreign competition and is just now getting its act back together. Poor service, however, can be harder to detect; it rarely even makes its way *onto* the issues list, let alone to the top of it.

Dartmouth professor James Brian Quinn concludes that the same inattention to quality that spelled near-disaster for American manufacturing is pervasive in the service industries today. It could have similar disastrous results for service companies that don't get with it. If Quinn's conclusion is right, the tragedy is due to the myopia of American leadership. Service companies have been under pressure from deregulation and heavy competition from the discounters. A natural reaction is to cut costs, which is to say cut service payroll, training, and the caliber of employees.

But service is like quality. There's every indication that it's a moneymaker. The most convincing evidence comes from The Strategic Planning Institute in Cambridge, Massachusetts, which tracks the fortunes of more than 2,500 business units worldwide. Using sophisticated statistical measures, they compare businesses producing high quality, or high service, with competitors in the same business who offer lower quality or lower service. The high-quality, high-service firms return, on average, twice as much on invested capital as do their typical low-end counterparts. The secret to success in the service business is simple: Offer service.

A frequent, and motivating, cause we heard was "be a winner." That cause appeals to our need to feel special, the positive side of Martin Luther King, Jr.'s "drum major instinct." When Peter Schutz left Cummins Engine to take over the helm of Porsche in Stuttgart, Porsche was on the verge of losing money for the first time in its history. The strategy Schutz inherited was to shrink the business, in hopes that, at some smaller size, Porsche could hang on to a profitable niche. Schutz believed that this cause would do nothing but breed losers. One day when he was talking with Professor Porsche, the visionary behind most of the Porsche line and the man who designed the Volkswagen Beetle, Schutz asked him: "What is the all-time best car? What is your personal favorite? Which car are you most proud of?" Porsche answered, "We haven't built it yet." It was then that Schutz began to believe he could restore the old spirit.

The winning cause began to infuse the Porsche team when Schutz asked a group of his managers to name the most important race of the year. They unanimously nominated the twenty-four-hour Le Mans Grand Prix. As usual, the company was planning to enter their 924 turbo in that race. When Schutz asked what their chances were of winning with that model, he was told they might be able to win within their class, but there was no chance of winning overall. At that point, he adjourned the meeting, saying, "As long as I'm in charge of the company, we won't talk about not winning."

Twenty-four hours later he called for another meeting, this time to talk about how they could win. According to Schutz, the interesting thing was how excited people got. In the past they had all been muttering under their breath about how they could win if someone in the company would only let them try. Now they had the chance. What they did not have was much time. There were two 936s in inventory. They figured they could take the transmission out of a 917, "kludge" together some other parts, and put together something that might win. This was just sixty-two days before the race. Two days later Schutz got a call from a fellow who had retired a couple of years previously as a race driver. He had heard via the grapevine what Porsche was doing, and he wanted to volunteer to drive whatever they came up with.

They did win that race and were on the way to restoring both a winning spirit and profitability.

Cost reduction is another common issue for the renewing companies. No cause may be more crucial to top management than lowering costs or increasing productivity. But it's a more difficult one to make meaningful than quality or service. It usually means lost jobs. Too often managers avoid the problem of trying to explain it, or they explain it in a way that relates only to the needs of the organization and not to the needs of the people who work there. One boss decided that a sense of discipline might instill pride in his employees. The discipline he used was to clock the employees' arrival time. Anyone getting to work later than 8:00 A.M. would get a demerit. Three demerits and you work on Saturday. This company is on the ropes. It desperately needs renewal. Getting to work at 8:00 is not a cause that will help turn it around.

Other companies have been able to define the cost issue in terms of a cause that has some nobility, integrity, and urgency by letting everyone know what will happen to the enterprise—and jobs in the long run—if the issue is not met head-on. We found managers who had taken workers and union leadership to Japan or Korea so they could see firsthand what they were up against. At Ford, Brunswick, Nucor, and Wells Fargo, we found people up and down the line who were highly motivated to control costs. Management had spent countless hours explaining to them the importance of productivity to the viability of the company.

Another common theme for renewal, which can become a cause, is technology. By definition it's important in the high-tech companies—HP, Digital, Olivetti, IBM. But technology was a theme for renewal in steelmaking at Nucor, in truck-parts manufacture at Dana, in printing at Quad/Graphics, in papermaking at both James River and Potlatch, and in banking at Citicorp. There, CEO John Reed made his mark by automating the so-called "back-office" operations. Information technology has become a cornerstone of much of the change happening at Morgan, where executives told us that one of every six people there is in programming, systems design, or related technical fields.

Cost control, productivity, technology, and certain other causes that pop out of the issues list can be meaningful for a while.

However, the most motivating causes focus on *quality products, service, and the customer*—making the work people do seem worth the effort—and *people quality*—making people believe in their individual worth. These causes are motivating because they relate equally to people and the organization. In all the other issues and causes, the organization comes first and the individual is secondary. An important leadership challenge is to find ways of articulating causes so that they make meaning for people. Causes that speak only to the needs of the organization—or to individual needs—are not the stuff of permanent renewal. A cause, put forward with some inspiration, can be what turns the dreary issue into a catalyst for renewal.

Adventure Capital

Erich Fromm comments: "Man is not free to choose between having or not having 'ideals,' but he is free to choose between different kinds of ideals, between being devoted to the worship of power and destruction and being devoted to reason and love." In a very similar way, it is not just the existence of a cause that engenders renewal in a company; the nature of the cause counts for a great deal. If the history of nations, governments, or companies has done nothing else, it has taught us that wrongly intentioned leaders can rally people to loathsome causes as well as to noble ones. Dictatorial regimes can change organizations quickly, but often for the worse, and certainly without the ability to renew.

But companies can find worthwhile causes to engage. That's the way manufacturing czar Jack Kuehler describes his company. "One unique feature of IBM is our ability to articulate causes and let them become the next mountain to climb." In the early 1980s, IBM recognized that the company no longer stood for quality in the way IBMers felt it should. Back then, regardless of the accuracy of public perceptions, many believed that the Japanese made a better-quality computer than IBM's. Kuehler says, "We decided to do everything we could to improve both the reality and perception of IBM's quality." As Hewlett-Packard did with the TQC program, the whole company recommitted to quality and to a new set of quality objectives—in development, in manufacturing, in accounting, and even in the handling of paperwork and documentation.

When there is a choice, part of the magic a leader can lend to the cause is to find adventure in it. We see a little of this in the GE story. For all their problems, there is a sense of adventure at Appliance Park. Demolishing the matrix organization. Convincing Welch that Project C could work. Roger Schipke recalls: "I argued that nothing better had been offered to him, so he might as well let me try it. He answered, 'It's going to fail. You guys in Louisville can't walk and chew gum at the same time. What's different about this?' " Making it work: "Project C was like changing a fan belt on a running engine. We built six hundred thousand dishwashers while we were modernizing the factory." It *was* an adventure, and behind it lies Schipke's willingness to risk a little.

Even in less dire circumstances, making work meaningful is closely related to the ability to find and articulate *adventure* in work. Often you will meet someone you haven't seen in years. Sometimes you take up right where you left off; the bond is still there. Other times, the person is a stranger, someone you knew once but don't know anymore. One difference seems to be whether you've had some kind of adventure together. Have you tried something, risked a little bit, done something you weren't sure you could do? The *size* of the adventure doesn't seem to matter much. A pickup game of touch football might do it. So might making a joint investment in a small project. The *content* of the adventure does matter; it has to be something positive, something that seems worthwhile, noble in its own small way.

Adventure and risk go together. One man's risk is another's terror, and if the risk is too high, adventure becomes disaster. We don't learn, and we don't renew. Behind the ability to risk has to be a basis for security. Friendly facts. Healthy people policies. Tolerance for mistakes. Safety nets.

At Porsche, Peter Schutz subscribes to the adventure theory in an interesting way. First, he says that one of the things you look for in the people you hire is courage. You can't teach them that. Second, he declares that money alone won't keep good people. You may attract them that way, but you hold them by giving them interesting work. One of the specific things that keeps the Porsche engineering staff tuned up, in touch, and turned on is doing contract engineering work for others. When I talked to Schutz his engineers had just helped design the airbus, they were working with the Russians on designing small automobiles, and they were developing a fuel-injection motor for a car to be manufactured in Spain. They were also developing a Formula 1 racing car.

One of the bigger adventure-filled causes we ran into was across town from Appliance Park in Louisville. Tired of taking the kind of flak that says for-profit hospitals don't serve the community, Humana decided to assume the management of Louisville's General Hospital. At the time, the hospital was providing indigent care and serving as a teaching facility for the University of Louisville's medical school. Facing a projected 1981 deficit of $3.6 million, the hospital eliminated jobs, reduced services, and began turning away the indigents it was supposed to serve. Despite these cost-saving measures, the situation grew worse. A year later, upon completion of a new facility to replace an old one that was actually crumbling, the hospital was projecting a $10 million loss.

Conditions were awful. Ann Powell, director of surgery, remembers all too clearly: "The old facility had added no new capital equipment in ten years. Daily we ran out of essential supplies. The hospital couldn't pay its bills without additional money from somewhere, so suppliers refused to send us anything more. Between 1980 and 1983 we had three layoffs. That left us with five people to cover twenty-four hours a day, seven days a week—and that wasn't just for the recovery room; we were also used for intensive care. We called the ICU 'pre-mortem'—it was that bad. I can't imagine more horrible environmental conditions. Needless to say, we couldn't recruit or retain quality staff." Mary Bennett, head RN for the trauma center, chimes in: "During the summer at the old hospital some of the wards reached a hundred and five degrees. Patients were perspiring so much we had to use a lot more IV fluid than normal. It was medicine from another era."

Humana approached the University of Louisville. David Jones and Wendell Cherry offered to lease the new hospital complex, purchase equipment, support medical education, and underwrite indigent-care deficits. The university would receive 20 percent of the hospital's pretax profits. In return Humana got a new 404-bed facility and the "opportunity" to make a profit if it could survive the challenge of this unusual public-private partnership.

Jones and Cherry might have appeared foolhardy hanging the General Hospital albatross around their necks. But in truth, they were relatively certain Humana's expertise in hospital administration could turn the place around. By taking on this particular cause, Humana could reaffirm its public commitment to improving the existing health-care delivery system and prove that public/private partnerships can work. Furthermore, Jones and Cherry would be able to show that for-profit businessmen aren't the heartless ogres the medical establishment has portrayed them to be.

The speed of the turnaround surprised everyone, even Humana. By fiscal year 1985 the hospital realized a $3.7 millon profit, despite an 11.6 percent increase in indigent use that cost Humana over $6 million. Gary Sherlock, who runs the facility, is modest about what he did. He admits it sounds a little too simple to be true, but there were really only four factors. First, he brought in business practices that had worked for Humana elsewhere, and they yielded the same results they had produced elsewhere—more service, lower cost. The second factor was treating people—both staff and patients—with dignity. Third, he encouraged open and honest communication with lots of feedback. Fourth was his continuing belief that people want to think well of themselves, and thus are motivated more by the vision of what could be than the need to make immediate profit.

The numbers depict the magnitude of the change, but to get a real sense of it you have to be there, to talk to some of the people who had seen it before and after. Dr. Donald Thomas, chairman of the department of emergency medicine, says, "Now we're both more efficient and more oriented to patient care. We no longer have to turn patients away. Instead of being in wards with thirty to forty others, patients are in double rooms. Nursing is on flexible hours now. Managers are more accessible, and they are willing to act if you convince them something should be done." Ann Powell declares that Humana's presence hasn't just improved the hospital; it has turned around her life. "We've got a happy bunch of people around here—productive people with creative ideas. Our education budget is twice that of other Humana hospitals, because people here are so interested in furthering their education. We do unique things here because of our equipment, personnel competence, and the aura of the place."

There is no magic in the way Humana turned the place around. It was work, but they simply did the thing they do well. For Humana the magic is in the adventure of taking a risk that nobody on the outside thinks possible, turning it into a cause, making it work, and enabling the whole organization to feel proud of itself for doing so well. The issue: the poor public image of for-profit hospitals. The cause: Louisville General Hospital. The adventure: Could anyone turn it around, let alone make a profit, given its abysmal situation? The continuing challenge: finding more ways to improve service to patients, support medical education and research, and cut costs.

Commitment

Causes and commitment are the core of renewal—both individual and institutional. Stating an organization-wide cause is one thing, but the words mean nothing unless people get committed. The rub is that you can't legislate commitment, and at some level you can't quite manage it, either. Commitment is an individual state of mind, something that falls into place person-by-person.

It isn't all that easy. Our society is very outspoken on the need for individual rights and freedom. But we have trouble thinking and talking clearly about how to balance individual freedom on the one hand and organizational commitment on the other. We are suspicious of causes; they dilute autonomy and sometimes compromise individual freedom for broader purposes that are questionable. We think it's better to keep our options open than to make a commitment we may regret later.

The below-the-surface conflict between rugged individualism and social commitment that many Americans experience is the subject of the recent book *Habits of the Heart*. Interviewing hundreds of people throughout the United States, the authors (five sociologists) uncovered a "classic case of ambivalence" between our need for both freedom and commitment. We feel the need for freedom so deeply, we have trouble making commitments. We all can recognize a part of ourselves reflected in the mirror *Habits of the Heart* holds up. The authors observe:

W*e found all the classic polarities of American individualism still operating: the deep desire for autonomy and self-reliance combined with an equally deep conviction that life has no meaning unless shared with others in the context of community; a commitment to the equal right to dignity of every individual combined with an effort to justify inequality of reward, which, when extreme, may deprive people of dignity; an insistence that life requires practical effectiveness and "realism" combined with the feeling that compromise is ethically fatal. . . . We deeply feel the emptiness of a life without sustaining social commitments. Yet we are hesitant to articulate our sense that we need one another as much as we need to stand alone, for fear that if we did we would lose our independence altogether. The tensions of our lives would be even greater if we did not, in fact, engage in practices that constantly limit the effects of an isolating individualism, even though we cannot articulate those practices nearly as well as we can the quest for autonomy.*

Today, in the context of many organizations, this polarity becomes even more confusing. People relinquish a great deal of autonomy in order to hold down a job. They earn a paycheck in return. In contrast to previous generations, they feel that a salary alone is small compensation if they have no sense that their work isn't contributing to the greater good. Even worse, many believe that their work is accomplishing the reverse. As metaphor for the conflict, the authors of *Habits of the Heart* pick the modern American hero: the hard-boiled detective. Whether the detective is Sam Spade, Travis McGee, Columbo, or Serpico, "When [he] begins his quest, it [the crime] appears to be an isolated incident.

But as it develops, the case turns out to be linked to the powerful and privileged of the community. Society, particularly 'high society,' is corrupt to the core."

All of us make commitments. They may erode our freedom to act autonomously, but in return they provide some meaning in our lives and on the job. What we need are causes that we can identify with—ones we believe are worth supporting. James Brian Quinn notes which goals work best: "To forge a common bond among individuals with widely diverse personal values, expectations and capacities ... goals must ... satisfy people's more basic psychological needs: to produce something worthwhile, to help others, to obtain recognition, to be free or innovative, to achieve security, to beat an opponent, or to earn community respect."

Besides defining causes in a relevant, exciting way, it's necessary to give people a choice about whether or not they will commit. Nothing engenders resentment—or limp submission—more quickly than ordering someone to be committed. When people have no choice in the matter, they're not likely to make a genuine commitment. Organizational theorist Gerald Salancik argues that "Volition ... is the cement that binds the action to the person and that motivates him to accept the implications of his acts. ... Without volition, a behavior is not necessarily committing, for the person can always assert that he really did not cause the behavior himself." In other words, if someone cannot choose *not* to commit, he probably won't take responsibility for his actions. The natural fallback position in this case is: "I was forced to do it."

The turnaround at Zebco,* Brunswick Corporation's fishing reel manufacturing division in Tulsa, Oklahoma, can be attributed to the choice every employee made to commit to improving quality and productivity. Faced with near-annihilation by off-shore competitors, Zebco's management decided to take the matter to the people. They understood that gains were impossible if employees on the line weren't aware of the situation and what each of them individually could do about it.

---

* Originally the Zero Hour Bomb Company. They made bombs for fracturing oil wells. One day a man who invented the fishing reel they now make showed up and asked the company if they wanted to manufacture it. A man in the toolroom took it out to the parking lot and tried it for ten minutes. He opined that it looked good. That was the strategy that launched Zebco.

Zebco had enjoyed twenty-five years of solid success after its beginnings in 1949. But the oil crisis of 1974 changed all that. People quit buying additional fishing reels, and the bottom fell out of the market. To make matters worse, the foreign manufacturers Zebco was competing with didn't turn off the switch. Between 1982 and 1985 an excess of 8 million rods poured into the U.S. market. The wholesale price of fishing reels was $9.50, and they retailed for $9.99.

By 1980, Zebco division manager John Charvat was convinced that the company couldn't survive if it didn't reduce costs. Zebco was driven initially by a survival-based cause; foreign competition was making Zebco's prices noncompetitive. But it was redefined into something positive and more meaningful to everyone: increase quality and productivity. The hope was that it would cut costs.

Charvat knew that *communication* was the crucial link between this cause and individual commitment to it. Every employee needed to understand that Zebco's foreign competitors were here to stay, but that there still was plenty of room for improvement on their own home court. The situation was bad, but the game wasn't lost yet.

Jim Dawson, vice-president of manufacturing, offered to get this message across to everyone. He didn't do it by scheduling one big "something's gotta give" session. Instead, he started having two-hour meetings with people in groups of four, explaining to them that the only way they could stay in business was to improve quality while they increased productivity and kept the costs down. Charvat comments: "We took the time to visit with the people and let them know what we were doing and why. We taught them that quality starts within and that they should try to work smarter, not harder." It took two years for Dawson to meet with all of the employees.

Those get-togethers were supplemented by plant meetings. Charvat explains: "We asked everyone what they needed to be able to do their job better. They told us: 'Give us better parts and tools, and have them here when we need them.' We discovered that 85 percent of the problems were rooted in bad parts from suppliers." Zebco began working with suppliers and developed a vendor certification program. That corrected much of the difficulty, but lots of other measures were needed. For example, now employees can stop the line themselves if they see there's a problem with quality control.

There are three notable aspects to this story. For one, Charvat's management approach reflects his belief that "everyone wants to contribute and be recognized." So the obvious place to begin was in helping each employee understand the gravity of the situation *and* the degree to which he or she could help turn it around. Charvat was convinced that employee attitudes were the key to the quality and productivity improvements he was looking for. And those attitudes couldn't be legislated; they had to be nurtured. This is very similar to Gary Sherlock's approach at Humana Hospital University.

Second, the link between an overriding cause and individual commitment to it doesn't appear automatically. It has to be forged over time by honest, consistent communication. Charvat and Dawson went about persuading the staff to make a commitment to their cause by talking straight to them, face-to-face and in small-group meetings that were long enough to be both informative and convincing. They didn't threaten, cajole, or use any "motivational" techniques. Dialogue continues all the time at Zebco—not just during scheduled meetings. As Charvat comments: "The people on the line are quick to tell us when there's a problem. They listen to us, and we listen to them." Again the similarities: Sherlock's emphasis on communication at Humana Hospital University; Jaguar's quality program, which demanded face-to-face discussion directly with the work force, not through the unions; musicians serving on the San Francisco Symphony's Long Range Planning Committee.

Third, things improved at Zebco. Commitment to a cause will wane if people see that it's all rhetoric and no action. But the employees at Zebco recognized that they began to get better service from suppliers; they had evidence that quality was going up, and productivity was rising at an astonishing rate. Management asked them for their advice, then listened to it and made the necessary changes. Today, everyone still sees a direct link between his or her ideas and actions and the success of the company. Commitment has never been higher. More similarities: At Wells Fargo, Carl Reichardt told us that real commitment to cost control occurred when everyone started seeing the impact of their cost-cutting program on Wells Fargo's stock price.

Since Zebco began its quality assurance and productivity programs in 1981, the number of reels assembled per person per day has almost tripled. The company cut costs four years straight. Charvat is like a proud father: "When a line meets its quota, everyone yells. Everyone wants to do better and better, mostly because of the sheer pride that comes from it."

On the surface, the renewal we found in the municipal offices of Scottsdale, Arizona, seems at best a distant cousin to Zebco's. But both hinge on their leaders' success in articulating a cause and then creating lots of opportunities for everyone to get behind it. Six years ago the Scottsdale City Council brought in city manager Roy Pederson from California to heal some deep wounds. We/ they barriers existed between managers and employees, who were a step away from unionization. The Fraternal Order of Police was becoming such a militant organization that it had taken the city to court. Interdepartmental conflict pulled people's attention away from their work. According to Pederson: "Some departments were being run like Prussian regiments and some were totally loose—country clubs."

Pederson inherited an organization that had been drifting for years without a sense of purpose. His challenge was to revitalize a demoralized, uncommitted staff, overhaul outmoded management practices, and develop organization-wide commitment to the cause of providing the best possible service for the community. Rather than hiding behind all the reasons something *couldn't* be changed, Pederson assumed that most things *could* be significantly improved.

After spending six months just talking to people all over the city offices, Pederson knew that the place to start was with the management team. They had a history of working at cross-purposes, and, with a few notable exceptions, they seemed adamantly resistant to change. Pederson saw an immediate, overriding need to refocus their attention on the organization's fundamental purpose of community service. Beyond that, he wanted to articulate new shared values that every manager would be expected to commit to. He had to smoke out the members of the top management team who couldn't or wouldn't get on board with the cause and values that he wanted to establish organization-wide.

To accomplish this, Pederson scheduled what he now calls a "Come to Jesus" meeting for all the department and division heads, where he stated the cause—serve the people in Scottsdale—and its supporting values: Be the best source of information, be cost-conscious, support city policy, plan, and treat people decently. What was the group's response? Pederson remembers: "There were no comments or questions afterwards. On the negative side, people could see I had decided it was time to get tough. On the positive side, I had made some moves toward a main thrust for the organization. About twenty-five percent of the managers were taking me seriously, fifty percent had decided to wait me out [they had seen other city managers come and go], and another twenty-five percent said, 'To hell with this.' They began to polish up their resumés."

Pederson had plenty of reason to believe that a number of managers would not at the outset be willing to get behind a broad-based renewal effort. Once he was ready to establish the new cause and set the necessary course to get there, his top priority was to give everyone on the management team an opportunity to sign up. But he also wanted to let them know that it would be tough for them to stay on the team if they chose not to support him.

Choice is crucial to commitment. So every leader must face the possibility that some managers will choose not to support the cause he or she has in mind. What should the leader do in that case? If the most competent and trusted people won't commit, the leader should take another look at the cause itself. It may be ill-conceived or stated in a misleading way. If the cause still seems worthy of pursuing, then he or she has to make it very hard for people who don't go along with it to stick around.

The leader must decide on the cause and the values. He or she should be open to question and challenge, but then be ready to commit. Once the leader commits to the cause, the top management team divides into three camps: strong supporters; no problem there. Strong opponents; they have to go. And the "mug-wumps," the fence-sitters with their "mug" on one side and their "wump" on the other; they seem committed, yet they fight the program. One executive advises: "Invent tests that force them to commit or to leave."*

A manager's responsibility is to get things done. He simply can't carry people who choose not to support a major mission. The members of the team may disagree on occasion about how to reach the goal. That's inevitable in a group of committed, yet free, thinkers. But if there's dissent at the outset over the cause itself, it's unlikely the team will ever be able to join together in reaching it. One weak link on the team—one uncommitted person—can create an enormous energy leak that's both distracting and debilitating. All the key players must choose to be on board from the beginning. Pederson understood that.

But so far, all Pederson had in Scottsdale was a management team that knew they'd better buy in or move out. He still had the problem of how to gain commitment from the eight hundred people who worked within the departments. Given their old habits, the past friction, the lingering hostility in some cases, and downright sloth in others, Pederson sensed that more might be needed than an inspiring cause and a gospel meeting.

He made the shift from cause to widespread commitment in two ways. First, he enlisted the help of two people who have turned out to be key lieutenants, Tom Davis and Dick Bowers, to spend seemingly endless hours talking with everyone. This step is a direct parallel to the process for gaining commitment we saw at Zebco, Jaguar, and a host of others.

But as powerful a force as it is, communication intensity alone may not have been enough to move this tar pit of lost causes. The second approach was inspired. Pederson, Davis, and Bowers, along with the department heads, found, invented, borrowed, and supported a cornucopia of small things that people in every nook and cranny of the organization could do. Taken one at a time, each seems too small, too gimmicky, too corny, or too insignificant to make a difference. But looking at them this way would miss the point on two counts. First, from an organizational perspective they aren't taken one at a time; hundreds of things are

---

* This sounds antithetical to my earlier statements that you can't order people to be committed. The difference is subtle. Here I'm talking about the leadership team. They do have a choice, though not a pleasant one: Get committed or get out.

going on that are directionally right. Second, it is precisely the smallness of the step that leads to commitment.

Here's what is going on: People use their own actions as a way of discovering what they believe in the first place. "Did I do that? There must have been a reason. Oh yes, here's why. . . ." If people act slightly differently from the way they have in the past, what psychologists call "cognitive dissonance" sets in. People are uncomfortable with dissonance. They can't undo the act, so they modify their beliefs a little to make them more consistent with what they just did. Dissonance reduction is one of the prime reasons that the most avid readers of automobile advertising are people who have just bought the car. They are looking for support for their decision.

Now, let's look at this process at work in Scottsdale. Community Development is the department that reviews and approves all building construction. Their typical turnaround time on any project was two months. They were so accustomed to working at cross-purposes, their automatic attitude toward anything new was to stonewall it. Tom Davis, who spearheaded the transformation of this department, told us, "When developers called to check on how far along their application had gotten in the approval process, there was no record of where it was." Davis tried a number of different ways to get them moving; nothing worked. He finally got the staff off the dime with a suggestion program for cleaning up red tape that encouraged employees to challenge outmoded or unnecessary procedures. People were asked to complete, in writing, the sentence "This seems stupid to me," whenever they came across "a dumb thing we'd been doing for a long time." People liked that idea and started writing about dumb things. A tiny action, almost trivial, yet the very act of doing it started a change in mind-set.

In the same department Davis also set up a One Stop Shop. Developers used to have to go to multiple locations to nurse their applications through the process. Now they get everything processed at one location. The service-driven values for the One Stop Shop: It is unforgivable not to make a decision; unless written policy says no, say yes; if written policy says no, ask yourself if that makes sense [and presumably, if it doesn't, fill out a "this seems stupid" letter]; each employee is allowed only two no's a week. Community Development now turns around developers' plans in five days.

When Deputy City Manager Dick Bowers said that he had collected some "artifacts" of the change process from the different departments, he didn't turn up with just T-shirts and some award certificates. Instead, there were turtle-adorned note pads and pins (WE STICK OUR NECK OUT FOR YOU) and lunch bags emblazoned with the maintenance department's slogan: WHERE WE DO COMMON THINGS UNCOMMONLY WELL. The formerly recalcitrant police department decided to affirm Scottsdale's new shared values with a KEEP THE PEACE AND SET THE PACE theme on everything from brochures to coffee mugs.

Scottsdale's motto for gaining commitment might have been "No step too small." One project that is nothing but a collection of tiny actions by everyone on the staff is called "Employees Yielding Effective Savings." The acronym is EYES; if anyone sees something anywhere in the city that needs maintenance, they're encouraged to send a notice to field operations. In stark relief to the "it's not my job" attitude that used to prevail, 5,200 two-part EYES suggestion forms were submitted last year. The bottom part of the EYES forms are collected for an annual drawing, with first prize a reconditioned city pickup truck that was scheduled to be cycled out of service. But the real incentive comes when an employee who has reported a pothole that needs to be fixed drives by a week later and sees that the job has been done. That person knows it wouldn't have happened as quickly without his or her contribution.

The seemingly cornball continues: Scottsdale has its own Emmy awards. The project behind it is serious. When a cable TV channel approached the city for approval, they were told they could have it. But in exchange they were asked to open a channel for the city. Its use would be training and internal staff development. There was no money to produce the programs, but seventy employees volunteered their free time to be trained and then create the videos, doing the filming, editing, and voice-overs. Every year at the Emmy awards ceremony the volunteers receive the recognition they deserve, along with hats, jackets, and certificates.

This kind of thing is exactly what develops commitment. The

overall causes are training, staff development, service. But Scottsdale found a way to turn the abstraction into something people can do. In producing the shows, they do something meaningful for the organization, and in turn find more meaning in their work.

Public offices don't usually budget funds for apparent "frills." But Pederson and his crew understand the mileage you can get with even a small line-item amount for awards. Dick Bowers uses $20 bills to reward people he "catches doing something right." About once a week he writes a note mentioning the "something right," tucks the note and a crisp $20 bill in an envelope, and pops it in interoffice mail. Bowers has found another small way of reinforcing the cause and a big way of paying attention.

Scottsdale is a great example of how commitment can emerge from a lackluster staff when every person is given a chance to do something that contributes to the cause. Here's an interesting case where the public sector has a thing or two to teach the private sector. Unlike many companies that—although they are in the growing service sector of the economy—still don't serve, Scottsdale has brought that intangible called "service" to life. The thousands of little things make the difference. It's similar to the earlier message on small wins. The overall impact looks big; the magic is in the minutiae. The people in the Scottsdale city offices believe they are living and serving a "world-class" city, and they are doing it in a world-class way.

These items may seem flaky at first glance—more the residue of empty-headed hoopla than meaningful activity. But that couldn't be further from the truth. Instead, they are evidence of Scottsdale's continuing effort to introduce lots of little ways for everyone in the organization to make a difference. And it all seems to increase commitment exponentially. Every time people can contribute successfully to the cause of serving the community, they become even more committed to it.

Commitment Traps

Commitment does have its downside. In fact, research on commitment contains more reports on the uses of commitment to manipulate than on its power to motivate. The challenge for all of us is to recognize when commitment is a trap and not a source of renewal.

Scottsdale shows how lots of little actions that support a cause can increase each person's commitment to it. There's enormous incremental power in making it possible for people to succeed—to experience small wins—in ways that move directionally toward renewal. In fact, that's an almost sure-fire way to assure down-the-line support for a cause people can believe in. Both Zebco and Scottsdale are great examples of the meaning and motivation that can result from enabling everyone to act in many small, committed ways.

But there's a significant down side to this process of escalating commitment. It can be used over time to manipulate unsuspecting people into making a much bigger commitment than they really had in mind. Psychologist Irving Janis calls these "commitment traps for the unwary." He says, "Occasionally even the most vigilant decision-maker becomes trapped in a network of decisional obligations never imagined, let alone contemplated, when the commitment was made." That's how the United States became so inextricably enmeshed in the Vietnam War. The trap builds over time, piece by piece, the cumulative effect of lots of seemingly insignificant decisions.

A related trap commits the unwary when he or she takes a public stand on an issue. Visible announcements of opinion or intention greatly increase commitment to the chosen action; it's not as easy for the person to deny or forget that it occurred. As organizational theorist Jeffrey Pfeffer observes, companies make some decisions noticeably public in order to manage the amount of commitment they engender. It's a variation on Citicorp's Larry Small's theme of "selling forward." Writes Pfeffer: "When a new associate joins a law or an investment banking firm, advertisements may be taken out and announcements mailed. This publicly associates the person with the firm, thereby committing him or her more firmly to it."

Apparently, the power of commitment to influence behavior—especially if the commitment is made publicly—is a function of our nearly obsessive desire to be (and to appear) consistent with what we have already decided to do. From our commitments we create "consistency tapes" which serve as shortcuts; they keep us from having to rethink our decisions on the basis of new information.

These tapes may save us time and trouble, but they can also be quite harmful if we use them to filter out things that challenge our commitments. Robert Cialdini, in a fascinating book called *Influence,* describes ways in which we go so far as to actively reject information indicating that a commitment we made may not have been the most appropriate thing to do. We tend to discredit feedback that tells us a commitment we've made may have been misguided.

Cialdini describes some remarkable research on commitment done by psychologists Jonathan Freedman and Scott Fraser in the mid-1960s. They started by making an outrageous request of a group of California homeowners. Would they put a very large, poorly lettered sign that said DRIVE CAREFULLY on their front lawn? Most said no. Then they ran a second experiment with a similar sample of homeowners, only this time they asked them first to put up a small, unobtrusive sign urging safe driving. Of those who agreed to do that, 70 percent later were willing to put up the outrageous sign.

But the researchers didn't stop there. They wanted to know if making an even smaller commitment first—signing a petition that said "Keep California Beautiful"—would influence whether or not people would later be willing to put the outrageous sign in their front yard. Surprisingly, they got almost the same result. Reports Cialdini: "At first, even Freedman and Fraser were bewildered by their findings. Why should the little act of signing a petition supporting state beautification cause people to be so willing to perform a different and much larger favor? After considering and discarding other explanations, Freedman and Fraser came upon one that offered a solution to the puzzle: Signing the beautification petition changed the view these people had of themselves. They saw themselves as public-spirited citizens who acted on their civic principles. When, two weeks later, they were asked to perform another public service by displaying the outrageous DRIVE CAREFULLY sign, they complied in order to be consistent with their newly formed self-images."

Commitment traps can be as tricky as those Chinese finger traps where the harder you struggle to pull your fingers out of the woven tube, the more trapped you are. Not only do we sometimes discount information that runs counter to a commitment we've made, but that very information can act as catalyst for us to commit even further to the chosen course of action. That heightened investment of effort and resources leads us to become even *more* favorably inclined toward something that wasn't working out in the first place! As James Brian Quinn notes: "As a consequence, people doggedly prolong outmoded—but publicly committed—goals, rather than swallow losses and move on."

The best any of us can do is realize that there are two sides to the commitment coin. This awareness can help us strengthen the positive attributes of commitments that are related to worthy causes, and minimize the effects of the ones that are questionable at best.

Steps for Getting There

1. Once a year, at least, generate or update a list of the problems and opportunities you face. Sort through them and set priorities. Top-priority issues generally have the following characteristics: a) They are easy to solve; you might as well get on with them; b) something disastrous will happen if they aren't dealt with soon; c) they present a unique opportunity; grab it while you can; d) combinations of the above. Maybe an issue is closely related to an existing cause and can be addressed that way. Don't treat the issues list as static. The moveable part of the issues list is a powerful source of continuing renewal.
2. Decide your appropriate role in relation to the issues. Think of the management process as being issue-brokering

as much as, or more than, issue-resolving. One of the most difficult things for some people to do is relinquish the reins to others who have the time and talent to tackle a problem. Delegating an issue to the people who are best equipped to handle it frees you to do what you're being paid to do: keep your finger on the pulse of what's going on inside and outside the organization. If you don't do that well, you won't know about half of the issues that are floating around, and you won't be able to recognize the important ones when you see them.

3. Find ways to turn dreary issues into interesting causes. Some—quality, service, employee involvement—are inspiriting in themselves. Others, like cost cutting, may have to be related to some broader organizational purpose to build inspiration. Add a dash of adventure. Strive to be the best at something. Attack an issue in a way that's never been tried before. Some may be slightly outrageous with just enough risk and plenty of fun. Take the time to state the cause in a moving, nonbureaucratic way. (Read Churchill for inspiration along that line.) Use metaphor: Don't break rocks; build cathedrals.

4. Take a close look at what your company stands for. Can your staff both agree on and identify with the causes that set your overall direction? Can you? If the answer is no, what's the reason? Are people getting mixed signals? Are they disillusioned with the end product of their work? Have they become apathetic because their repeated efforts to do their best have met with opposition—implicit or explicit? If you are convinced that your causes need to be redefined or revitalized, the time to start is now.

5. Check to see if the causes you can identify are good for both your company *and* the people who work there. Lopsided causes will skew the course your company is on and jeopardize its values, not to mention its future. In such cases, neither your organization nor your people benefit. Don't tread on individual dignity. That's what happened when companies sacrificed quality for volume, and it backfired. When you have to cut costs or automate, make that a cause by building safety nets for the

people and by letting them know why it's necessary and how they can help.

6. Do some soul-searching about whether or not the causes you and your company are promoting reflect a winning attitude. Is there a chance that you are signaling a "we're only number two (or ten), so we *don't* try harder" approach to things? If your staff does not exhibit a winning attitude, what can you do to light a fire under them?

   Sometimes all it takes to shake people out of the "loser" doldrums is a well-placed question or two. Remember Petersen's "Would you want this car parked in your driveway?" question at Ford, and Schutz's inquiry about the best car Professor Porsche had ever designed. In both cases the implied message was: "If we're not already making a first-rate product, or providing first-rate service, we can be."

7. Look for adventure in business. It's always there, even though our entrenched work ethic makes it difficult to see things that way; we all tend to assume that we can't have fun and earn money at the same time. But there *is* a definite link between adventure and renewal. The adventure should be neither so foolhardy that it introduces undue risks nor so laughably timid that it is more embarrassing than inspiring.

8. Once you've identified an overriding cause you want to introduce (or resurrect), at some point you're going to have to determine whether or not your core group of managers can get behind it one hundred percent. Those who aren't on board can create an enormous energy leak, both within the group itself and among the staff they supervise. You simply can't afford to tolerate a bunch of naysayers. If your team resists, double-check the cause. If the cause still seems right, force the issue. Expect that people will get forced out from time to time, and build safety nets for them (early retirement, assistance in finding jobs) that help keep their dignity intact. Be tough only when you have to, but keep in mind that disorder at the top means chaos below.

9. Communicate extensively to create the link between causes and the commitment individual employees make to them. You can't force people to be committed; neither can you control whether or not they stay committed. The best approach is to be the source of clear, consistent, honest information. When in doubt, tell people too much. The more they know about your cause, the more they can help in ways you wouldn't have expected. The more they find they can help, the more commitment they feel. Respect people enough to be straight with them about the down side as well as the up side; that, too, strengthens commitment.

   Remember that commitment can be a trap for the wrong cause. As commitment increases, people become less willing to acknowledge that it may be inappropriate. Listen to your own "consistency tapes" and those you hear from others around you. Find different mirrors that will tell you what you or your organization is really committed to; examine the underlying moral implications. Are your de facto commitments either ignoble or the traps that will stop renewal? If so, you have a new, high priority that ought to move some of the others aside.

10. Keep reminding yourself of the fact that renewal comes about because everyone in your company—not just the managers—has had a chance to commit and contribute to it. Progress is the result of thousands of things done differently, not a few big management decisions. To build commitment, give people something they can do to act in alignment with the cause. Remember the Scottsdale story: Small individual actions add up to commitment.

11. Recognize the interrelationship of issues, causes, and commitment. Causes spearhead renewal; they identify a new vision for the future that is both noble and attainable. But the causes must be seen to be relevant to the important business issues. And it's the commitment people make to those causes that transforms them from concept to reality. Remember, a cause without committed people gets nowhere, and committed people without a

unifying cause go nowhere. The renewing companies use issues, causes, and commitment to forge a common bond among the diverse people who work for them.

12. Make sure that your causes are related to the shared values of the organization. Even more important, they must square with the dignity of the individual. Continually examine the causes and commitments that engage you, and the ones you ask of your people, to ensure their basic worth, humanity, and integrity.

CONCLUSION

Change breeds opportunity. The renewal factor is the opportunity that transforms threat into issue, issue into cause, cause into quest. The complacent manager merely presides. The renewing manager is engaged in a daily effort to fight corporate entropy, to welcome change, to uproot habits, and to use renewal to build the future.

Most of us fear change. Even when our minds say change is normal, our stomachs quiver at the prospect. But for leaders and managers today, there is no choice but to change. Every business has been profoundly affected—and some industries radically altered—by the forces of oil shocks, global competition, deregulation, takeovers, and spinoffs. Managers in the nonprofit sector have experienced comparable shocks—reduced funding, new technologies, increased demands for accountability to their constituencies. A manager must build the renewal factor into his or her organization to keep the competitive edge. No renewal ... no excellence. In fact, for many organizations, no renewal ... no future.

When Don Petersen asked Ford engineers about the kind of car they really wanted to build, he was asking them to join him in a daring act. He was daring to put an element of fun, of adventure, into the engineers' jobs. The result was a product that has propelled Ford to leadership of its industry. Renewal can be the adventure that puts the excitement back into business. Energy that was expressing itself as fear gets redirected into a revitalizing force—a commitment, a cause.

Organizations—which, after all, are merely collections of people—exist for only one purpose: to help people reach ends together that they could not achieve individually. Most leaders in renewing organizations share a belief that the organization stands in service to the individual. When the organization starts getting in the way, they change it.

As most of us know, often from bitter experience, organizations can slither out of their servile role and seize unwarranted domain. The servant becomes the suppressor. Thoreau talked about men leading lives of quiet desperation. For too many of us that statement is as true today as when he wrote it, not because the desperate person wants it that way but because he or she is trapped by society's institutions.

Dreams, not desperation, move organizations to the highest levels of performance. Our dream ought to be institutions that work for, not against, our needs. That is the hope, the power, the dream, and the challenge in renewal.

APPENDIX

Our Research

Because little practical material exists on managing change and renewal, we wanted to focus, in this book, on the process of renewal over time rather than the characteristics of excellent companies (though many of the excellent company traits are also sources of renewal). My own experiences and observations from over two decades with McKinsey & Company, the management consulting firm, would serve as background and middle distance for this research. In the foreground would be our original research on more than forty companies in the United States and Europe during 1985 and 1986.

Our approach to the research was similar to the one Tom Peters and I followed in *In Search of Excellence:* We identified organizations that are top performers in relation to their industry or field, reviewed published articles about each company, then interviewed their executives and employees to uncover what it is about their approach to renewal that is so effective.

As in our earlier search for excellence, we were not trying to come up with formulas for success. At its best and finest, management is art, not science. Just as excellence defies prescription, so does renewal. By taking a look at organizations with a great track record for managing renewal—one way or another—we hoped to identify best practices. This book is as much a handbook of ideas for the practicing executive as it is a study of the factors that help organizations renew.

Casting the Net

To begin the search we cast a broad net, covering the performance of more than five hundred companies in fifty-three industries. For industry groupings we used *Forbes* magazine's "Annual Report on American Industry." That list seemed to us the best for comparing like with like, especially since *Forbes* estimates the percentage of business each company does in its industry grouping.

Our decision to group and analyze companies by industry reflected our awareness that growth and rates of return vary among industries, depending on different factors—everything from the overall growth in a market served by an industry to the varying investment requirements needed to generate payroll or sales dollar. Just looking at the different problems facing managers in the steel industry compared to the personal computer business brings this point home.

To narrow the field we collected financial data from the preceding decade on every company on the *Forbes* list. We used the *Value Line Investment Survey* as our main information source, because it contains data on sales, returns, and stock market performance, adjusted for stock splits and dividends. Other sources go back further but are less consistent, and we decided to go with consistency.

Then we compared each company with its industry, using four financial criteria. We reasoned that a successful company is characterized by high rates of return and superior growth. These four measures:

Total return to shareholders—the appreciation in stock price plus the dividends (assuming reinvestment) over a given period—provides an objective measure of a company's performance from the shareholder's point of view.

Rate of return on capital—earnings before interest and after taxes, divided by total stockholder equity and debt—measures how productively a company puts its investment to work.

Rate of growth in total sales—the annual percentage growth in a company's total revenues—evaluates a company's ability to sustain growth.

Rate of return on sales—net income divided by total revenues—shows how well a company can control its costs and maintain its prices.

Because the goal of this research was to study organizations that have successfully managed renewal, we decided to look at two kinds of companies. First were the ones that had consistently performed well over the last ten years. Our heroic assumption was that to have done well during that tumultuous time was to have changed and renewed. Second, we wanted to include organizations that had significantly improved their performance over the last decade. Thus, for each of the four performance measures, we calculated a ten-year average and two sets of five-year averages, the latter to help smoke out examples of good companies that got better.

The first step in our selection process, then, was fairly tight, heavily quantitative. Ninety-three companies surfaced from our industry-based statistical screen. Although this financial analysis was useful in helping us narrow the field, it was not a final determinant of the companies we ultimately studied.

Beyond the Numbers

The eventual choice of companies we visited was a decidedly nonstatistical, subjective judgment call. In some industries the choice was obvious. One or two companies clearly outperformed the rest on both the ten-year averages and the five-year improvement measures.

In other cases the results of the financial screening were ambiguous. We looked beyond the summary rankings, examining in detail more performance measures for each company, reading about the companies, and seeking the opinions of knowledgeable parties: customers, suppliers, competitors, business journalists. Surveys like *Fortune* magazine's "Most Admired Companies" were helpful, although each poll had its own set of limitations and biases. We were looking for the firms that might teach us the most about managing renewal, rather than statistical winners of corporate beauty contests.

In some industries our screening had identified two or three top performers that were all deserving of being included in the research. In such cases we selected the company that seemed to provide the most interesting or striking example of renewal.

By the time we had finished this second phase of the selection process, the initial list of ninety-three organizations had been pared to about forty. We started reviewing the literature on them and making initial contact with their home offices. Frequently we knew the top people and could approach them with a phone call. In others we wrote "blind" to the chief executive, explaining our research effort and asking for the company's cooperation.

Our investment in doing on-site interviews at any one company varied from two to ten person-days. Typically, we spent a total of fifteen days doing research on each company: a couple of days gathering and reading materials before the interviews, six days interviewing, one or two days in transit, and another six days or so writing our interview notes and sharing our impressions with one another.

Once we arrived on-site at a company, our research approach followed a predictable pattern. We asked for one- to two-hour interviews with each of the company's top people. We specifically wanted to include the chief executive and chief operating officer in these interviews. Although we arrived prepared with a list of general questions about renewal, and more specific ones about the company, our interviews with individual people were informal. We introduced the renewal theme and then opened the topic for discussion, enabling the managers to choose whatever they wanted to talk about. That approach kept us from biasing the direction of the interviews in favor of our own preconceptions about the renewal process. Most of the people we interviewed were extraordinarily forthcoming.

In many cases, after the executive interviews we spent time at a plant or in the field visiting the operating level of the organization—verifying, elaborating, and sometimes contradicting what we had heard from the people at the top. During these visits, what we had heard earlier from top management came alive for us in ways that would have been impossible otherwise.

In the early phases of our fieldwork we took extensive notes, believing that a tape recorder would be too obtrusive. Besides, it didn't seem worth the time it would take later to listen to all those tapes. But after a few excursions on-site, we decided to try taping anyway. We found that most of our subjects didn't mind being taped at all, and listening to the tapes afterward enabled us to pick up on themes that we might have missed otherwise in the intensity of the "live" interview. We ended up listening to a lot of tapes.

As the fieldwork progressed, we added companies that had not emerged from the initial financial screens. For example, someone would mention that we should look at what Ford has done on quality and employee involvement. Someone else would mention Ford and rave about the way they went about the design of the Taurus/Sable. We had been looking for a good non-Chrysler example of change from the American automobile industry, anyway. So Ford went on the list of companies to contact. This flexibility served to strengthen the quality and diversity of the companies included in the research.

In addition to the American companies we studied, we included some examples from Europe, one example from Japan, and a few nonprofit organizations. We could not do the same kind of financial analysis for these organizations that we did for American companies. In the case of European companies, we picked examples on the advice of my former McKinsey colleagues. Generally, these companies met two criteria: They had renewed, like Olivetti, or they seemed to be continuously renewing, like Swissair; and they are well known internationally, therefore familiar to readers in the United States and other countries.

The Japanese company, Sanwa Bank, is one I know well. The nonprofits include Children's Television Workshop, an organization that seems always to stay fresh, and the San Francisco Symphony and the City of Scottsdale—two organizations that have made clear advances toward excellence in recent years.

In the end we followed some forty-five organizations in depth through the literature, through analysts' reports, and through our own original research. We spent six months—more hours than we want to count—on airplanes, crisscrossing the United States to visit the executive suites, plants, and field locations of thirty-four of these organizations. In between was an occasional trip to Europe. We estimate that we spent more than 1,500 person-hours in interviews and at least twice that reviewing interview notes, listening to tapes, and writing up the interviews in some detail. I'm not sure whether we should take pride in this or not, but in the end our single-spaced interview notes summed to 1,100 pages, 660,000 words.

NOTES

CHAPTER 1: RENEWAL: THE CHALLENGE

Page

5 Albert Bandura, *Social Learning Theory* (Englewood Cliffs, NJ: Prentice-Hall, 1977), p. 12.

5 *Ibid.*, p. 22.

10 "Oldest US Officer Retires," *San Francisco Chronicle*, August 15, 1986.

10 "Admiral Hopper's Farewell," *The New York Times*, August 14, 1986.

12 Peter Jenkins, "Patient Britain," *The New Republic*, December 23, 1985, p. 15.

14 Walter Wriston, *Risk and Other Four-Letter Words* (New York: Harper & Row, 1986), p. 70.

15 John W. Gardner, *Self-Renewal: The Individual and the Innovative Society*, rev. ed. (New York: W. W. Norton & Company, 1981).

16 Robert E. Ornstein, *The Psychology of Consciousness*, 2d ed. (San Diego: Harcourt Brace Jovanovich, 1977), p. 56.

17 William James, *The Principles of Psychology* (Cambridge, MA: Harvard University Press, 1983), p. 125.

18 Berkshire Hathaway, Inc., *Letters to Shareholders 1977–1984*, p. 98.

19 Boyce Rensberger, *How the World Works: A Guide to Science's Greatest Discoveries* (New York: William Morrow, 1986), p. 139.

20 John W. Gardner, *loc. cit.*, pp. xii–xiii.

20 Myron Magnet, "Restructuring Really Works," *Fortune*, March 2, 1987, p. 38.

22 Berkshire Hathaway, Inc., *1985 Annual Report to the Stockholders*, p. 3 and p. 20.

CHAPTER 2: THE INFORMED OPPORTUNISTS

Page
25 *The New Yorker,* August 4, 1986, p. 19.
27 Herbert A. Simon, *The Sciences of the Artificial* (Cambridge, MA: MIT Press, 1984), p. 63.
31 "Dan Lundberg, Oil Analyst, Dies: Forecast 1979 Gasoline Shortage," *The New York Times,* August 6, 1986, p. 24.
32 John von Neumann and Oskar Morganstern, *The Theory of Games and Economic Behavior* (Princeton, NJ: Princeton University Press, 1944).
32 Simon, *loc. cit.,* pp. 44–45.
32 Kevin McKean, "Decisions, Decisions," *Discover,* June 1985, p. 26.
40 William R. Hewlett, *Inventions of Opportunity: Matching Technology with Market Needs* (Palo Alto, CA: Hewlett-Packard Company, 1983), p. vii.
42 Ralph E. Gomory, "Technology Development," *Science,* vol. 220, May 6, 1983, p. 578.
43 Roy Rowan, *The Intuitive Manager* (Boston: Little, Brown, 1986), p. 9.
44 Harvey M. Wagner, *Principles of Operations Research with Applications to Managerial Decisions* (Englewood Cliffs, NJ: Prentice-Hall, 1969), p. 7.
44 Arthur Koestler, *The Act of Creation* (London: Hutchinson, 1964).
45 Rowan, *loc. cit.,* p. 118.
45 Willis W. Harman, "Creativity and Intuition in Business: The Unconscious Mind and Management Effectiveness," Report No. 715, Winter 1984–85 (Menlo Park, CA: SRI International, 1985), p. 10.
45 Raymond Corsini, ed., *Encyclopedia of Psychology,* vol. 2 (New York: John Wiley, 1984), pp. 252–254.
45 "Rocket Engineers Tell of Pressure for Launching," *The New York Times,* February 26, 1986, p. 17.
46 W. R. Hartson and P. C. Watson, *The Psychology of Chess* (New York: Facts on File, 1984), p. 59.
46 David Ogilvy, *Ogilvy on Advertising* (New York: Crown Publishers, 1983), p. 16.
48 Amar Bhide, "Hustle as Strategy," *Harvard Business Review,* September–October 1986, p. 59.
49 Berkshire Hathaway, Inc., *Letters to Shareholders 1977–1984,* p. 85.
50 Berkshire Hathaway, Inc., *1985 Annual Report to the Stockholders,* p. 22.
51 S. I. Hayakawa, *Language in Thought and Action,* 4th ed. (San Diego, CA: Harcourt Brace Jovanovich, 1978), p. 154.

66 Garrett Hardin, *Filters Against Folly* (New York: Viking Press, 1985), p. 210.

66 Karl E. Weick, *The Social Psychology of Organizing* (Reading, MA: Addison-Wesley, 1979), p. 2.

67 Daniel Kahneman and Amos Tversky, "The Psychology of Preferences," *Scientific American*, vol. 246, no. 1, January 1982, pp. 160–73.

68 Ronald Clark, *Einstein: The Life and Times* (New York: World Publishing, 1966), p. 6.

CHAPTER 3: DIRECTION AND EMPOWERMENT

Page
73 Edward Scharff, *Worldly Power: The Making of The Wall Street Journal* (Beaufort, SC: Beaufort Books, 1986), pp. 184–185.

73 William Styles, "Ideas Cut Procter & Gamble Costs by Millions," *Cincinnati Post*, August 23, 1983.

74 *IBM 1985 Annual Report*, p. 23.

74 "John Psarouthakis: Whipping Underdog Companies into Shape," *Business Week*, August 11, 1986, p. 74.

74 Editors of *Fortune*, *Working Smarter* (New York: Viking Press, 1982), pp. viii–ix.

77 James O'Toole, *Making America Work: Productivity and Responsibility* (New York: Continuum, 1981), pp. 69–70.

77 "High Technology: Clash of the Titans," *The Economist*, August 23, 1986, p. 4.

78 *Ibid.*

78 *Ibid.*

82 Interview with Lew Veraldi, "News from the World of Ford," February 1, 1985, p. 1.

83 *Motor Trend*, February 1986.

85 Philip Caldwell, "Cultivating Human Potential at Ford," *The Journal of Business Strategy*, Spring 1984, p. 75.

87 David L. Bradford and Allen R. Cohen, *Managing for Excellence* (New York: John Wiley & Sons, 1984), p. 28.

87 *Ibid.*, p. 27.

88 "Management by Walking Away," *Inc.*, October 1983, pp. 67–68.

92 Karl E. Weick, "Organization Design: Organizations as Self-Designing Systems," *Organizational Dynamics*, Autumn 1977, pp. 31–32.

96 James F. Fixx, *The Complete Book of Running* (New York: Random House, 1977), pp. 254–255.

100 Karl Weick, *loc. cit.*, p. 31.

102 Philip Caldwell, "Excellence—Ford's Mandate: The Lessons of Yesterday . . . the Strategy for Tomorrow," Keynote Address at the Ford Worldwide Management Meeting, Boca Raton, Florida, November 19, 1984, p. 14 and p. 10.

CHAPTER 4: FRIENDLY FACTS, CONGENIAL CONTROLS

Page

104 Milton Moskowitz, *et al.*, *Everybody's Business: The Irreverent Guide to Corporate America* (New York: Harper & Row, 1980), p. 283.

105 Geoffrey N. Smith, "The Yankee Samurai," *Forbes*, July 14, 1986, pp. 82–83.

105 *Ibid.*

107 Abraham Maslow, "A Theory of Human Motivation," *Readings in Managerial Psychology*, 3d ed., Harold J. Leavitt, *et al.*, eds. (Chicago: University of Chicago Press, 1980), pp. 5–22.

111 Lee Iacocca, *Iacocca: An Autobiography* (New York: Bantam Books, 1984), p. 154.

112 Robert J. Conrads, "It's Time to Stop Raiding IBM," *Electronic Business*, April 1, 1986, pp. 54–57.

116 Herbert Simon, *Administrative Behavior*, 3d ed. (New York: Free Press, 1976), pp. 1–19.

116 "Bill and Ebenezer," *The Economist*, April 26, 1968, p. 13.

117 Brenton R. Schlender, "Daisy Admits Guilt in Tax Case Filed by Massachusetts," *The Wall Street Journal*, October 21, 1986.

117 Letters to the Editor, *The Wall Street Journal*, November 24, 1986.

122 Robert Townsend, *Further Up the Organization* (New York: Knopf, 1984), p. 43.

123 Peter Drucker, *Managing for Results: Economic Tasks and Risk-Taking Decisions* (New York: Harper & Row, 1964).

124 Gregory Bateson, *Steps to an Ecology of Mind* (New York: Ballantine Books, 1972), p. 451.

124 *Ibid.*, p. 481.

124 Ian I. Mitroff, "Teaching Corporate America to Think about Crisis Prevention," *The Journal of Business Strategy*, Spring 1986, p. 41.

125 Sir Arthur Conan Doyle, "Silver Blaze," *The Complete Sherlock Holmes* (Garden City, NY: Doubleday, 1926), p. 347.

127 Roy Rowan, *The Intuitive Manager* (Boston: Little, Brown, 1986), p. 153.

CHAPTER 5: A DIFFERENT MIRROR

Page

137 "GM Hasn't Bought Much Peace," *Business Week,* December 15, 1986, pp. 24–27.

138 *Car and Driver,* January 1986, p. 40.

138 "The Best: Outstanding Achievements of 1986," *Business Week,* January 12, 1987, p. 123.

140 Michael Edwardes, *Back from the Brink* (London: Pan Books, 1984), p. 13.

140 Lee Iacocca, *Iacocca: An Autobiography* (New York: Bantam Books, 1984), p. 144.

140 *Ibid.,* p. 147.

142 Graham T. Allison, *Essence of Decision: Explaining the Cuban Missile Crisis* (Boston: Little, Brown, 1971).

143 Arthur Schlesinger, Jr., *The Imperial Presidency,* cited by Chris Argyris, "Single-Loop and Double-Loop Models in Research on Decision Making," *Administrative Science Quarterly,* vol. 21, September 1976, p. 366.

143 Jonathan L. Freedman, *Introductory Psychology,* 2d ed. (Reading, MA: Addison-Wesley, 1982), p. 370.

143 Elisabeth Kübler-Ross, *On Death and Dying* (New York: Macmillan, 1969), pp. 38–39.

143 Walter Laqueur, *A World of Secrets: The Uses and Limits of Intelligence* (New York: Basic Books, 1985), pp. 279–280.

144 *Ibid.,* p. 280.

144 G. C. Allen, *The British Disease,* 2d. ed. (London, England: The Institute of Economic Affairs, 1979), p. 70.

145 Irving L. Janis, "Groupthink," *Readings in Managerial Psychology,* 3d ed., Harold J. Leavitt, *et al.,* eds. (Chicago: University of Chicago Press, 1980), p. 439.

145 *Ibid.*

146 *Ibid.,* p. 442.

147 Chris Argyris, "Single-Loop and Double-Loop Models in Research on Decision Making," *Administrative Science Quarterly,* vol. 21, September 1976, pp. 363–377.

148 Chris Argyris, "How Learning and Reasoning Processes Affect Organizational Change," in Paul S. Goodman and Associates, *Change in Organizations* (San Francisco: Jossey-Bass, 1982), pp. 47–86.

153 David D. Connell and Edward L. Palmer, "Sesame Street—A Case Study," Seminar Presentation, Leicester, England, University of Leicester, December 19, 1970, p. 19.

154 *Fortune,* January 19, 1987, p. 35.

156 Michael E. Porter, *Competitive Advantage: Creating and Sustaining Superior Performance* (New York: Free Press, 1985), p. xvi.

174 Albert O. Hirschman, *Exit, Voice and Loyalty: Responses to Decline in Firms, Organizations, and States* (Cambridge, MA: Harvard University Press, 1970).

CHAPTER 6: TEAMWORK, TRUST, POLITICS, AND POWER

Page

179 *The Wall Street Journal*, January 20, 1987.

182 Lowell Cohn, "Is Will Really Such a Thrill?" *San Francisco Chronicle*, September 11, 1986, p. 69.

189 Martin Luther King, Jr., speech delivered on February 4, 1968, at Ebenezer Baptist Church, Atlanta, Georgia.

195 Frank J. Burge, "Why IBM Wins," *Electronic Engineering Times*, April 14, 1986, p. 26.

195 Alfie Kohn, "How to Succeed Without Even Vying," *Psychology Today*, September 1986, p. 24.

196 *Ibid.*

196 *Ibid.*

196 *Ibid.*, pp. 27–28.

196 Jeffrey Z. Rubin, "Psychological Traps," *Psychology Today*, March 1981, p. 59.

200 Graham T. Allison, *Essence of Decision: Explaining the Cuban Missile Crisis* (Boston: Little, Brown, 1971), p. 145.

202 Count Carlo Sforza, *The Living Thoughts of Machiavelli* (Westport, CT: Greenwood Press, 1940), p. 89.

203 James MacGregor Burns, *Leadership* (New York: Harper Torch books, 1978), p. 258.

203 *Ibid.*, p. 425.

203 *Ibid.*, p. 426.

204 *Ibid.*, pp. 426–427

207 Roger Fisher and William Ury, *Getting to Yes* (Harmondsworth, Middlesex: Penguin Books, 1981).

CHAPTER 7: STABILITY IN MOTION

Page

213 John W. Gardner, *Self-Renewal: The Individual and the Innovative Society*, rev. ed. (New York: W.W. Norton, 1981), p. 7.

217 Peter Drucker, *The Frontiers of Management* (New York: Dutton, 1986), p. 265.

222 Harold J. Leavitt, *Corporate Pathfinders* (Homewood, IL: Dow Jones-Irwin, 1986), pp. 10–11.

223 *Ibid.,* p. 126.
225 Karl E. Weick, "Small Wins: Redefining the Scale of Social Problems," *American Psychologist,* January 1984, p. 40.
225 *Ibid.*
228 *Ibid.,* p. 42.
230 Harrison Kinney, "A Matter of Balance," *Think,* vol. 52, no. 2, 1986, p. 6.
231 *Ibid.,* p. 5.
241 John W. Gardner, *loc. cit.,* 2d ed. (New York: W.W. Norton, 1981), p. 5.

CHAPTER 8: ATTITUDES AND ATTENTION

Page
246 John W. Gardner, *Self-Renewal: The Individual and the Innovative Society* (New York: W.W. Norton, 1981), p. xiii and p. 105.
249 Michael Novak, *The American Vision: An Essay on the Future of Democratic Capitalism* (Washington, D.C.: American Enterprise Institute for Public Policy Research, 1978), pp. 10–11.
249 *Ibid.,* p. 12.
252 Fritz J. Rothlisberger and William J. Dickson, *Management and the Worker: An Account of a Research Program Conducted by the Western Electric Company, Hawthorne Works, Chicago* (Cambridge, MA: Harvard University Press, 1967).
252 Jeffrey Pfeffer, "Management as Symbolic Action: The Creation and Maintenance of Organizational Paradigms," *Research in Organizational Behavior,* vol. 3, 1981, p. 35.
262 Robert Rosenthal and Lenore Jacobson, *Pygmalion in the Classroom* (New York: Holt, Rinehart & Winston, 1968).
262 Robert K. Merton, "The Self-fulfilling Prophecy," *Antioch Review,* vol. 8, 1948, pp. 193–210.
262 Robert Rosenthal, "The Pygmalion Effect," *Psychology Today,* September 1973, p. 58.
263 *Ibid.*
263 *Ibid.,* p. 62.
263 Rom J. Markin and Charles M. Lillis, "Sales Managers Get What They Expect," *Business Horizons,* June 1975, p. 54.
266 Robert Sobel, *IBM vs. Japan: The Struggle for the Future* (Briarcliff Manor, NY: Stein and Day, 1986), pp. 86–87.
267 Thomas J. Peters and Robert H. Waterman, Jr., *In Search of Excellence: Lessons from America's Best-Run Companies* (New York: Harper & Row, 1982), p. 245.

268 Richard I. Kirkland, Jr., "Pilgrims' Profits at Nucor," *Fortune,* April 6, 1981. p. 44.

269 Joanne Martin, *et al.,* "The Uniqueness Paradox in Organizational Stories," *Administrative Science Quarterly,* vol. 28, September 1983, pp. 438–453.

271 Edward E. Scharff, *Worldly Power: The Making of The Wall Street Journal* (Beaufort, S. C.: Beaufort Books, 1986), p. 156.

271 Lamar Alexander, *Steps Along the Way: A Governor's Scrapbook* (Nashville: Thomas Nelson, 1986), p. 108.

273 Warren Bennis and Burt Nanus, *Leaders* (New York: Harper & Row, 1985), p. 69.

CHAPTER 9: CAUSES AND COMMITMENT

Page

276 Michael D. Cohen, James G. March, and Johan P. Olsen, "A Garbage Can Model of Organizational Choice," *Administrative Science Quarterly,* vol. 17, March 1972, pp. 1–25.

276 Karl E. Weick, *The Social Psychology of Organizing,* 2d ed. (Reading, MA: Addison-Wesley, 1979), pp. 194–204.

276 Viktor Frankl, *Man's Search for Meaning,* 3d ed. (New York: Simon & Schuster, 1984).

286 James Brian Quinn and Christopher E. Gagnon, "Will Services Follow Manufacturing into Decline?" *Harvard Business Review,* November–December 1986, pp. 95–103.

289 Erich Fromm, *Man for Himself: An Inquiry into the Psychology of Ethics* (Greenwich, CT: Fawcett Publications, 1947), p. 58.

294 Robert N. Bellah, *et al.,* *Habits of the Heart: Individualism and Commitment in American Life* (New York: Harper & Row, 1985), pp. 150–151.

295 *Ibid.,* p. 145.

295 James Brian Quinn, "Strategic Goals: Process and Politics," *Sloan Management Review,* Fall 1977, p. 26.

295 Barry M. Staw and Gerald R. Salancik, *New Directions in Organizational Behavior* (Chicago: St. Clair Press, 1977), p. 69.

304 Irving L. Janis and Leon Mann, *Decision Making* (New York: Free Press, 1977), p. 287.

304 Jeffrey Pfeffer, *Power in Organizations* (Boston: Pitman, 1981), p. 292.

305 Robert B. Cialdini, *Influence: The New Psychology of Modern Persuasion* (New York: Morrow Quill, 1984), pp. 66–114.

305 *Ibid.,* p. 80.

306 James Brian Quinn, *loc. cit.,* p. 23.

INDEX

Accounting systems, 122–23
Achievement, and competition,
   196–97
Acquisitions and mergers, 130–32
Administrative Behavior (Simon),
   116
Adventure, 289–93, 308
Airline industry, deregulation, 73
Akers, John (IBM), 10, 31, 48, 49,
   51–52, 54, 140, 154, 159,
   181–82, 205, 216, 248, 280
Alcoholics Anonymous (AA), 228
Alexander, Lamar, 206, 271
Allen, G.C., 144
Allen, Jim (GE), 185–86
Allison, Graham, 142, 199–200
American Broadcasting Companies
   (ABC), 50
American Express, 205, 243–44
American Medical Association
   (AMA), 80
American Telephone & Telegraph
   (AT&T), 18–19, 205
American Vision, The (Novak), 249
Anderson, Larry (Super Valu), 267
Anosognosia, 143
Answer Center (GE), 168–69
Apple computer, 218
Argyris, Chris, 147–48
Armour, Larry (Dow Jones), 170
Armstrong, Louis, 20
Art of Japanese Management, The
   (Athos and Pascale), *56n*

Athos, Tony, 19, *56n*, 69, 116
Atlantic Richfield, 34
Attention
   and measurement systems,
      255–61, 274
   and productivity, 251–56
   through symbolism, 265–71, 275
   to quality, 257–61, 263–65
   to R & D, 252–54
   to workers, 252–65, 272
Attitudes
   toward controls, 132
   optimism, 244–51
   and positive expectations, 11,
      261–65, 272
   see also Attention
Automation, 76, 250
Automobile industry, 81, 138–39
   see also names of specific
      companies and cars
Autonomy, directed, 75–80, 86–94
Aviall, 33–34
Aycock, Dave (Nucor), 181

Back From the Brink (Edwardes),
   140
Bandura, Albert, 4–5
Bankers Trust Company, 83–84,
   268
Banking industry
   competitive analysis, 155
   control systems, 131–32
   deregulation, 7–8, 14, 25, 37, 83

Banking industry *(continued)*
  outside U.S., 88–90
  see also names of specific banks
    and institutions
Bateson, Gregory, 124
Behavior modification, 4–5
Bell System. *See* American Tele-
  phone & Telegraph
Bennett, Mary (Humana), 291
Bennis, Warren, 273
Berkshire Hathaway, 22*n*, 49–50
Berra, Yogi, 39
Best of the Breed (IBM), 153–54,
  158–60
Best of Class (Ford), 156–58
Bhide, Amar, 48
Blackburn, Charlie (Diamond
  Shamrock Exploration), 28,
  29
Blair Marketing, John, Inc., 38–39
Blau, Peter, 195
Board of directors, 171–72
Bobnar, Joe (Ford), 86, 191
Boker knife, 163
Boundaries. *See* Autonomy, directed
Bowers, Dick (City of Scottsdale),
  300, 302, 303
"Bowery El effect," 16–17
Bradford, David, 87
Brain hemispheres, 43–44, 69
Breckenridge, Bruce (Morgan), 197,
  198
Briggs, Mary (IBM), 251
British Airways, 171
British Disease, The (Allen), 144
British Leyland Ltd., 140, 185*n*,
  279, 283
Britt, David (CTW), 155–16, 133
Brubaker, Terry (James River),
  108–109, 145–46
Brunswick Corp., 3, 109–10, 117,
  144, 288
BSN (French consumer goods
  company), 46–47
Buchanan, Peter (First Boston), 182,
  242–43
Buffet, Warren E. (Berkshire
  Hathaway), 18, 22, 49–50
Bullitt, Mrs. Stimson (King
  Broadcasting), 206
Bureaucracy-busting, 10, 216–20,
  237, 247
Burge, Frank J., 194

Burke, Dick (GE), 284–85
Burns, James MacGregor, 203–204
Burns, Tony (Ryder), 33, 104,
  221–22
Business Week (publication), 74,
  138

Caldwell, Philip (Ford), 85, 102,
  180, 203, 222
Capability building, 60–62
Capital Cities Communications, 50
Carnegie Foundation, 151
Cary, Frank (IBM), 48
Cassady, Ken (Union president,
  GE Appliance Park), 185
Causes, 11–12, 276–93, 306–10
  and adventure, 289–93, 308
  breaking down we/they barriers
    as, 281
  changing, 282–89
  commitment to, 293–306, 309
  cost reduction as, 288
  customer as, 280–81, 289
  individual and, 276–78
  issues and, 278–82, 309–10
  meaningful work and, 276–78,
    285
  motivating, 289
  and planning, 61
  quality as, 278–79, 285–86, 289
  service as, 286, 289
  technology as, 288
  volume as, 283–85
  winning attitude as, 281, 287,
    308
  See also Commitment
CEOs, 171–72, 179–83
  see also specific names
Challenger (space shuttle), 45
Change, 20, 213–41
  balance and, 214
  bureaucracy-busting, 216–20, 237
  employment security and, 228–36,
    240
  in leadership, 233–36, 240
  as norm, 214–16
  resistance to, 12–16
  tiny steps toward, 225–28,
    239–40
  values shared and, 220–25, 238,
    239
Chantiers Beneteau (French
  Shipbuilder), 3–4

Charvat, John (Zebco), 296, 297, 298
Chatterjee, P.C. (McKinsey), 178
Cherry, Wendell (Humana), 35, 255, 291
Chief executive officers. *See* CEOs; specific names
Children's Television Workshop (CTW), 92, 115–16, 135, 283
see also Sesame Street
Chrysler Corp., 111, 140
Cialdini, Robert, 305
Citicorp, 30, 33, 55–56, 120–21, 122, 127–28, 155, 179, 193, 211, 271, 288
change at, 215–16
integrity at, 198–99
job performance at, 233
value system at, 224
Club Med, 11, 169, 232
Cognitive dissonance, 301
Cohen, Michael, 276
Cohn, Lowell, 182
Colby, William, 137
Colombo factor, 44, 68
Commitment, 11–12, 293–310
and choice, 299
cognitive dissonance and, 301
communication and, 296–97, 309
developing, 301–303
freedom and, 294–95
individual, 278, 293
meaningful work and, 276–78, 285, 290
and planning, 61
traps, 304–306, 309
Communication
commitment and, 296–97, 309
of the facts, 133
listening to, 137–38
strategic planning and, 50–55, 60
for teamwork, 208–209
with work force, 189
Competitive advantage, sustainable, 60
Competitiveness
and achievement, 196–97
vs. cooperation, 195–97
within work force, 195–97
Competitors, business, 153–60
Connolly, J. Wray (Heinz), 234, 235

Conrads, Bob (McKinsey), 112
Conrail, 17
Consultants, 170, 210, 239
Contention system, 54–55
Controls, 103–135
comparison, use for 124–26, 135
congenial, 107–10, 119–21
cost, 104–107, 109–10
feedforward, 126–28
friendly facts, 105–107
good use of, 7–8
imperative, 130–32
lack of, 116–19
overhead, 104–107, 109–10
and planning, 61–62
quality, 108–109
in service sector, 119–21
Total Quality Control (TQC) program, 257–61, 274
for turnarounds, 111–16
Cooley, Richard (Wells Fargo), 47
Cooney, Joan Ganz (CTW), 150–53
Cooper, Howard (Steelcase), 147
Cooperation, 195–97
Coors, Bill (Coors beer), 149
Corddry, Paul (Heinz), 38, 162, 234, 235, 253–54
Cost
control, 21, 104–107, 132
reduction, 288
Crisis
and competition, 154–60
groupthink and, 145–47
heading off, 153
leadership change from, 233–36
management isolation and, 140–44
new approach resulting from, 136–40
reality and, 140–44
anticipating the "what-if" analyses, 61
see also Turnarounds
Crocker, Jack (Super Valu), 215
Crocker Bank, 6, 25, 36–37
Crump, Barry (IBM), 251
CTW. *See* Children's Television Workshop
Culture. *See* Values, shared
Cummins Engine, 104–107, 144, 176
Curiosity, 137
Customer feedback, 139, 149, 150–53

Daisy Systems Corp., 117
Dana Corp., 9, 10, 11–12, 95–96,
   160, 192, 211, 229, 235,
   288
Dannon (BSN), 46–47
Data. *See* Facts
Davidow, Bill, 129, 130
Davis, Murray, 124
Davis, Tom (City of Scottsdale),
   300, 301
Dawson, Jim (Zebco), 296, 297
De Benedetti, Carlo (Olivetti), 11,
   111–12, 134, 156, 232, 243,
   245–46, 267, 272
de Gaulle, Charles, 127
Dekko, Tom (Super Valu), 79
Delayering (corporate staff), 95–96
Delta Airlines, 73
Demerit system, 231
Deming, W. Edwards, 74–75, 99,
   170
Deming Award, 74
Denial, 143–44
Deregulation
   and airlines, 14, 73
   and banks, 7–8, 14, 25, 37, 83
   and telecommunications, 14,
   18–19
   and trucking, 14
Dickson, William, 252
Digital Equipment Corp., 31, 56,
   246–48
Directed autonomy. *See* Autonomy,
   directed
Dissent, 54–55
Dissonance reduction, 301
Divisiveness. *See* We/they split
Double-loop learning, 147–50, 174,
   247
Dow Jones, 52, 72–73, 170, 270
   employee involvement at, 72–73
   reader response surveys at,
   168–70
Doyle, Arthur Conan, 125
Doyle, John (Hewlett-Packard),
   126, 228
Drews, Rudy (McKesson), 113
Drexel Burnham Lambert, 131
Dreyer's Grand Ice Cream Co.,
   25–26, 43
Drohan, Tom (McKesson), 114
Drucker, Peter, 123, 170, 217, 255,
   262n

Drum major instinct, 189–90, 287
Duerr, Fred (Kona Villlage), 1, 167
Dunn, Bill (Dow Jones), 129–30
Durbrow, Philip (Landor Associates),
   170–71, 175

Economist, The (publication),
   77–78, 116
Edwardes, Sir Michael, 140, 185n
Egan, John (Jaguar), 279, 283, 286
EG&G, 49, 268
Einstein, Albert, 68
Electric Company (tv show), 153
Electronic Business (publication),
   112
Electronic Engineering Times
   (publication), 194
Electronic industry, change in,
   226–27
Electronic spreadsheet, 129–30, 135
Elliott, J.H., 12–13
Emerson, Ralph Waldo, 179, 254
Employee
   attention to, 252–65
   empowerment, 72–75, 84–86
   individual renewal, 96–98
   job security, 228–33, 248–51
   listening to, 160–66
Employee Involvement (EI) 84–86
Employee stock ownership plan
   (ESOP), 277n
Empowerment, 72–75, 84–86
Enders, Bruce (GE), 149, 155
Entropy, 19
Entry Systems Division (IBM),
   218–19
Essence of Decision (Allison), 142,
   199–200
Estridge, Don (IBM), 218–19
Exit, Voice and Loyalty (Hirschman),
   174
Expectations, 262
Experience, value of, 69

Fact base, 122–24
   comparisons, 124–26, 135
   friendly facts, 105–107
   See also Information
Facilitators, 208n
Fact pack, 53, 133
Falotti, Pier-Carlo (Digital
   Equipment), 246
Feedforward, 126–28, 130

Fellows programs, 219, 244, 252–54
Ferris, John (Super Valu), 79
Financial strategy, 35
Fireman's Fund Insurance Co., 204, 243
First Boston Corp., 3, 155, 182, 242–43
First Law of Ecology (Hardin), 66
Fischer, Jim (Hewlett-Packard), 259
Flynn, George (Dow Jones), 73
Fontaine, Ed (Newmont Mining), 35
Fontanet, Xavier (Chantiers Beneteau), 3–4
Foodways National, 126
Forbes (publication), 314
Ford Motor Co., 2, 3, 11, 81–82, 83n, 100, 140, 285, 288
    attitude shift at, 188–89
    competitor analysis at, 157–58
    employee involvement program, 85–86, 91
    management control at, 86–87
    symbolism at, 270
    top-level teamwork at, 180–81
    turnaround, 138–40, 170, 311
    vision at, 222–24
Forecasting, 32
    "what-if" analyses, 58, 61, 128–30, 135
Foreign trade, 13–14
Foremost Dairies, 113
Fortune (publication), 18, 20, 74, 101, 154, 315
Frankl, Viktor, 276–77
Fraser, Scott, 305
Freedman, Jonathan, 143, 305
Freedman, Louis, 151
Fret factor, 153–54
Fromm, Erich, 289
Fry, Art (3M), 26–27
FUD (fear, uncertainty, and doubt) factor, 248
Further Up the Organization (Townsend), 122–23

Gagliardi (frozen-food co.), 38
Game theory, 32
Gardner, John, 15, 20, 213, 241, 246, 282
GE Answer Center, 168–69
Geneen, Harold (ITT), 108

General Electric (GE), 2–3, 11, 108, 149, 155, 179, 220, 278, 290
    Answer Center, 168–69
    customer relations/suggestions, 167–69
    Pygmalion effect at, 263–65
    teamwork at, 184–88
    trust at, 194
    volume vs. quality at, 284–85
General Motors (GM), 137–38, 201n
    "doubling" at, 76–77
"Gin rummy management," 22
Gomory, Ralph (IBM), 42, 153, 225–27
Gookin, Burt (Heinz), 234
Greenmail tactics, 21
Gresham's Law, 49
Groupthink, 145–47
Gubert, Walter (Morgan), 193

Habits
    breaking, 8, 9–10, 55
    in organizations, 142
    trap of, 16–19, 142–43
Habits of the Heart (Bellah, *et al*), 293
Habituation, 16
Haire, Mason, 255
Hardin, Garrett, 66
Harlan, Neil (McKesson), 113–14
Harman, Willis, 45
Hartson, William, 46
Hawthorne effect, 251–52
Hayakawa, S.I., 51
Hazen, Paul (Wells Fargo), 37
Health care industry, 34–35, 80, 255–56, 291–93
Heinz
    acquisitions by, 37–38
    management changes at, 234–35
    see also Ore-Ida
Helmreich, Robert, 196
Henderson, Jim (Cummins Engine), 106
Hendricks, Maureen (Morgan), 146, 190
Herman Miller (co.), 75
Herrick, Gerry (Ore-Ida), 234, 235
Hewlett, Bill (Hewlett-Packard), 40, 267
Hewlett-Packard (HP)
    diversification at, 14, 66, 190

Hewlett-Packard (HP) (continued)
    employee policy at, 10, 229, 232, 267, 285
    inventions, 40
    quality program at, 257–61, 274
    skill building at, 56
    TQC program, 257–61, 274
Hierarchy of needs, 107–108
Hirschman, Albert O., 174
Hoffman, Gene (Super Valu), 215
"Holding-company syndrome," 140
Holtz, Lou, 244–45, 272
Hopper, Grace (retired Navy Rear-Admiral), 10
Hospitals. See Health care industry
Howard, Merrell & Partners, 163
Huber, Dick (Citicorp), 31, 155, 177, 178, 215–16, 271
Humana Corp., 2, 34–35, 163–64, 170, 255–56, 291–93, 297
Humor, 174–75

Iacocca, Lee, 111, 134, 140, 158, 203
Iacocca: An Autobiography (Iacocca), 111
Independent Business Unit (IBU), 66, 218–19
Imitative learning, 4–5
Implementation (parallel), 80–86
Individual renewal, 95–98
Infighting, 211
Influence (Cialdini), 305
Information
    and communication, 50–55
    forecasting and, 30–35
    innovation and, 40–43
    intuition and, 43–47, 69
    keeping up with, 36–40
    opportunity and, 49–50, 60
    for strategy, 24–30, 39, 47–48, 122
Informed opportunism
    through acquisition, 25–26, 33–34, 36–39
    definition of, 6, 28
    and exploration, 28–29
    and innovation, 40–43
    and market research, 29–30
    and strategic planning, 36–40, 64–65
Innovation, 40–43, 190–91
In Search of Excellence (Peters and Waterman), 28n, 34, 108, 267, 313
    7-S framework in, 56–58
Integrity, 193, 198–99, 202, 211
International Business Machines (IBM), 8, 16, 31, 179, 194, 209, 211, 220
    bureaucracy-busting at, 216–17, 218–20
    competitor analysis, 158–60
    contention system at, 54–55
    diversification at, 56, 66
    employee contributions at, 73–74, 99–100
    employment policy at, 229–31, 248–49, 250–51
    incrementalism at, 225–27
    Fortune survey rankings, 154
    fret factor at, 153–54
    internal management shifts in, 232–33
    issues at, 280, 285
    Lexington (Ky.) plant, 249–50
    optimism at, 248–49
    quality at, 289–90
    research at, 42
    skill building at, 56
    strategic planning at, 48, 51, 65
    top-level teamwork at, 181
    "what if?" analyses at, 128–30
    white shirt symbol at, 266
Intuition, 43–47, 69
Intuitive Manager, The (Rowan), 127
Inventions of Opportunity (Hewlett), 40
Isolation, management, 140–44, 149, 175
Issues, 278–82, 309–10
It All Depends, 184n
Iverson, Ken (Nucor), 125–26, 134, 170, 181, 268

Jacobson, Lenore, 261, 263
Jaguar (car), 279, 283, 284, 285, 286
James, William, 17–18
James River (co.), 10, 21, 69, 108–109, 145–46, 173, 288
Janis, Irving, 145, 146, 304
Japan
    banking industry in, 88–90
    bureaucracy-busting in, 217–18

Japan *(continued)*
  cost-cutting in U.S., 104–105, 107
  Hewlett-Packard venture, 257–61
  outside cultures' influence on, 144*n*
  productivity in, 74–75
  vs. American workers, 13, 78
Jewkes, John, 41
Job rotation, 190
Jobs, Steven (Apple), 220*n*, 226
Johnson & Johnson, 190
Jones, David (Humana), 8, 35, 164, 255, 291
Jordan, Dick (Mercury Marine), 109–10, 117
Junk bonds, 131
Juran, Joseph M., 74–75, 99, 170

Kahneman, Daniel, 32, 67
Kelley, Don (GE), 11, 194, 263–65
Kennedy, Donald, 174
Kennedy, John F., 143, 145
Kilgore, Barney (Dow Jones), 73, 270–71
King, Martin Luther, Jr., 189–90, 287
King Broadcasting, 206
Kluth, Dietmar (Ore-Ida), 162
Kodachrome, 41
Koestler, Arthur, 44–45
Kohn, Alfie, 195, 196
Kona Village, 1, 167
Krowe, Allen (IBM), 140–41, 159, 266, 266*n*
Krumm, Daniel (Maytag), 132, 220
Kübler-Ross, Elisabeth, 143
Kuehler, Jack (IBM), 219–20, 220*n*, 289

Labor relations, 185, 187, 189–90
Land, Edwin, 45
Landor Associates, 170–71
Language in Thought and Action (Hayakawa), 51
Laqueur, Walter, 143–44
Lassetter, Ted (IBM), 250
Leadership
  commitment of, 299–300
  and change, 214–16
  changing, 233–36
  effective, 204–207
  pathfinding, 222–25

  transactional/transforming, 203–204
  see also CEOs; Management
Leadership (Burns), 203–204
learning
  single- and double-loop, 147–50, 174, 247
  types of, 4–5, 43–44, 69
Learson, Vincent (IBM), 140
Leavitt, Hal, 222, 223
Lee, Will (*Sesame Street*), 92–93
Lefton, Robert (Psychological Associates), 179
Lindsay, Robert V. (Morgan), 190–91
Liptak, Tom (IBM), 54–55, 159–60, 216–17, 233
Listening
  Best of Breed (IBM), 153–54, 158–60
  Best of Class (Ford), 156–58
  to board of directors, 171–72
  to competitors, 153–60, 162, 166, 175
  to consultants, 170
  to customers, 139, 149, 150–53, 163–69
  to dealers, 164–65
  to design firms, 170–71
  to employees, 160–67
  to new ideas, 150–53
  techniques, 160–76
  to technology, 170
Long-range planning. *See* Strategic planning
Loops, single- and double-, 147–50, 174, 247
Louisville General Hospital, 291–93
Lundberg, Dan, 31

MacAllister, Jack (US West), 18–19, 96–98, 102, 146, 205
Machiavelli, Niccolo, 202
Madden, Dick (Potlatch), 91, 94, 101, 172, 217, 227–28, 232
Maisonrouge, Jacques (IBM), 154
Malozemoff, Plato (Newmont Mining), 35
Management, 71–101
  arrogance of, 284–85
  "big brain" school of, 84
  "gin rummy," 22
  isolation of top, 140–44

Management (continued)
  replacement of, 232–36
  types of, 7, 22–23
  see also Leadership
Managing for Results (Drucker),
  123
Man's Search for Meaning (Frankl),
  276
March, James, 276
Market research
  competitors' products as form of,
    155–56, 162
  customers' views in, 163, 166–69,
    170
  focus groups, 139
Marriott, Bill, 176
Martin, Jack (Dana Corp.), 235
Martin, Joanne, 269
Maslow, Abraham, 107–108, 134
Matrix organization, 184–85
Mayo, Elton, 252
Maytag, 7, 8, 10, 78, 100, 146,
    189, 220, 229, 285
  employee involvement at, 189
  listening channels, 165–67
McCormick, Bill (Fireman's Fund),
    204, 205–206, 243–44, 272
McKesson Corp., 80, 112–14
McKinsey & Co., 112, 122, 253,
    313
McPherson, Rene (Dana Corp.), 235
Meaning, need for, 276–77, 290
Measurement systems, 255–61, 274
Measurex, 228
Mellinger, John (Maytag), 166
Melville Co., 262n
Mercury Sable (car), 138–40
Mercury Marine, 109–10
Mergers. See Acquisitions and
    mergers; specific co. names
Merlotti, Frank (Steelcase), 161,
    165, 180, 230, 231
Merrell, Mac (Howard, Merrell &
    Partners), 163
Merton, Robert, 262
Midland Bank, 37
Milken, Mike (Drexel Burnham
    Lambert), 131
Miller, J. Irwin (Cummins Engine),
    104, 105
Milliken and Co., 121
Minnesota Mining & Manufactur-
    ing. See 3M

Misawa, Chiyoshi (Misawa Homes),
    217
Mitchell, Gerry (Dana Corp.), 50,
    95, 160–61, 192
Mitroff, Ian, 124
Mogensen, Allan H., 74, 75, 99
Morcott, Woody (Dana Corp.), 95,
    192
Moret, Marc (Sandoz), 236
J.P. Morgan and Company, 7–8,
    10, 18, 55, 120, 134, 146,
    155, 174, 179, 190, 233, 248
  issues at, 279–80
  teamwork at, 197–98
  trust at, 192–94, 211
Morgenstern, Oskar, 32
Morison, Bill (McKesson), 113
Morton Thiokol, 45
Moskowitz, Milton, 104
Motivation and Personality
    (Maslow), 107–108
Moveable issues, 278–82
Müller, Alex, 226n
Multifactor productivity, 78

Nanus, Burt, 273
Needs hierarchy, 107–108
Negotiation, 207, 210
Networking, 209
Newhouse, Sy (Newhouse
    Publishing), 266–67
Newmont Mining, 35
New Yorker, The (publication), 25
NIH (not invented here) factor, 81
No-layoff policies, 228–33
Nomura Securities, 217
Nonprofit organizations, 201
Novak, Michael, 249
Nucor Corp., 2, 10, 78, 95–96,
    125–26, 134, 170, 181, 268,
    288
  no-layoff policy, 229
Nunn, Ralph (Maytag), 146, 166

Ogilvy, David, 46
Ohmae, Kenichi (McKinsey), 217
O'Keefe, Bernard (EG&G), 49, 65,
    165, 268–69
Oliver, Barney (Hewlett-Packard),
    40
Olivetti Corp., 11, 111–12, 156,
    232, 243, 245–46, 262
Opel, John (IBM), 48, 233

Opportunity generation, 49–50
  and research, 42–43, 68–69
Ore-Ida, 10, 38, 69, 126, 162, 170,
  219
  Fellows program, 244, 252–54
  management changes at, 234–35
O'Reilly, Tony (Heinz), 38
Organization skill-building, 55–58
O'Toole, James, 76

Palmer, Dr. Edward (CTW), 151
Pascale, Richard, 56*n*, 84
Pathfinding, 222–25
Patterns of Winning and Losing
  (Peters), 225*n*
PC (personal computer), 129,
  218–19
Pearson, Andy (PepsiCo), 29, 90,
  101, 155–56, 157, 278
Pedersen, Bob (Heinz), 234
Pederson, Roy (City of Scottsdale),
  298–99, 300, 303
PepsiCo, 155–56
Perot, H. Ross., 43, 137–38, 201*n*,
  282
Persuasion, 209
Peters, Tom, 28*n*, 56*n*, 255*n*, 313
Petersen, Don (Ford), 139, 180,
  203, 222–24, 238, 308, 311
Petso, Richard J., 117
Pew, Bob (Steelcase), 161, 180,
  214–15
Pfeffer, Jeffrey, 252, 304
"Phenomenon-limited repertoires,"
  142
Philip, Peter (Newmont Mining), 68
Phillips, Lynn (Stanford), 30, 31
Phillips, Warren (Dow Jones), 68,
  169, 220
Phypers, Dean (IBM), 129
Planning
  and communication, 50–55, 60
  control and, 61–62
  crisis points, 61
  defining, 34, 57, 58–59
  implementation of, 64–70
  issues in, 61
  problems with, 31–32
  purposes of, 58–59
  strategy formulation, 32, 34, 35,
    50–55
Poling, Harold "Red" (Ford), 180,
  223

Politics, 199–207
  in nonprofit organizations, 201
  positive, 203–207
Porsche, 6, 283, 287–88, 290–91
Porsche, Prof. Ferdinand, 287, 308
Porter, Michael, 156–57
Potlatch Corp., 91, 172, 227–28,
  232, 288
Powell, Ann (Humana), 291, 292
Powers, J.D. (Company), 285–86
Pragmatism, 249
Precision Steel, 22*n*
Preston, Lew (Morgan), 18, 198
Pribram, Karl, 16, 127
Pricing, 125, 187
Prince, The (Machiavelli), 202
Prince tennis rackets, 29–30
Priorities. *See* Moveable issues
Probability
  use of, 67
  determining, 32–33
  and strategy, 35
Proctor & Gamble, 73, 99
Productivity, 77–78, 252
"Profit-centeritis," 197
Psarouthakis, John, 74
Psychological Associates, 179
"Psychology of Preferences, The"
  (Kahneman and Tversky),
  67*n*
"Psychology of Thinking, The"
  (Simon), 27
Puckett, Bernard (IBM), 49, 52–53,
  280
Pulp and paper industry, 227–28
Pygmalion effect, 11, 261–65
Pygmalion in the Classroom
  (Rosenthal and Jacobson),
  261– 63

Quad/Graphics, 38–39, 141,
  161–62, 194, 267, 288
Quadracci, Harry (Quad/Graphics),
  10, 38–39, 87–88, 141,
  161–62, 180, 194, 267
Quality
  as cause, 274, 279, 285–86
  employee contribution to, 72
  improvement, 264–65
  recommitment to, 11, 285–86,
    289–90
  reputation for, 220
  in service industries, 286

Quality (continued)
    TQC program, 257–61, 274
    volume vs., 284–85
Quinn, James Brian, 286, 306

Random events. See Stochastic
    shocks
Reed, John (Citicorp), 288
Reichardt, Carl (Wells Fargo), 25,
    36–37, 47, 58, 118–19, 124,
    297
Reichert, Jack (Brunswick),
    109–10
Rensberger, Boyce, 19
Repression. see Denial
Research, importance of, 42–43,
    68–69
"Revolving-door capitalists," 22
Rhind, Ridley (Ampex), 114
Riboud, Antoine (BSN), 47
Risk aversion, 28n
Risk taking, 289–90
Risk, John (Ford), 82–83, 158
Robotics, 192
Roethlisberger, Fritz, 252
Rogers, Art (Morgan), 192–93
Rogers, Gary (Dreyers' Grand Ice
    Cream), 26, 43, 45
Rosenthal, Robert, 261, 262–63
Ross, Dick (Ford), 86, 188–89
Roti Roti, Jim (UAW local), 83n
Rowan, Roy, 127
Ruffle, Jack (Morgan), 120, 134,
    191, 197, 198, 248
Ryder System Inc., 107, 170
    acquisition strategy, 33–34, 131
    change at, 221–22
    financial strategy, 103–104

Sable (car), 138–40
Saito, Ken (YHP), 257
Salancik, Gerald, 295
Sanawa Bank, 88–90
Sandoz (Swiss drug co.), 236
San Francisco Fine Arts Museum,
    53–54, 297
San Francisco Symphony, 12,
    114–15, 130, 135, 281–82
Savings and loan industry, 14, 132
Sayer, Duane (Steelcase), 231
Schacht, Henry (Cummins Engine
    Co.), 43, 104, 105, 106, 107
Scharff, Ed, 73

Schipke, Roger (GE), 3, 108,
    167–68, 184–86, 186n, 202,
    203, 205, 209, 263, 285, 290
Schlesinger, Arthur, Jr., 143, 145
Schumpeter, Josef, 30n
Schutz, Peter (Porsche), 6, 283, 287,
    290–91
Scottsdale, Ariz., city government
    of, 3, 298–303
"Self-actualization," 107
Self-Renewal (Gardner), 15, 241,
    246
Service industry
    controls and, 119–21, 134
    quality and, 286–87
Sesame Street (tv show), 2, 92–93
    conception and success, 150–53
    solution space at, 92–93
    see also Children's Television
        Workshop
7-C framework, 59–70
7-S framework, 56–58, 62–64, 70
Shares values. See Values, shared
Shaw, Ray (Dow Jones), 52
Sheehan, George A., 96
Shell Oil Co., 28, 29
Shoemaker, Alvin V. (First Boston),
    182
Shostack, Lynn (Bankers Trust), 83,
    137
Siegel, Sam (Nucor), 181
Silver, Spence (3M), 27
Simon, Herbert, 27–28, 29, 32,
    39–40, 116
Sherlock, Gary (Humana), 292,
    297
Single-loop learning, 147–50,
    174
"65 Billion Man Hours" (Mogensen),
    74
Skill building, 55–58, 70
Skylab, 92
Small, Larry (Citicorp), 117, 121,
    127–28, 198–99, 215, 224,
    304
"Small wins", 225–28
Smith, Adam, 60
Smith, Alex (Kona Village), 1, 167
Snodgrass, Warren (Steelcase), 165
Sobel, Robert, 266
Solution space, 90–94
Sources of Invention, The (Jewkes),
    41

Southern California Edison, 73
Space industry, 45, 92
Spreadsheet software, 129–30, 135
Stability from shared values,
220–222
Steak-Umm, 38
Steelcase, 2, 161, 220
change at, 214–15
customer relations at, 8, 164–65
dealer/designer relations, 165
employee contributions to,
75–76, 91, 99
facility size at, 8
hiring practices of, 75–76
information sharing, 147
management style of, 7
no-layoff policy at, 229–30, 231
strategic Planning at, 50, 52
symbolism, 269–70
top teamwork at, 180
Steps to an Ecology of Mind
(Bateson), 124
Stochastic shocks, 30–31, 36, 41,
68
Strategy (simple), 47–48
see also Planning
Strategic Planning Institute, 286
Strauss, Charlie, 38
Subsidiarity (concept), 94, 101
Superconductivity, 226*n*
Super Valu, 2, 10, 78–80,
180, 215, 232, 267
Suppliers, 187, 191–92, 195
Sustainable competitive advantage,
60
Swanger, Sterling (Maytag),
189
Swissair, 167
Symbols, 11, 57, 265–71, 275
organizational stories, 269–70
unintended results of, 270–271
Systems integration, 280

Takeovers. *See* Acquisitions and
mergers; specific company names
Taurus (Ford car)
competitor analysis and, 157–58
consumer reaction, 170
development of, 3, 8, 41, 100,
138–40, 157–58
employee contributions to, 7,
82–83, 84
team effort, 81–83, 180–81, 188

Taylor, N. Powell (GE), 168
Teamwork, 9, 138, 179–212
competition vs. cooperation,
195–99
politics and, 199–207
top management level, 179–83,
197–98
trust and, 192–95, 211
Telnack, Jack (Ford), 91, 222, 223
Terkel, Studs, 283
Terry, Bill (Hewlett-Packard), 260
Theobald, Tom (Citicorp), 30, 31,
43, 100–101, 209
Think (IBM publication), 230
Thomas, Dr. Donald (Humana),
292
Thousand Days, A (Schlesinger),
145
3M (Minnesota Mining &
Manufacturing)
diversification at, 66, 190
Post-it note development by,
26–27
3-2-1 Contact (tv show), 283
Toshiba, 217–18
Toughminded optimism, 244–51
Townsend, Robert, 122–23
TQC program, 257–61, 274
Train, Russell (World Wildlife
Fund), 104
Training programs, 193–94, 209
Transforming vs. transactional
leadership, 203–204
Trigano, Gerard (Club Med), 169,
232–33
Trucking industry
change and, 221–22
deregulation in, 14, 33, 103–104
U.S. vs. Japan, 105–106
Trust, 9, 192–95, 211
Turnarounds, 111–16
see also specific company names
Tversky, Amos, 32–33, 67
Twain, Mark, 17

University of Louisville, 291–92
University of Minnesota football
team, 245
US West, 18–19, 52, 96–97

Values, shared, 57, 62, 220–25,
238, 239
Van Arden, Paul (GE), 186

Veraldi, Lew (Ford Taurus), 82, 83, 157–58
Videotape, for communication, 133, 221
Vietnam, 13
Vision. *See* Pathfinding
Von Neumann, John, 32
Von Neumann and Morganstern (Game theory), 32

Wagner, Harvey, 44
Walleck, Steve (McKinsey), 191–92
Wall Street Journal, The, 72–73, 117, 169, 270–71
Walter, Craig (Hewlett-Packard), 257, 258, 259
Watson, Peter, 46
Watson, Thomas, Sr. (IBM), 219, 270
Watson, Thomas, Jr. (IBM), 220, 266
Weatherstone, Dennis (Morgan), 18
Weick, Karl, 66, 100, 225, 228
Welch, Jack (GE), 185, 186
Wells Fargo Bank, 124
  acquisitions by, 6, 25, 36–37
  deregulation and, 7–8
  financial strategy of, 25, 36–37, 47–48, 65, 118–19, 288, 297–98

  skill building at, 58
Western Electric Co., 252
We/they split, 183–92, 208–209, 223, 281, 298
"What-if?" analyses, 58, 61, 128–30, 135
Whittaker Corp., 109–10
Willemssen, John (US West), 50
Williams, Bob (James River), 127, 173
Willoughby, Mimi, 193
Wilson Sporting Goods, 29
Witting, Paul (Steelcase), 52
Word processing, 227
Working (Terkel), 283
Worldly Power: The Making of The Wall Street Journal (Scharft), 73
Wright, Mike (Super Valu), 79, 80, 180, 215

Yankelovich, 170
Yokogawa-Hewlett-Packard (YHP), 257–61
Young, John (Hewlett-Packard), 258–59, 260, 274

Zebco, 295–98